W0207354

BRITAIN

Oxford University Press
Great Clarendon Street, Oxford OX2 6DP

Oxford New York
Athens Auckland Bangkok Bogotá
Buenos Aires Calcutta Cape Town Chennai
Dar es Salaam Delhi Florence Hong Kong
Istanbul Karachi Kuala Lumpur Madrid Melbourne
Mexico City Mumbai Nairobi Paris São Paulo
Singapore Taipei Tokyo Toronto Warsaw

and associated companies in
Berlin Ibadan

OXFORD and OXFORD ENGLISH
are trade marks of Oxford University Press.

ISBN 0 19 432429 X

First published 1995
Sixth impression 2000

Typeset in Joanna and Gill Sans by Selwood Systems, Midsomer Norton

Printed in China

ACKNOWLEDGEMENTS

The publisher and author would like to thank the following for their permission to use extracts from copyright material:

BBC Enterprises Ltd for extracts from *Yes, Prime Minister* by Jonathan Lynn and Antony Jay.

Cambridge University Press for extracts from 'The Invisible Scot' in *English Today* 18 April 1989.

Penguin Books Ltd for extracts from *How to be Inimitable* by George Mikes (Penguin Books 1966, first published by André Deutsch) copyright © George Mikes, 1960.

Radio Times/BBC Magazines for extract from 'Peter Snow's Armchair Guide,' *Radio Times*, April 1992.

Reed Consumer Books for extracts from *The Queen and I* by Sue Townsend (Methuen, London), © 1992 by Sue Townsend.

Times Newspapers Ltd for extracts from 'Mad about plaid' by A A Gill, *The Sunday Times*, London, 23 January 1994, © Times Newspapers Ltd 1994: 'Who gives a caber toss?' by Harry Ritchie, *The Sunday Times*, London, 23 January 1994, © Times Newspapers Ltd 1994: 'Defiant English hold out against Welsh arsonists' by Stuart Wavell, *The Sunday Times*, London, 15 November 1992, © Times Newspapers Ltd 1992: and 'Britain bans EC Medals' from News Digest, *The Sunday Times*, 18 April 1993, © Times Newspapers Ltd 1993.

A P Watt Ltd on behalf of The National Trust for extracts from 'The White Man's Burden' and 'Recessional' by Rudyard Kipling.

Cover photograph:
Collections Photo Library/Gary Smith

Illustrations by:
Bret Breckon pages 10, 13
Matthew Lawrence page 110
Alan Nanson all chapter openers
Oxford University Press cartographic department pages 9, 31, 34, 86, 87, 113, 209
Oxford University Press technical graphics department pages 32, 33, 46, 89, 91, 104, 108, 109, 121, 132, 133, 137, 143, 145, 146, 152, 153, 158, 160, 171, 180, 181, 195, 199, 202
Murray Zanoni pages 174, 176

Studio photography by:
Haddon Davies pages 118, 134, 155, 211

The publisher would like to thank the following for their permission to reproduce photographs and other copyright material:
Action Images page 199; AKG London page 21 (Henry VIII); Allsport Photo Library page 196 (R Cheyne); Aquarius Photo Library page 160; The Automobile Association (for use of their logo) page 162; BBC Photo Library pages 50, 103, (*old swingometer*), 107 (*Dixon of Dock Green*); Barclays Bank (for use of their logo) page 147; The Bridgeman Art Library/John Noot Galleries, Broadway page 23; Bryant Homes page 175; Collections Photo Library pages 15 (R Hallman), 37 (*Land's End*: P Watts), 138 (A Gordon), 209 (*rock shop*: A Le Garsmeur); Colorsport page 194; The Conservative Party (for use of their logo) page 73; Lupe Cunha page 172; Dominic Pictures page 213 (C Ashmore); The Environmental Picture Library page 197 (A Testa); Eye Ubiquitous page 37 (*farmland*: T Page); Garden News page 192 (T Sandall); Sally and Richard Greenhill Photo Library pages 182, 214; Sue Hallet page 202; House of Commons Press Office page 97 (*Black Rod*); Hulton Deutch Library page 27; Images/Landscape Only Photo Library pages 16, 40; The Independant page 129 (R Perry); The Kobal Collection page 17; The Labour Party (for use of their logo) page 73; The Liberal Democrats (for use of their logo) page 73; Life File pages 61 (*Polesden Lacey*: A Ward), 80 (I Richards), 156 (J Hoare); Lloyds Bank (for use of their logo) page 147; Lord Snooty, © DC Thompson and Co Ltd 1989 page 59; Magnum Photo Library pages 115 (C Steele-Perkins), 119 (*Free Derry*: L Freed), 131 (P Marlow), 187 (M Parr); Mary Evans Picture Library pages 10, 11, 21 (*Elizabeth I*); Midland Bank (for use of their logo) page 147; NatWest Bank (for use of their logo) page 147; Neal's Yard Remedies page 173; Network Photo Library pages 61 (*allotments*: H Sykes), 111 (M Abrahams), 119 (*Freedom Fighters mural*; G Mendel), 123 (both pics by H Sykes), 147 (B Lewis), 149 (Barry Lewis), 163 (B Lewis), 164 (*traffic cones*: H Sykes), (*beach*: P Jordan); The Performing Arts Library page 204 (C Barda); Photofusion pages 144 (J Martin), 189; Popperfoto pages 47 (D Joyner), 66, 79, 124; The Press Association pages 53, 74, 83, 95; Punch Publications Ltd page 190; RAC (for the use of their logo) page 162; RSPCA Photo Library page 64 (T Sambrook); The Retrograph Archive page 210; Rex Features pages 56, 69, 78 (D Hartley), 90, 97 (*state opening of Parliament*), 101 (J Bradley), 103 (*new swingometer*: P Brooker), 188, 206 (N Jorgensen); The Samaritans page 170; Scope Features page 107 (*The Bill*); Skyscan Balloon Photography page 178; Frank Spooner Pictures pages 33 (Gamma, T Bitchburn), 65 (K Bernstein/ESP), 91 (Gamma: K Bernstein), 114 (Gamma); The Still Moving Picture Company page 43; The Sun Newspaper/News International page 118; John Walmsley Photo Library pages 38, 44, 164 (*traffic warden*); Warwick University page 139.

We would also like to thank Gertrude Erbach at the reference library, News International for her help in obtaining illustrative material and Derek Heater, founder Chairman of the Politics Association, for his advice on the chapters concerning history and politics.

Britain

James O'Driscoll

Oxford University Press

Contents

Introduction

Who this book is for

This book is for learners of English as a foreign language, at any level of proficiency from intermediate upwards, who need to know more about Britain. It will be invaluable to students on British Studies courses and to those who are studying British culture as part of a general English course. It is for all people who recognize that a knowledge of British life is necessary to improve their understanding and use of the English language as it is spoken in Britain.

How many times have you not fully understood a phrase in a British text and found that the dictionary did not help? How many times have you understood every word that a British person has said but not understood what he or she *meant*? In any society, writers and speakers leave some things unsaid or unexplained because they assume that their readers and listeners are equipped with the basic knowledge which comes from sharing the same cultural background. You may have reached a high level of proficiency in English, but find British people hard to understand because you lack this background knowledge. This book aims to fill in the gaps so that, when you encounter British writers and speakers, you are closer to being in the same position as an averagely educated British person would be.

Of course, it is impossible for you to put yourself in exactly the same position as natives of Britain. They have been sharing many, distinctly British, experiences and influences ever since they were born. Therefore, this book also looks behind the facts and figures, so that you can begin to understand the British approach to life in general.

What this book is about

This book contains all the basic information you need about the structure of the British political system and other aspects of public life. But it has more than that. Throughout the book, particular attention is paid to the attitudes of British people. Knowledge of these is very important because they are what 'colour' the language used by British people. For example, to understand the word 'Catholic' as used in Britain, it is not enough to know the legal position of Catholicism and how many Catholics there are; you also have to know something about the general place of religion in British people's minds and how different religious groups in the country feel about each other (see chapter 13). Because attitudes are so important, there are two chapters concerned entirely with them: one is about how British people feel about themselves (chapter 4) and the other is about their attitudes to certain aspects of life in general (chapter 5).

All the pieces of information in this book are included for one or both of two possible reasons. Some of them, for example the mention of the Union Jack (see page 13), are there because they form part of a British person's general knowledge. But others, for example the description of the pairing system in Parliament (see page 72), are not so well-known. They are there to serve as illustrations of more general points.

This book is not an encyclopaedia. Britain shares many characteristics with other countries. This book concentrates on what makes Britain different.

Using this book

In each chapter there is a main text plus extra material in the margins and elsewhere, which is presented in various forms (tables, graphs, text, pictures etc). You will sometimes find an invitation in the main text to refer to this extra material, indicated by the symbol ▷. The information provided in this way may illustrate a point made in the main text, or add some extra detail, or introduce a related issue. The two types of material can be read independently.

As you read, remember that 'facts' are relative things. For example, when you read (on page 10) that St Andrew is the patron saint of Scotland, you are getting a hard-and-fast fact. However, some of the most important aspects of life cannot be described in terms of hard-and-fast facts. For example, this book refers to the importance of privacy in Britain. This is not a fact; it is only an interpretation of the facts. Of course, such comments have not been made lightly – and in most cases other commentators on Britain have made the same ones. But it is always possible that another commentator, looking at the same set of facts, might arrive at a different conclusion.

At the end of each chapter there is a *Questions* section. The questions are intended as 'taking off' points for discussion in class, as topics for written work, or simply to get you thinking about the various aspects of British life described in the chapter, particularly in comparison with life in your own country. You will sometimes also find suggestions for further reading and other activities.

A note on terminology

In this book you will encounter the words *state*, *country* and *nation*. These are similar in meaning but are not used interchangeably. The word *state* has a political meaning. It is used when referring to a unit of governmental authority. The word *nation* is used when referring to English, Scottish, Welsh or Irish people and when the focus is on the sense of identity which these people feel. The word *country* is used more generally, to refer to either Britain or one of its nations without specific allusion to either government or people.

1
Country and people

This is a book about Britain. But what exactly is Britain? And who are the British? The table below illustrates the problem. You might think that, when it comes to international sport, the situation would be simple – one country, one team. But you can see that this is definitely not the case with Britain. For each of the four sports or sporting events listed in the table, there are a different number of national teams which might be called 'British'. This chapter describes how this situation has come about and explains the different names which are used when people talk about Britain.

Geographically speaking

Lying off the north-west coast of Europe, there are two large islands and several much smaller ones. Collectively, they are known as *The British Isles*. The largest island is called *Great Britain*. The other large one is called *Ireland* (▷ *The British Isles*).

Politically speaking

In the British Isles there are two states. One of these governs most of the island of Ireland. This state is usually called *The Republic of Ireland*. It is also called 'Eire' (its Irish language name). Informally it is referred to as just 'Ireland' or 'the Republic'.

The other state has authority over the rest of the British Isles (the whole of Great Britain, the northeastern area of Ireland and most of the smaller islands). This is the country that is the main subject of this book. Its official name is *The United Kingdom of Great Britain and Northern*

▸ **National teams from the British Isles in selected sports**

	England	Wales	Scotland	Northern Ireland	Irish Republic
olympics	United Kingdom				Irish Republic
cricket	England		Scotland	Ireland	
rugby union	England	Wales	Scotland	Ireland	
football	England	Wales	Scotland	Northern Ireland	Irish Republic

Ireland although it is usually known by a shorter name. At the Eurovision Song Contest, at the United Nations and in the European Parliament, for instance, it is referred to as 'the United Kingdom'. In everyday speech this is often shortened to 'the UK'. In other contexts it is referred to as 'Great Britain'. This, for example, is the name you hear when a gold medal winner steps onto the rostrum at the Olympic Games. The stickers on cars ('GB') are another example of the use of this name. In writing and speaking that is not especially formal or informal, the name 'Britain' is used. The normal adjective, when talking about something to do with the UK, is 'British'.

▶ Crown dependencies

There are two small parts of the British Isles which have special political arrangements. These 'Crown dependencies' are the Channel Islands and the Isle of Man. Each has complete internal self-government, including its own Parliament and its own tax system. Both are 'ruled' by a Lieutenant Governor appointed by the British government.

Some historical and poetic names

Albion is a word used in some poetic or rhetorical contexts to refer to England. It was the original Roman name for Britain. It may come from the Latin word *albus*, meaning 'white'. The white chalk cliffs around Dover on the south coast are the first part of England to be seen when crossing the sea from the European mainland.

Britannia is the name that the Romans gave to their southern British province (which covered, approximately, the area of present-day England). It is also the name given to the female embodiment of Britain, always shown wearing a helmet and holding a trident (the symbol of power over the sea), hence the patriotic song which begins 'Rule Britannia, Britannia rule the waves'. The figure of Britannia has been on the reverse side of many British coins for more than 300 years.

Britannia

The four nations

People often refer to Britain by another name. They call it 'England'. But this is not strictly correct, and it can make some people angry. England is only one of the four nations of the British Isles (England, Scotland, Wales and Ireland). Their political unification was a gradual process that took several hundred years (see chapter 2). It was completed in 1800 when the Irish Parliament was joined with the Parliament for England, Scotland and Wales in Westminster, so that the whole of the British Isles became a single state – the United Kingdom of Great Britain and Ireland. However, in 1922, most of Ireland became a separate state (see chapter 12).

At one time the four nations were distinct from each other in almost every aspect of life. In the first place, they were different

▶ Identifying symbols of the four nations

	England	Wales	Scotland	Ireland
Flag	 St George's Cross	 Dragon of Cadwallader	 St Andrew's Cross	 St Patrick's Cross
			 Lion rampant	 Republic of Ireland
Plant	 Rose	 Leek/Daffodil[1]	 Thistle	 Shamrock
Colour[2]				
Patron saint	St George	St David	St Andrew	St Patrick
Saint's day	23 April	1 March	30 November	17 March

[1] There is some disagreement among Welsh people as to which is the real national plant, but the leek is the most well-known.

[2] As typically worn by sports teams of the different nations.

racially. The people in Ireland, Wales and highland Scotland belonged to the Celtic race; those in England and lowland Scotland were mainly of Germanic origin. This difference was reflected in the languages they spoke. People in the Celtic areas spoke Celtic languages: Irish Gaelic, Scottish Gaelic and Welsh. People in the Germanic areas spoke Germanic dialects (including the one which has developed into modern English). The nations also tended to have different economic, social and legal systems.

Today these differences have become blurred. But they have not completely disappeared. Although there is only one government for the whole of Britain, and people have the same passport regardless of where in Britain they live, some aspects of government are organized separately (and sometimes differently) in the four parts of the United Kingdom. Moreover, Welsh, Scottish and Irish people feel their identity very strongly.

John Bull is a fictional character who is supposed to personify Englishness and certain English virtues. (He can be compared to Uncle Sam in the USA.) He features in hundreds of nineteenth century cartoons. His appearance is typical of an eighteenth century country gentleman, evoking an idyllic rural past (see chapter 5).

John Bull

Other signs of national identity

The following are also associated by British people with one or more of the four nations.

Names
The prefix 'Mac' or 'Mc' in surnames (such as McCall, MacCarthy, MacDonald) is always either Scottish or Irish. The prefix 'O' (as in O'Brien, O'Hara) is distinctly Irish. A very large number of surnames (for example, Davis, Evans, Jones, Lloyd, Morgan, Price, Rees, Williams) suggest Welsh origin (although many of these are found throughout England). The most common surname in both England and Scotland is actually 'Smith'.

First names can also be indicative. The Scottish form of 'John' is 'Ian' and its Irish form is 'Sean' (although all three names are common throughout Britain). There are also nicknames for Scottish, Irish and Welsh men. For example, an English, Welsh or Irish person might refer to and address a Scottish friend as 'Jock', whatever his first name is. Irishmen are called 'Paddy' or 'Mick' and Welshmen are known as 'Dai' or 'Taffy'. If the person is not a friend the nickname can sound rather insulting.

Clothes
The kilt, a skirt with a tartan pattern worn by men, is a very well-known symbol of Scottishness (though it is hardly ever worn in everyday life).

Musical instruments
The harp is an emblem of both Wales and Ireland. The bagpipes are regarded as distinctively Scottish (though a smaller type is also used in traditional Irish music).

Characteristics
There are certain stereotypes of national character which are well-known in Britain. For instance, the Irish are supposed to be great talkers, the Scots have a reputation for being careful with money, and the Welsh are renowned for their singing ability. These characteristics are, of course, only caricatures and are not reliable descriptions of individual people from these countries. Nevertheless, they indicate some slight differences in the value attached to certain kinds of behaviour in the countries concerned.

Briton is a word used in official contexts and in formal writing to describe a citizen of the United Kingdom. 'Ancient Britons' is the name given to the race of people who lived in England before and during the Roman occupation (AD 43–410). These are the ancestors of the present-day Welsh people.

Caledonia, Cambria and **Hibernia** were the Roman names for Scotland, Wales and Ireland respectively. The words are commonly used today in scholarly classifications (for example, the type of English used in Ireland is sometimes called 'Hiberno-English') and for the names of organizations (for example, the airline 'British Caledonian').

Erin is a poetic name for Ireland. 'The Emerald Isle' is another way of referring to Ireland, evoking the lush greenery of its countryside.

▶ The invisible Scot

Here are some brief extracts from an article written by a Scotswoman, Janet Swinney, which expresses anger at how the dominance of England over Scotland is reflected in the way things are described.

First, there is 'domination by omission'. A map appeared in the *Observer* newspaper in May 1989 under the heading 'Britain's Dirty Rivers'. It showed only England and Wales. Janet Swinney says: 'What is the meaning of this illustration? Does Scotland have no rivers or no dirty rivers, or has someone simply used the word *Britain* to mean *England and Wales?*'

Second, she points out the common use of *England/English* to mean *Britain/British*: 'When I went to Turkey a few years ago with an assorted group of Britons, most of the English were happy to record their nationality on their embarkation cards as *English*, and saw nothing offensive about it. It's not unusual, either, for Scots to receive mail from elsewhere in the UK addressed *Scotland, England* . . . Last year, works of art from the Soviet Union intended for display at the Edinburgh International Festival were sent to the City Art Gallery addressed *Edinburgh, England*'.

A third aspect of domination can be seen in the names given to publications and organizations: 'The practice is to label anything that pertains to England and (usually) Wales as though it were the norm, and anything Scottish as though it were a deviation from it. Why else do we have *The Times Educational Supplement* and *The Times Educational Supplement (Scotland)*, the "National Trust" and the "National Trust for Scotland", the "Trades Union Congress" and the "Scottish Trades Union Congress"? In a society of equals, all these names would carry their geographical markers: *The Times Educational Supplement (England and Wales)* etc'.

J Swinney, 'The Invisible Scot', *English Today*, April 1989

The dominance of England

There is, perhaps, an excuse for people who use the word 'England' when they mean 'Britain'. It cannot be denied that the dominant culture of Britain today is specifically English. The system of politics that is used in all four nations today is of English origin, and English is the main language of all four nations. Many aspects of everyday life are organized according to English custom and practice. But the political unification of Britain was not achieved by mutual agreement. On the contrary. It happened because England was able to exert her economic and military power over the other three nations (see chapter 2).

Today English domination can be detected in the way in which various aspects of British public life are described (▷ *The invisible Scot*). For example, the supply of money in Britain is controlled by the Bank of England (there is no such thing as a 'Bank of Britain'). The present queen of the country is universally known as 'Elizabeth the Second', even though Scotland and Northern Ireland have never had an 'Elizabeth the First'! (Elizabeth I of England and Wales ruled from 1553 to 1603.) The term 'Anglo' is also commonly used. (The Angles were a Germanic tribe who settled in England in the fifth century. The word 'England' is derived from their name.) For example, newspapers and the television news talk about 'Anglo-American relations' to refer to relations between the governments of Britain and the USA (and not just those between England and the USA).

National loyalties

When you are talking to people from Britain, it is safest to use 'Britain' when talking about where they live and 'British' as the adjective to describe their nationality. This way you will be less likely to offend anyone. It is, of course, not wrong to talk about 'people in England' if that is what you mean – people who live within the geographical boundaries of England. After all, most British people live there (▷ *Populations in 1995*). But it should always be remembered that England does not make up the whole of the UK.

There has been a long history of migration from Scotland, Wales and Ireland to England. As a result there are millions of people who live in England but who would never describe themselves as English. They may have lived in England all their lives, but as far as they are concerned they are Scottish or Welsh or Irish – even if, in the last case, they are citizens of Britain and not of Eire. These people support the country of their parents or grandparents rather than England in sporting contests. They would also, given the chance, play for that country rather than England. If, for example, you had heard the members of the Republic of Ireland World Cup football team talking in 1994, you would have heard several different kinds of English accent and some Scottish accents, but only a few Irish accents. Most of the players did not live in Ireland and were not brought up in Ireland. Nevertheless, most of them would never have considered playing for any country other than Ireland!

The same holds true for the further millions of British citizens whose family origins lie outside the British Isles altogether. People of Caribbean or south Asian descent, for instance, do not mind being described as 'British' (many are proud of it), but many of them would not like to be called 'English'. And whenever the West Indian or Indian cricket team plays against England, it is certainly not England that they support!

There is, in fact, a complicated division of loyalties among many people in Britain, and especially in England. A black person whose family are from the Caribbean will passionately support the West Indies when they play cricket against England. But the same person is quite happy to support England just as passionately in a sport such as football, which the West Indies do not play. A person whose family are from Ireland but who has always lived in England would want Ireland to beat England at football but would want England to beat (for example) Italy just as much. This crossover of loyalties can work the other way as well. English people do not regard the Scottish, the Welsh or the Irish as 'foreigners' (or, at least, not as the same kind of foreigners as other foreigners!). An English commentator of a sporting event in which a Scottish, Irish or Welsh team is playing against a team from outside the British Isles tends to identify with that team as if it were English.

A wonderful example of double identity was heard on the BBC during the Eurovision Song Contest in 1992. The commentator for the BBC was Terry Wogan. Mr Wogan is an Irishman who had become Britain's most popular television talk-show host during the 1980s. Towards the end of the programme, with the voting for the songs nearly complete, it became clear that the contest (in which European countries compete to present the best new popular song) was going to be won by either Ireland or the United Kingdom. Within a five-minute period, Mr Wogan could be heard using the pronouns 'we' and 'us' several times; sometimes he meant the UK and sometimes he meant Ireland!

▶ Populations in 1995

England	48.9 million
Scotland	5.1 million
Wales	2.9 million
Northern Ireland	1.6 million
UK total	58.6 million

These figures are estimates provided by the Government Actuary's Department of the UK, based on the 1991 Census. It is expected that the total population of Britain will continue to rise by very small amounts until around the year 2025.

▶ The Union Jack

The Union Jack is the national flag of the UK. It is a combination of the cross of St George, the cross of St Andrew and the cross of St Patrick (▷ *Identifying symbols of the four nations*).

The Union Jack

QUESTIONS

1 Think of the most well-known symbols and tokens of nationality in your country. Are they the same *types* of real-life objects (e.g. plants, clothes) that are used in Britain?

2 In 1970, the BBC showed a series of programmes about the history of the British Empire. Before the series started, they advertised it. The advertisement mentioned 'England's history'. Within a few hours, the BBC had received thousands of angry calls of protest and it was forced to make an apology. Who do you think the angry callers were? Why did the BBC apologize?

3 In 1991, UEFA (the Union of European Football Associations) introduced a new regulation. This limited the number of foreign players who were allowed to play for a football club in European competitions. For example, a German club team could have only a certain number of players in it who were not German. Under the new regulation a player in the Liverpool team, Ian Rush, was classified as 'foreign', even though he was born only twenty miles from Liverpool and had lived in the same area all his life. Many other players of English club teams found themselves in the same position. Many people in England thought that this was ridiculous. How did this happen? Do *you* think it was ridiculous?

4 The dominance of England in Britain is reflected in the organization of the government. There are ministers for Scotland, Wales and Northern Ireland, but there is no minister for England. Do you think this is good for the people of the other British nations (they have special attention and recognition of their distinct identity) or is it bad (it gives them a kind of second-class, colonial status)?

5 Are there any distinct *national* loyalties in your country (or are they better described as regional loyalties)? If so, is the relationship between the 'nations' in any way similar to that between the nations in Britain? If not, can you think of any other countries where such loyalties exist? Do these loyalties cause problems in those countries?

SUGGESTIONS

- *Britain, an Official Handbook* (HMSO) is published annually and is prepared by the Central Office of Information. It includes facts and figures on aspects of British life such as politics and law, economic and social affairs, arts and sport.
- *Dictionary of Britain* by Adrian Room (Oxford University Press) is an alphabetical guide to well-known British organizations, people, events, traditions and other aspects of life in Britain.

2
History

Prehistory

Two thousand years ago there was an Iron Age Celtic culture throughout the British Isles. It seems that the Celts, who had been arriving from Europe from the eighth century BC onwards, intermingled with the peoples who were already there. We know that religious sites that had been built long before the arrival of the Celts continued to be used in the Celtic period.

For people in Britain today, the chief significance of the prehistoric period (for which no written records exist) is its sense of mystery. This sense finds its focus most easily in the astonishing monumental architecture of this period, the remains of which exist throughout the country. Wiltshire, in south-western England, has two spectacular examples: Silbury Hill, the largest burial mound in Europe, and Stonehenge (▷ *Stonehenge*). Such places have a special importance for anyone interested in the cultural and religious practices of prehistoric Britain. We know very little about these practices, but there are some organizations today (for example, the Order of Bards, Ovates and Druids – a small group of eccentric intellectuals and mystics) who base their beliefs on them.

Stonehenge

▶ Stonehenge

Stonehenge was built on Salisbury Plain some time between 3050 and 2300 BC. It is one of the most famous and mysterious archaeological sites in the world. One of its mysteries is how it was ever built at all with the technology of the time (the stones come from over 200 miles away in Wales). Another is its purpose. It appears to function as a kind of astronomical clock and we know it was used by the Druids for ceremonies marking the passing of the seasons. It has always exerted a fascination on the British imagination, and appears in a number of novels, such as Thomas Hardy's *Tess of the D'Urbevilles*.

These days Stonehenge is not only of interest to tourists, but is also a gathering point for certain minority groups such as hippies and 'New Age Travellers' (see chapter 13). It is now fenced off to protect it from damage.

▶ Hadrian's Wall

Hadrian's Wall was built by the Romans in the second century across the northern border of their province of Britannia (along nearly the same line as the present English-Scottish border) in order to protect their territory from attacks by the Scots and the Picts.

Hadrian's Wall

The Roman period (43–410)

The Roman province of Britannia covered most of present-day England and Wales. The Romans imposed their own way of life and culture, making use of the existing Celtic aristocracy to govern and encouraging this ruling class to adopt Roman dress and the Roman language (Latin). They exerted an influence, without actually governing there, over only the southern part of Scotland. It was during this time that a Celtic tribe called the Scots migrated from Ireland to Scotland, where they became allies of the Picts (another Celtic tribe) and opponents of the Romans. This division of the Celts into those who experienced direct Roman rule (the Britons in England and Wales) and those who did not (the Gaels in Ireland and Scotland) may help to explain the development of two distinct branches of the Celtic group of languages.

The remarkable thing about the Romans is that, despite their long occupation of Britain, they left very little behind. To many other parts of Europe they bequeathed a system of law and administration which forms the basis of the modern system and a language which developed into the modern Romance family of languages. In Britain, they left neither. Moreover, most of their villas, baths and temples, their impressive network of roads, and the cities they founded, including Londinium (London), were soon destroyed or fell into disrepair. Almost the only lasting reminder of their presence are place-names like Chester, Lancaster and Gloucester, which include variants of the Roman word *castra* (a military camp).

The Germanic invasions (410–1066)

One reason why Roman Britannia disappeared so quickly is probably that its influence was largely confined to the towns. In the countryside, where most people lived, farming methods had remained unchanged and Celtic speech continued to be dominant.

The Roman occupation had been a matter of colonial control rather than large-scale settlement. But, during the fifth century, a number of tribes from the north-western European mainland invaded and settled in large numbers. Two of these tribes were the Angles and

Some important dates in British history

55 BC*
The Roman general Julius Caesar lands in Britain with an expeditionary force, wins a battle and leaves. The first 'date' in popular British history.

AD 43
The Romans come to stay.

61
Queen Boudicca (or Boadicea) of the Iceni tribe leads a bloody revolt against the Roman occupation. It is suppressed. There is a statue of Boadicea, made in the nineteenth century, outside the Houses of Parliament. This has helped to keep the memory of her alive.

*BC means 'before Christ'. All the other dates are AD (Latin *anno Domini*), which signifies 'after the birth of Christ'.

the Saxons. These Anglo-Saxons soon had the south-east of the country in their grasp. In the west of the country their advance was temporarily halted by an army of (Celtic) Britons under the command of the legendary King Arthur (▷ *King Arthur*). Nevertheless, by the end of the sixth century, they and their way of life predominated in nearly all of England and in parts of southern Scotland. The Celtic Britons were either Saxonized or driven westwards, where their culture and language survived in south-west Scotland, Wales and Cornwall.

The Anglo-Saxons had little use for towns and cities. But they had a great effect on the countryside, where they introduced new farming methods and founded the thousands of self-sufficient villages which formed the basis of English society for the next thousand or so years.

The Anglo-Saxons were pagan when they came to Britain. Christianity spread throughout Britain from two different directions during the sixth and seventh centuries. It came directly from Rome when St Augustine arrived in 597 and established his headquarters at Canterbury in the south-east of England. It had already been introduced into Scotland and northern England from Ireland, which had become Christian more than 150 years earlier. Although Roman Christianity eventually took over the whole of the British Isles, the Celtic model persisted in Scotland and Ireland for several hundred years. It was less centrally organized, and had less need for a strong monarchy to support it. This partly explains why both secular and religious power in these two countries continued to be both more locally based and less secure than it was elsewhere in Britain throughout the medieval period.

Britain experienced another wave of Germanic invasions in the eighth century. These invaders, known as Vikings, Norsemen or Danes, came from Scandinavia. In the ninth century they conquered and settled the extreme north and west of Scotland, and also some coastal regions of Ireland. Their conquest of England was halted when they were defeated by King Alfred of the Saxon kingdom of Wessex (▷ *King Alfred*). This resulted in an agreement which divided England between Wessex, in the south and west, and the 'Danelaw' in the north and east.

▶ King Arthur

King Arthur provides a wonderful example of the distortions of popular history. In folklore and myth he is a great English hero, and he and his knights of the round table are regarded as the perfect example of medieval nobility and chivalry. In fact, he lived long before medieval times and was a Romanized Celt trying to hold back the advances of the Anglo-Saxons – the very people who became 'the English'!

King Arthur, Queen Guinevere and one of the knights of the round table, from the film 'Camelot'

410
The Romans leave Britain.

432
St Patrick converts Ireland to Christianity.

597
St Augustine arrives in England.

793
The great monastery on the island of Lindisfarne in northeast England is destroyed by Vikings and its monks killed.

878
The Peace of Edington partitions England between the Saxons, led by King Alfred, and the Danes.

973
Edgar, grandson of Alfred, becomes king of all England.

▶ King Alfred

King Alfred was not only an able warrior but also a dedicated scholar and a wise ruler. He is known as 'Alfred the Great' – the only monarch in English history to be given this title. He is also popularly known for the story of the burning of the cakes.

While Alfred was wandering around his country organizing resistance to the Viking invaders, he travelled in disguise. On one occasion, he stopped at a woman's house. The woman asked him to watch some cakes that were cooking to see that they did not burn, while she went off to get food. Alfred became lost in thought and the cakes burned. When the woman returned, she shouted angrily at Alfred and sent him away. Alfred never told her that he was her king.

▶ 1066

This is the most famous date in English history. On 14 October 1066 an invading army from Normandy defeated the English at the Battle of Hastings. The battle was close and extremely bloody. At the end of it, most of the best warriors in England were dead, including their leader, King Harold. On Christmas day that year the Norman leader, Duke William of Normandy, was crowned king of England. He is known in popular history as 'William the Conqueror'. The date is remembered for being the last time that England was successfully invaded.

However, the cultural differences between Anglo-Saxons and Danes were comparatively small. They led roughly the same way of life and spoke two varieties of the same Germanic tongue (which combined to form the basis of modern English). Moreover, the Danes soon converted to Christianity. These similarities made political unification easier, and by the end of the tenth century England was one kingdom with a Germanic culture throughout.

Most of modern-day Scotland was also united by this time, at least in name, in a (Celtic) Gaelic kingdom.

The medieval period (1066–1485)

The successful Norman invasion of England in 1066 (▷ 1066) brought Britain into the mainstream of western European culture. Previously most links had been with Scandinavia. Only in Scotland did this link survive; the western isles (until the thirteenth century) and the northern islands (until the fifteenth century) remaining under the control of Scandinavian kings. Throughout this period the English kings also ruled over areas of land on the continent and were often at war with the French kings in disputes over ownership.

Unlike the Germanic invasions, the Norman invasion was small-scale. There was no such thing as a Norman village or a Norman area of settlement. Instead, the Norman soldiers who had been part of the invading army were given the ownership of land – and of the people living on it. A strict feudal system was imposed. Great nobles, or barons, were responsible directly to the king; lesser lords, each owing a village, were directly responsible to a baron. Under them were the peasants, tied by a strict system of mutual duties and obligations to the local lord, and forbidden to travel without his permission. The peasants were the English-speaking Saxons. The lords and the barons were the French-speaking Normans. This was the beginning of the English class system (▷ *Language and class*).

The strong system of government which the Normans introduced meant that the Anglo-Norman kingdom was easily the most powerful political force in the British Isles. Not surprisingly therefore, the authority of the English monarch gradually extended to other parts of these islands in the next 250 years. By the end of the thirteenth century, a large part of eastern Ireland was controlled by Anglo-Norman lords in the name of the English king and the whole of Wales

1014
Brian Boru's Irish army defeats the Vikings at Clontarf (near modern Dublin). As a result, Viking settlement in Ireland remains limited and Ireland retains its Celtic identity, never becoming part of the Scandinavian empire.

1066
The Battle of Hastings (▷ 1066)

1086
King William's officials complete the Domesday Book, a very detailed, village-by-village record of the people and their possessions throughout his kingdom.

was under his direct rule (at which time the custom of naming the monarch's eldest son the 'Prince of Wales' began). Scotland managed to remain politically independent in the medieval period, but was obliged to fight occasional wars to do so.

The cultural story of this period is different. Two hundred and fifty years after the Norman Conquest, it was a Germanic language (Middle English) and not the Norman (French) language which had become the dominant one in all classes of society in England. Furthermore, it was the Anglo-Saxon concept of common law, and not Roman law, which formed the basis of the legal system.

Despite English rule, northern and central Wales was never settled in great numbers by Saxon or Norman. As a result the (Celtic) Welsh language and culture remained strong. Eisteddfods, national festivals of Welsh song and poetry, continued throughout the medieval period and still take place today. The Anglo-Norman lords of eastern Ireland remained loyal to the English king but, despite laws to the contrary, mostly adopted the Gaelic language and customs.

The political independence of Scotland did not prevent a gradual switch to English language and customs in the lowland (southern) part of the country. First, the Anglo-Saxon element here was strengthened by the arrival of many Saxon aristocrats fleeing the Norman conquest of England. Second, the Celtic kings saw that the adoption of an Anglo-Norman style of government would strengthen royal power. By the end of this period a cultural split had developed between the lowlands, where the way of life and language was similar to that in England, and the highlands, where (Celtic) Gaelic culture and language prevailed – and where, because of the mountainous landscape, the authority of the king was hard to enforce.

It was in this period that Parliament began its gradual evolution into the democratic body which it is today. The word 'parliament', which comes from the French word *parler* (to speak), was first used in England in the thirteenth century to describe an assembly of nobles called together by the king. In 1295, the Model Parliament set the pattern for the future by including elected representatives from urban and rural areas.

▶ Language and class

The existence of two words for the larger farm animals in modern English is a result of the class divisions established by the Norman conquest. There are the words for the living animals (e.g. *cow, pig, sheep*), which have their origins in Anglo-Saxon, and the words for the meat from the animals (e.g. *beef, pork, mutton*), which have their origins in the French language that the Normans brought to England. Only the Normans normally ate meat; the poor Anglo-Saxon peasants did not!

▶ Robin Hood

Robin Hood is a legendary folk hero. King Richard I (1189–99) spent most of his reign fighting in the crusades (the wars between Christians and Muslims in the Middle East). While Richard was away, England was governed by his brother John, who was unpopular because of all the taxes he imposed. According to legend, Robin Hood lived with his band of 'merry men' in Sherwood Forest outside Nottingham, stealing from the rich and giving to the poor. He was constantly hunted by the local sheriff (the royal representative) but was never captured.

1170

The murder of Thomas Becket, the Archbishop of Canterbury, by soldiers of King Henry II. Becket (also known as Thomas à Becket) was made a saint and his grave was visited by pilgrims for hundreds of years. *The Canterbury Tales*, written by Geoffrey Chaucer in the fourteenth century, recounts the stories told by a fictional group of pilgrims on their way to Canterbury.

1171

The Norman baron known as Strongbow and his followers settle in Ireland.

1215

An alliance of aristocracy, Church and merchants force King John to agree to the *Magna Carta* (Great Charter), a document in which the king agrees to follow certain rules of government. In fact, neither John nor his successors entirely followed them, but *Magna Carta* is remembered as the first time a monarch agreed in writing to abide by formal procedures.

The sixteenth century

The power of the English monarch increased in this period. The strength of the great barons had been greatly weakened by the Wars of the Roses (▷ *The Wars of the Roses*). Bubonic plague (known in England as the Black Death) contributed to the reduction of their power. It killed about a third of the population in its first outbreak in England in the middle of the fourteenth century and continued to reappear periodically for another 300 years. The shortage of labour which this caused, and the increasing importance of trade in the towns, helped to weaken the traditional ties between feudal lord and peasant.

The Tudor dynasty (1485–1603) established a system of government departments, staffed by professionals who depended for their position on the monarch. As a result, the feudal barons were no longer needed for implementing government policy. They were also needed less for making government policy. Parliament was traditionally split into two 'Houses'. The House of Lords consisted of the feudal aristocracy and the leaders of the Church; the House of Commons consisted of representatives from the towns and the less important landowners in rural areas. It was now more important for monarchs to get the agreement of the Commons for policy-making because that was where the newly powerful merchants and landowners (the people with the money) were represented.

Unlike in much of the rest of Europe, the direct cause of the rise of Protestantism in England was political and personal rather than doctrinal (▷ *Henry VIII*). Henry VIII wanted a divorce which the Pope would not give him. Also, by making himself head of the 'Church of England', independent of Rome, all church lands came under his control and gave him a large new source of income.

This rejection of the Roman Church accorded with a new spirit of patriotic confidence in England. The country had finally lost any realistic claim to lands in France, thus becoming more consciously a distinct 'island nation'. At the same time, increasing European exploration of the Americas and other parts of the world meant that

▶ The Wars of the Roses

During the fifteenth century the throne of England was claimed by representatives of two rival groups. The power of the greatest nobles, who had their own private armies, meant that constant challenges to the position of the monarch were possible. The Lancastrians, whose symbol was a red rose, supported the descendants of the Duke of Lancaster, and the Yorkists, whose symbol was a white rose, supported the descendants of the Duke of York. The struggle for power led to the 'Wars of the Roses' between 1455 and 1485. They ended when Henry VII defeated and killed Richard III at the Battle of Bosworth Field and were followed by an era of stability and strong government which was welcomed by those weakened and impoverished by decades of war.

▶ Off with his head!

Being an important person in the sixteenth century was not a safe position to be in. The Tudor monarchs were disloyal to their officials and merciless to any nobles who opposed them. More than half of the most famous people of the period finished their lives by being executed as traitors. Few people who were taken through Traitor's Gate to become prisoners in the Tower of London came out again alive.

1275
Llewellyn, a Welsh prince, refuses to submit to the authority of the English monarch.

1284
The Statute of Wales puts the whole of that country under the control of the English monarch.

1328
After several years of war between the Scottish and English kingdoms, Scotland is recognized as an independent kingdom.

1534
The Act of Supremacy declares Henry VIII to be the supreme head of the Church in England.

1536
The administration of government and law in Wales is reformed so that it is exactly the same as it is in England.

England was closer to the geographical centre of western civilisation instead of being, as previously, on the edge of it. It was in the last quarter of this adventurous and optimistic century that Shakespeare began writing his famous plays.

It was therefore patriotism as much as religious conviction that had caused Protestantism to become the majority religion in England by the end of the century. It took a form known as Anglicanism, which was not so very different from Catholicism in its organization and ritual. But in the lowlands of Scotland it took a more idealistic form. Calvinism, with its strict insistence on simplicity and its dislike of ritual and celebration, became the dominant religion. It is from this date that the stereotype of the dour, thrifty Scot developed. However, the Scottish highlands remained Catholic and so further widened the gulf between the two parts of the nation. Ireland also remained Catholic. There, Protestantism was identified with the English, who at that time were making further attempts to control the whole of the country.

▶ Henry VIII

Henry VIII is one of the most well-known monarchs in English history, chiefly because he took six wives during his life. It was during his reign that the Reformation took place. In the 1530s, Henry used Parliament to pass laws which swept away the power of the Roman Church in England. His quarrel with Rome was nothing to do with doctrine (it was because he wanted to be free to marry again and to appoint who he wished as leaders of the Church in England). In the same decade, he had a law passed which demanded complete adherence to Catholic belief and practice. He had also previously written a polemic against Protestantism, for which the pope gave him the title *Fidei Defensor* (Defender of the Faith). The initials FD still appear on British coins today.

▶ Elizabeth I

Elizabeth I, daughter of Henry VIII, (▷ *Henry VIII*) was the first of three long-reigning queens in British history (the other two are Queen Victoria and Elizabeth II). During her long reign she established, by skilful diplomacy, a reasonable degree of internal stability in a firmly Protestant England, allowing the growth of a spirit of patriotism and general confidence. She never married, but used its possibility as a diplomatic tool. She became known as 'the virgin queen'. The area which later became the state of Virginia in the USA was named after her by one of the many English explorers of the time (Sir Walter Raleigh).

Elizabeth I

Henry VIII

1538
An English language version of the Bible replaces Latin bibles in every church in the land.

1560
The Scottish Parliament abolishes the authority of the Pope and forbids the Latin mass.

1580
Sir Francis Drake completes the first voyage round the world by an Englishman.

1588
The Spanish Armada, a fleet of ships sent by the Catholic King Philip of Spain to help invade England, is defeated by the English navy (with the help of a violent storm!).

1603
James VI of Scotland becomes James I of England.

1605
The Gunpowder Plot: a group of Catholics fail in their attempt to blow up the king in Parliament (see chapter 23).

The seventeenth century

When James I became the first English king of the Stuart dynasty, he was already king of Scotland, so the crowns of these two countries were united. Although their parliaments and administrative and judicial systems continued to be separate, their linguistic differences were lessened in this century. The kind of Middle English spoken in lowland Scotland had developed into a written language known as 'Scots'. However, the Scottish Protestant church adopted English rather than Scots bibles. This, and the glamour of the English court where the king now sat, caused modern English to become the written standard in Scotland as well.

In the sixteenth century religion and politics became inextricably linked. This link became even more intense in the seventeenth century. At the beginning of the century, some people tried to kill the king because he wasn't Catholic *enough* (see chapter 23). By the end of the century, another king *had* been killed, partly because he seemed *too* Catholic, and yet another had been forced into exile for the same reason.

This was the context in which, during the century, Parliament established its supremacy over the monarchy in Britain. Anger grew in the country at the way that the Stuart monarchs raised money, especially because they did not get the agreement of the House of Commons to do so first. This was against ancient tradition. In addition, ideological Protestantism, especially Puritanism, had grown in England. Puritans regarded many of the practices of the Anglican Church, and also its hierarchical structure, as immoral. Some of them thought the luxurious lifestyle of the king and his followers was immoral too. They were also fiercely anti-Catholic and suspicious of the apparent sympathy towards Catholicism of the Stuart monarchs.

This conflict led to the Civil War (▷ *The Civil War*), which ended with complete victory for the parliamentary forces. The king (Charles I) was captured and became the first monarch in Europe to be executed after a formal trial for crimes against his people. The leader of the parliamentary army, Oliver Cromwell, became 'Lord Protector' of a republic with a military government which, after he had brutally crushed resistance in Ireland, effectively encompassed the whole of the British Isles.

But when Cromwell died, he, his system of government, and the puritan ethics that went with it (theatres and other forms of amusement had been banned) had become so unpopular that the son of the executed king was asked to return and take the throne. The Anglican

▶ The Civil War

This is popularly remembered as a contest between fun-loving, aristocratic, royalist 'Cavaliers', who nevertheless were 'wrong' in their beliefs, and over-serious, puritan parliamentarian 'Roundheads' (because of the style of their haircuts), who nevertheless had right on their side. The Roundheads were victorious by 1645, although the war periodically started up again until 1649.

1642
The Civil War begins (▷ *The Civil War*).

1649
Charles I is executed. For the first and only time, Britain briefly becomes a republic and is called 'the Commonwealth'.

1660
The monarchy and the Anglican religion are restored.

A nineteenth-century painting of victorious Roundheads with two captured Cavaliers after the battle of Naseby in 1645

Church was restored. However, the conflict between monarch and Parliament soon re-emerged. The monarch, James II, tried to give full rights to Catholics, and to promote them in his government.

The 'Glorious Revolution' ('glorious' because it was bloodless) followed, in which Prince William of Orange, ruler of the Netherlands, and his Stuart wife Mary, accepted Parliament's invitation to become king and queen. In this way it was established that a monarch could rule only with the support of Parliament. Parliament immediately drew up a Bill of Rights, which limited some of the powers of the monarch (notably, the power to dismiss judges). It also allowed Dissenters (those who did not agree with the practices of Anglicanism) to practise their religion freely. This meant that the Presbyterian Church, to which the majority of the lowland Scottish belonged, was guaranteed its legality. However, Dissenters were not allowed to hold government posts or be Members of Parliament.

James II, meanwhile, had fled to Ireland. But the Catholic Irish army he gathered there was defeated. Laws were then passed forbidding Catholics to vote or even own land. In Ulster, in the north of the country, large numbers of fiercely anti-Catholic Scottish Presbyterians settled (in possession of all the land). The descendants of these people are still known today as Orangemen (after their patron William of Orange). They form one half of the tragic split in society in modern Northern Ireland, the other half being the 'native' Irish Catholics (see chapter 13).

Ring-a-ring-a-roses

Ring-a-ring-a-roses
A pocket full of posies
Atishoo! Atishoo!
We all fall down.

This is a well-known children's nursery rhyme today. It comes from the time of the Great Plague of 1665, which was the last outbreak of bubonic plague in Britain. The ring of roses refers to the pattern of red spots on a sufferer's body. The posies (bags of herbs) were thought to give protection from the disease. 'Atishoo' represents the sound of sneezing, one of the signs of the disease, after which a person could sometimes 'fall down' dead in a few hours.

1666

The Great Fire of London destroys most of the city's old wooden buildings. It also destroys bubonic plague, which never reappears. Most of the city's finest churches, including St Paul's Cathedral, date from the period of rebuilding which follows.

1688

The Glorious Revolution

1690

The Presbyterian Church becomes the official 'Church of Scotland'.

The Battle of the Boyne, in which William III and the Ulster Protestants defeat James II and the Irish Catholics.

The eighteenth century

Politically, this century was stable. Monarch and Parliament got on quite well together. One reason for this was that the monarch's favourite politicians, through the royal power of patronage (the ability to give people jobs), were able to control the election and voting habits of a large number of Members of Parliament (MPs) in the House of Commons.

Within Parliament the divisions of the previous century, though far less bitter than before, were echoed in the formation of two vaguely opposed loose collections of allies. One group, the Whigs, were the political 'descendants' of the parliamentarians. They supported the Protestant values of hard work and thrift, were sympathetic to Dissenters and believed in government by monarch and aristocracy together. The other group, the Tories, had a greater respect for the idea of the monarchy and the importance of the Anglican Church (and sometimes even a little sympathy for Catholics and the Stuarts). The two terms, Whig and Tory, had in fact first been used in the late 1670s and allegiance to one side or the other was more often the result of family or regional loyalty than of political beliefs. This could be said, however, to be the beginning of the party system in Britain (see chapter 6).

The modern system of an annual budget drawn up by the monarch's Treasury officials for the approval of Parliament was established during this century. So, too, was the habit of the monarch appointing one principal, or 'Prime', Minister from the ranks of Parliament to head his government.

At the beginning of the century, by agreement, the Scottish Parliament joined with the English and Welsh Parliament at Westminster in London. However, Scotland retained its own system of law, more similar to continental European systems than to that of England. It does so to this day.

The only part of Britain to change radically as a result of political forces in this century was the highlands area of Scotland. This area twice supported failed attempts to put a (Catholic) Stuart monarch back on the throne by force. After the second attempt, many

1707
The Act of Union joins the Parliament of Scotland with that of England and Wales.

1708
The last occasion on which a British monarch refuses to accept a bill which has been passed by Parliament.

1746
At the Battle of Culloden, a government army of English and lowland Scots defeats the highland army of Charles Edward, who, as grandson of the last Stuart king, claimed the British throne. Although he made no attempt to protect his supporters from revenge afterwards, he is still a popular romantic figure in the highlands, and is known as 'Bonnie Prince Charlie'.

1771
For the first time, Parliament allows written records of its debates to be published freely.

1782
James Watt invents the first steam engine.

1783
After a war, Britain recognizes the independence of the American colonies.

inhabitants of the highlands were killed or sent away from Britain and the wearing of highland dress (the tartan kilt) was banned. The Celtic way of life was effectively destroyed.

It was cultural change that was most marked in this century. Britain gradually expanded its empire in the Americas, along the west African coast and in India. The increased trade which resulted from the links with these new markets was one factor which led to the Industrial Revolution. The many technical innovations in the areas of manufacturing and transport during this period were also important contributing factors.

In England, the growth of the industrial mode of production, together with advances in agriculture, caused the greatest upheaval in the pattern of everyday life since the Anglo-Saxon invasions. Areas of common land, which had been available for use by everybody in a village for the grazing of animals since Anglo-Saxon times, disappeared as landowners incorporated them into their increasingly large and more efficient farms. (Some pieces of common land remain in Britain today, used mainly as public parks. They are often called 'the common'.) Hundreds of thousands of people moved from rural areas into new towns and cities. Most of these new towns and cities were in the north of England, where the raw materials for industry were available. In this way, the north, which had previously been economically backward compared to the south, became the industrial heartland of the country. The right conditions for industrialisation also existed in lowland Scotland and south Wales, which accentuated the differences between those parts of these countries and their non-industrialised areas.

In the south of England, London came to dominate, not as an industrial centre but as a business and trading centre. By the end of the century, it had a population close to a million.

Despite all the urban development, social power and prestige rested on the possession of land in the countryside. The outward sign of this prestige was the ownership of a country seat – a gracious country mansion with land attached. More than a thousand such mansions were built in the eighteenth century.

1788

The first British settlers (convicts and soldiers) arrive in Australia.

1800

The separate Irish Parliament is closed and the United Kingdom of Great Britain and Ireland is formed.

1805

A British fleet under the command of Admiral Horatio Nelson defeats Napoleon's French fleet at the Battle of Trafalgar. Nelson's Column in Trafalgar Square in London commemorates this national hero, who died during the battle.

1829

Robert Peel, a government minister, organizes the first modern police force. The police are still sometimes known today as 'bobbies'. ('Bobby' is a short form of the name 'Robert'.)

Catholics and non-Anglican Protestants are given the right to hold government posts and become MPs.

The nineteenth century

Not long before this century began, Britain had lost its most important American colonies in a war of independence. When the century began, the country was locked in a war with France, during which an invasion by a French army was a real possibility. Soon after the end of the century, Britain controlled the biggest empire the world had ever seen (see chapter 12).

One section of this empire was Ireland. During this century it was, in fact, part of the UK itself, and it was during this century that the British culture and way of life came to predominate in Ireland. In the 1840s, the potato crop failed two years in a row and there was a terrible famine. Millions of peasants, those with Irish Gaelic language and customs, either died or emigrated. By the end of the century almost the whole of the remaining population were using English as their first language.

Another part of the empire was made up of Canada, Australia and New Zealand, where settlers from the British Isles formed the majority of the population. These countries had complete internal self-government but recognized the overall authority of the British government. Another was India, an enormous country with a culture more ancient than Britain's. Tens of thousands of British civil servants and troops were used to govern it. At the head of this administration was a viceroy (governor) whose position within the country was similar to the monarch's in Britain itself. Because India was so far away, and the journey from Britain took so long, these British officials spent most of their working lives there and so developed a distinctly Anglo-Indian way of life. They imposed British institutions and methods of government on the country, and returned to Britain when they retired. Large parts of Africa also belonged to the empire. Except for South Africa, where there was some British settlement, most of Britain's African colonies started as trading bases on the coast, and were only incorporated into the empire at the end of the century.

As well as these areas (Canada, Australia, New Zealand, India and Africa), the empire included numerous smaller areas and islands.

1833

The first law regulating factory working conditions is passed. (It set a limit on the number of hours that children could work.)

Slavery is made illegal throughout the British Empire.

1868

The TUC (Trades Union Congress) is formed.

1870

Free primary education (up to the age of eleven) is established.

1886

After much debate, an atheist is allowed to sit in the House of Commons.

1893

The first socialist, Keir Hardie, is elected to Parliament. He enters the House of Commons for the first time wearing a cloth cap (which remained a symbol of the British working man until the 1960s).

Queen Victoria, Prince Albert, and their nine children, photographed in 1857

Some, such as those in the Caribbean, were the result of earlier British settlement, but most were acquired because of their strategic position along trading routes.

A change in attitude in Britain towards colonization during the nineteenth century gave new encouragement to the empire builders. Previously, colonization had been seen as a matter of settlement, of commerce, or of military strategy. The aim was simply to possess territory, but not necessarily to govern it. By the end of the century, colonization was seen as a matter of destiny. There was an enormous increase in wealth during the century, so that Britain became the world's foremost economic power. This, together with long years of political stability unequalled anywhere else in Europe, gave the British a sense of supreme confidence, even arrogance, about their culture and civilization. The British came to see themselves as having a duty to spread this culture and civilization around the world. Being

▶ Queen Victoria

Queen Victoria reigned from 1837 to 1901. During her reign, although the modern powerlessness of the monarch was confirmed (she was often forced to accept as Prime Ministers people she personally disliked), she herself became an increasingly popular symbol of Britain's success in the world. As a hard-working, religious mother of nine children, devoted to her husband, Prince Albert, she was regarded as the personification of contemporary morals. The idea that the monarch should set an example to the people in such matters was unknown before this time and created problems for the monarchy in the twentieth century (see chapter 7).

1902
Nationwide selective secondary education is introduced.

1908
The first old-age pensions are introduced.

1911
The power of the House of Lords is severely reduced.
Sick pay for most workers is introduced.

1914
Britain declares war on Germany. Until the 1940s, the First World War was known in Britain as 'the Great War'.

1916
The 'Easter Rising' in Ireland against British rule is suppressed. Its leaders are executed.

1918
The right to vote is extended to include women over the age of thirty.

1920
The British government partitions Ireland.

the rulers of an empire was therefore a matter of moral obligation. It was, in fact, known as 'the white man's burden' (▷ *The White Man's Burden*).

There were great changes in social structure. Most people now lived in towns and cities. They no longer depended on country landowners for their living but rather on the owners of industries. These factory owners held the real power in the country, along with the new and growing middle class of tradespeople. As they established their power, so they established a set of values which emphasized hard work, thrift, religious observance, family life, an awareness of one's duty, absolute honesty in public life and extreme respectability in sexual matters. This is the set of values which we now call Victorian.

Middle-class religious conviction, together with a conscious belief that reform was better than revolution, allowed reforms in political and public life to take place. Britain was gradually turning into something resembling a modern state. There were not only political reforms, but also reforms which recognized some human rights (as we now call them). Slavery and the laws against people on the basis of religion were abolished, and laws were made to protect workers from some of the worst forms of exploitation resulting from the industrial mode of production. Public services such as the police force were set up.

Despite reform, the nature of the new industrial society forced many people to live and work in very unpleasant conditions. Writers and intellectuals of this period either protested against the horrors of this new style of life (as Dickens did) or simply ignored it. Many, especially the Romantic poets, praised the beauties of the countryside and the simplicity of country life. This was a new development. In previous centuries the countryside had just existed, and it wasn't something to be discussed or admired. But from this time on, most British people developed a sentimental attachment to the idea of the countryside (see chapter 5).

▶ The White Man's Burden

Here are some lines from the poem of this title by Rudyard Kipling (1865–1936), who is sometimes referred to as 'the poet of imperialism'.

Take up the White Man's burden –
Send forth the best ye breed –
Go, bind your sons to exile
To serve your captives' need;
To wait in heavy harness
On fluttered folk and wild –
Your new-caught, sullen peoples,
Half-devil and half-child.

Other races, the poem says, are 'wild' and have a 'need' to be civilized. The white man's noble duty is to 'serve' in this role. This is not a quest for mere power. The duty is bestowed by God, whom Kipling invokes in another poem (Recessional) in a reference to the British empire in tropical lands;

God of our fathers, known of old,
Lord of our far-flung battle-line,
Beneath whose awful hand we hold
Dominion over palm and pine –

1921
Treaty between Britain and the Irish Parliament in Dublin is signed.

1922
The Irish Free State is born.

1926
General Strike

1928
The right to vote is extended again. All men and women over the age of twenty-one can now vote.

1939
Britain declares war on Germany.

1944
Free compulsory secondary education (up to the age of fifteen) is established and secondary modern schools are set up (see chapter 14).

1946
The National Health Service is established (see chapter 18).
Coal mines and railways are nationalized. Other industries follow (see chapter 15).

1949
Ireland becomes a republic.

1953
Coronation of Elizabeth II

1958
The Clean Air Act is the first law of widespread application to attempt to control pollution (see chapter 3).

1959
The first motorway is opened (see chapter 17).

The twentieth century

By the beginning of this century, Britain was no longer the world's richest country. Perhaps this caused Victorian confidence in gradual reform to weaken. Whatever the reason, the first twenty years of the century were a period of extremism in Britain. The Suffragettes, women demanding the right to vote, were prepared both to damage property and to die for their beliefs; the problem of Ulster in the north of Ireland led to a situation in which some sections of the army appeared ready to disobey the government; and the government's introduction of new types and levels of taxation was opposed so absolutely by the House of Lords that even Parliament, the foundation of the political system, seemed to have an uncertain future in its traditional form. But by the end of the First World War, two of these issues had been resolved to most people's satisfaction (the Irish problem remained) and the rather un-British climate of extremism died out.

The significant changes that took place in the twentieth century are dealt with elsewhere in this book. Just one thing should be noted here. It was from the beginning of this century that the urban working class (the majority of the population) finally began to make its voice heard. In Parliament, the Labour party gradually replaced the Liberals (the 'descendants' of the Whigs) as the main opposition to the Conservatives (the 'descendants' of the Tories). In addition, trade unions managed to organize themselves. In 1926, they were powerful enough to hold a General Strike, and from the 1930s until the 1980s the Trades Union Congress (see chapter 14) was probably the single most powerful political force outside the institutions of government and Parliament.

1963
The school-leaving age is raised to sixteen.

1968
The 'age of majority' (the age at which somebody legally becomes an adult) is reduced from twenty-one to eighteen.

1969
British troops are sent to Northern Ireland.
Capital punishment is abolished.

1971
Decimal currency is introduced (see chapter 15).

1973
Britain joins the European Economic Community.

1981
Marriage of Prince Charles and Lady Diana Spencer.

1982
Falklands War (see chapter 12)

1984
Privatization of British Telecom. This is the first time that shares in a nationalized company are sold direct to the public (see chapter 15).

1990
Gulf War (see chapter 12)

1994
Channel tunnel opens.

QUESTIONS

1 1066 *And All That* is the title of a well-known joke history book published before the Second World War which satirizes the way that history was taught in British schools at the time. This typically involved memorizing lots of dates. Why, do you think, did the writers choose this title?

2 In 1986, the BBC released a computer-video package of detailed information about every place in Britain. It took a long time to prepare this package but the decision to publish it in 1986 (and not, for example, 1985 or 1987) was deliberate. What is significant about the date?

3 Which of the famous names in popular British history could be described as 'resistance fighters'?

4 Around the year 1500, about 5 million people used the English language – less than the population of Britain at the time. Today, it is estimated that at least 600 million people use English regularly in everyday life – at least ten times the present population of Britain. Why has the use of English expanded so much in the last 500 years?

5 How would you describe the changing relationship between religion and politics in British history? Are the changes that have taken place similar to those that have occurred in your country?

6 Britain is unusual among European countries in that, for more than 300 years now, there has not been a single revolution or civil war. What reasons can you find in this chapter which might help to explain this stability?

SUGGESTIONS

- *Understanding Britain* by John Randle (Basil Blackwell, Oxford) is a very readable history of Britain, written with the student in mind.
- *The Story of English* is a BBC series of nine programmes which is available on video. Episodes 2–4 are largely historical in content and very interesting.
- There is a strong tradition of historical novels in English (set at various times in Britain's history). The writings of Georgette Heyer, Norah Lofts, Jean Plaidy, Rosemary Sutcliffe and Henry and Geoffrey Treece are good examples.

3
Geography

It has been claimed that the British love of compromise is the result of the country's physical geography. This may or may not be true, but it is certainly true that the land and climate in Britain have a notable lack of extremes. Britain has mountains, but none of them are very high; it also has flat land, but you cannot travel far without encountering hills; it has no really big rivers; it doesn't usually get very cold in the winter or very hot in the summer; it has no active volcanoes, and an earth tremor which does no more than rattle teacups in a few houses is reported in the national news media.

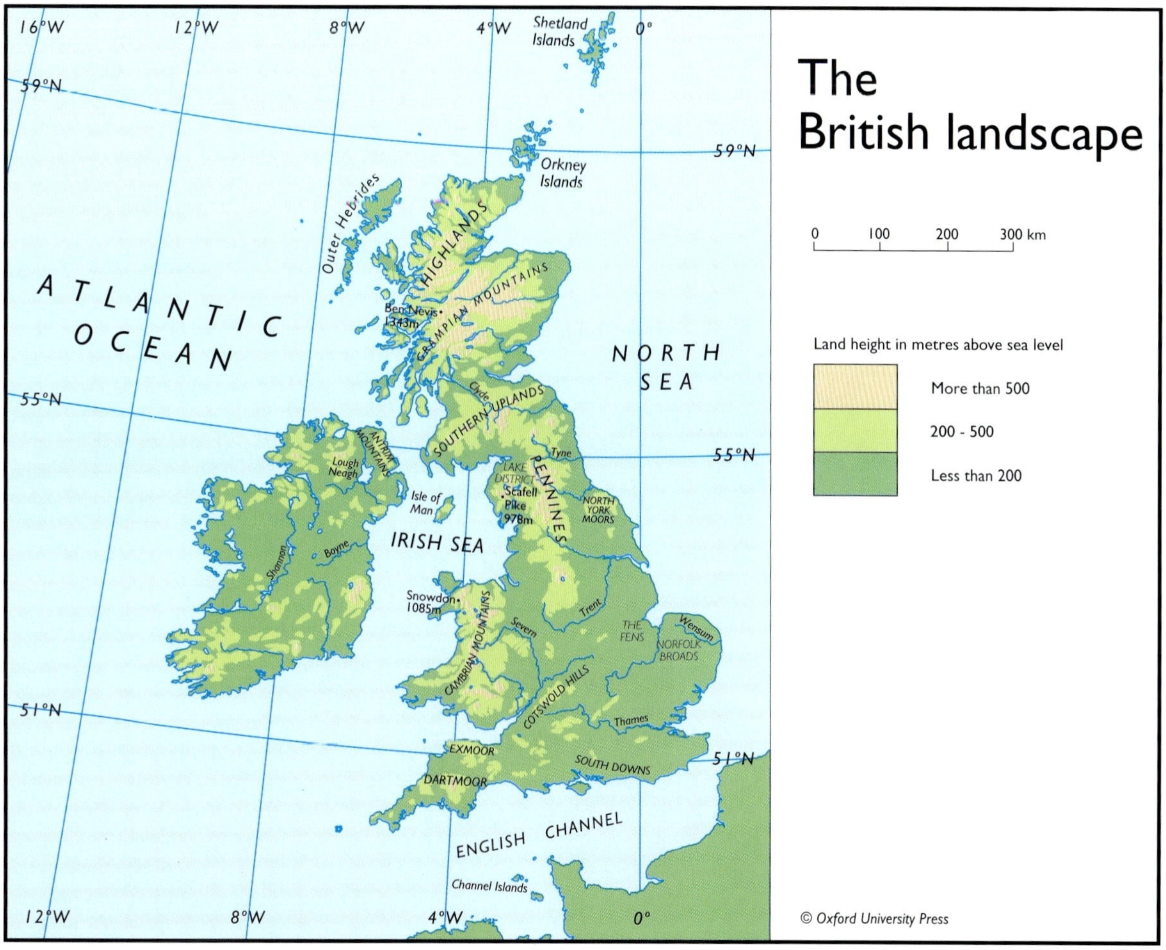

The British landscape

Climate

The climate of Britain is more or less the same as that of the north-western part of the European mainland. The popular belief that it rains all the time in Britain is simply not true. The image of a wet, foggy land was created two thousand years ago by the invading Romans and has been perpetuated in modern times by Hollywood. In fact, London gets no more rain in a year than most other major European cities, and less than some (▷ *How wet is Britain?*).

The amount of rain that falls on a town in Britain depends on where it is. Generally speaking, the further west you go, the more rain you get. The mild winters mean that snow is a regular feature of the higher areas only. Occasionally, a whole winter goes by in lower-lying parts without any snow at all. The winters are in general a bit colder in the east of the country than they are in the west, while in summer, the south is slightly warmer and sunnier than the north.

Why has Britain's climate got such a bad reputation? Perhaps it is for the same reason that British people always seem to be talking about the weather. This is its changeability. There is a saying that Britain doesn't have a climate, it only has weather. It may not rain very much altogether, but you can never be sure of a dry day; there can be cool (even cold) days in July and some quite warm days in January.

The lack of extremes is the reason why, on the few occasions when it gets genuinely hot or freezing cold, the country seems to be totally unprepared for it. A bit of snow and a few days of frost and the trains stop working and the roads are blocked; if the thermometer goes above 80°F (27°C) (▷ *How hot or cold is Britain?*), people behave as if they were in the Sahara and the temperature makes front-page headlines. These things happen so rarely that it is not worth organizing life to be ready for them.

▶ How wet is Britain?

Annual total rainfall (approximate) in some European cities

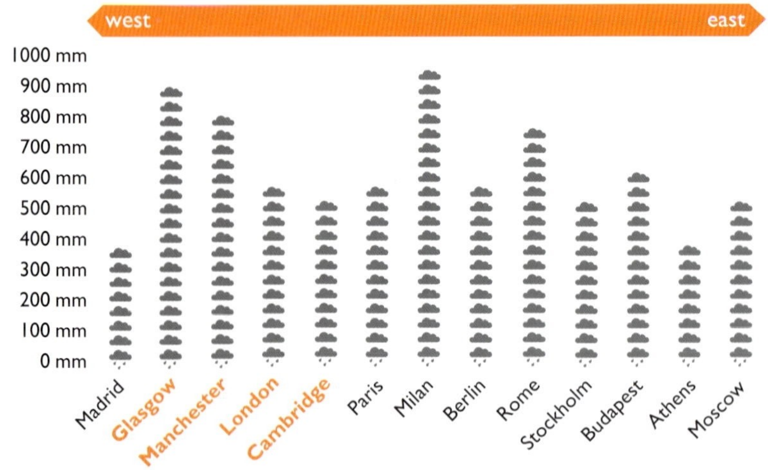

Land and settlement

Britain has neither towering mountain ranges, nor impressively large rivers, plains or forests. But this does not mean that its landscape is boring. What it lacks in grandeur it makes up for in variety. The scenery changes noticeably over quite short distances. It has often been remarked that a journey of 100 miles (160 kilometres) can, as a result, seem twice as far. Overall, the south and east of the country is comparatively low-lying, consisting of either flat plains or gently rolling hills. Mountainous areas are found only in the north and west, although these regions also have flat areas (▷ *The British landscape*).

Human influence has been extensive. The forests that once covered the land have largely disappeared. Britain has a greater proportion of grassland than any other country in Europe except the Republic of Ireland. One distinctive human influence, especially common in southern England, is the enclosure of fields with hedgerows. This feature increases the impression of variety. Although many hedgerows have disappeared in the second half of the twentieth century (farmers have dug them up to increase the size of their fields and become more efficient), there are still enough of them to support a great variety of bird-life.

▶ How hot or cold is Britain?

Annual temperature range (from hottest month to coldest month) in some European cities

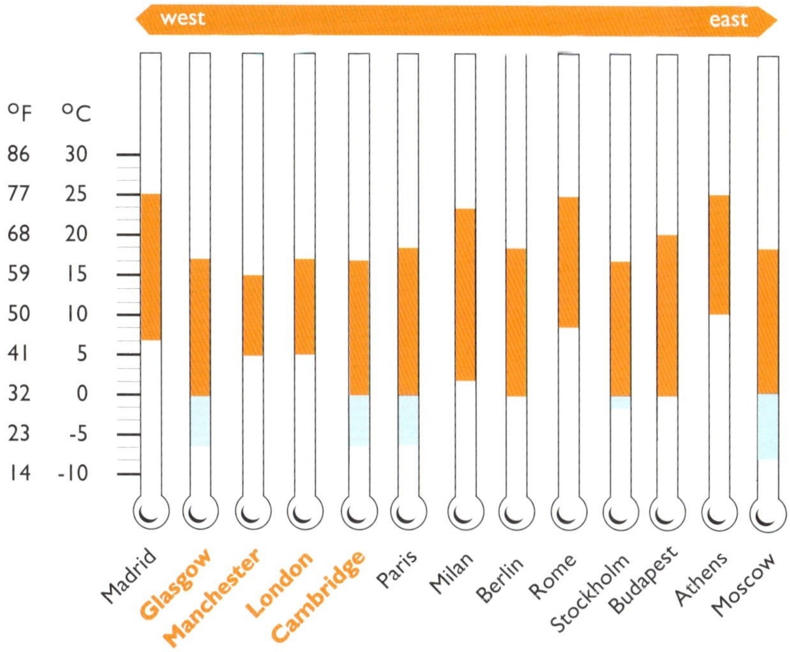

Most people in Britain are happier using the Fahrenheit scale of measurement (F). To them, a temperature 'in the upper twenties' means that it is freezing and one 'in the low seventies' will not kill you – it is just pleasantly warm.

▶ The vanishing coastline

Britain is an island under constant attack from the surrounding sea. Every year, little bits of the east coast vanish into the North Sea. Sometimes the land slips away slowly. But at other times it slips away very suddenly. In 1993 a dramatic example of this process occurred near the town of Scarborough in Yorkshire.

The Holbeck Hotel, built on a clifftop overlooking the sea, had been the best hotel in town for 110 years. But on the morning of 4 June, guests awoke to find cracks in the walls and the doors stuck. When they looked out of the window, instead of seeing fifteen metres of hotel garden, they saw nothing – except the sea. There was no time to collect their belongings. They had to leave the hotel immediately. During the day various rooms of the hotel started leaning at odd angles and then slipped down the cliff. The Holbeck Hotel's role in the tourism industry was over. However, by 'dying' so dramatically, it provided one last great sight for tourists. Hundreds of them watched the action throughout the day.

The Holbeck Hotel falling into the sea

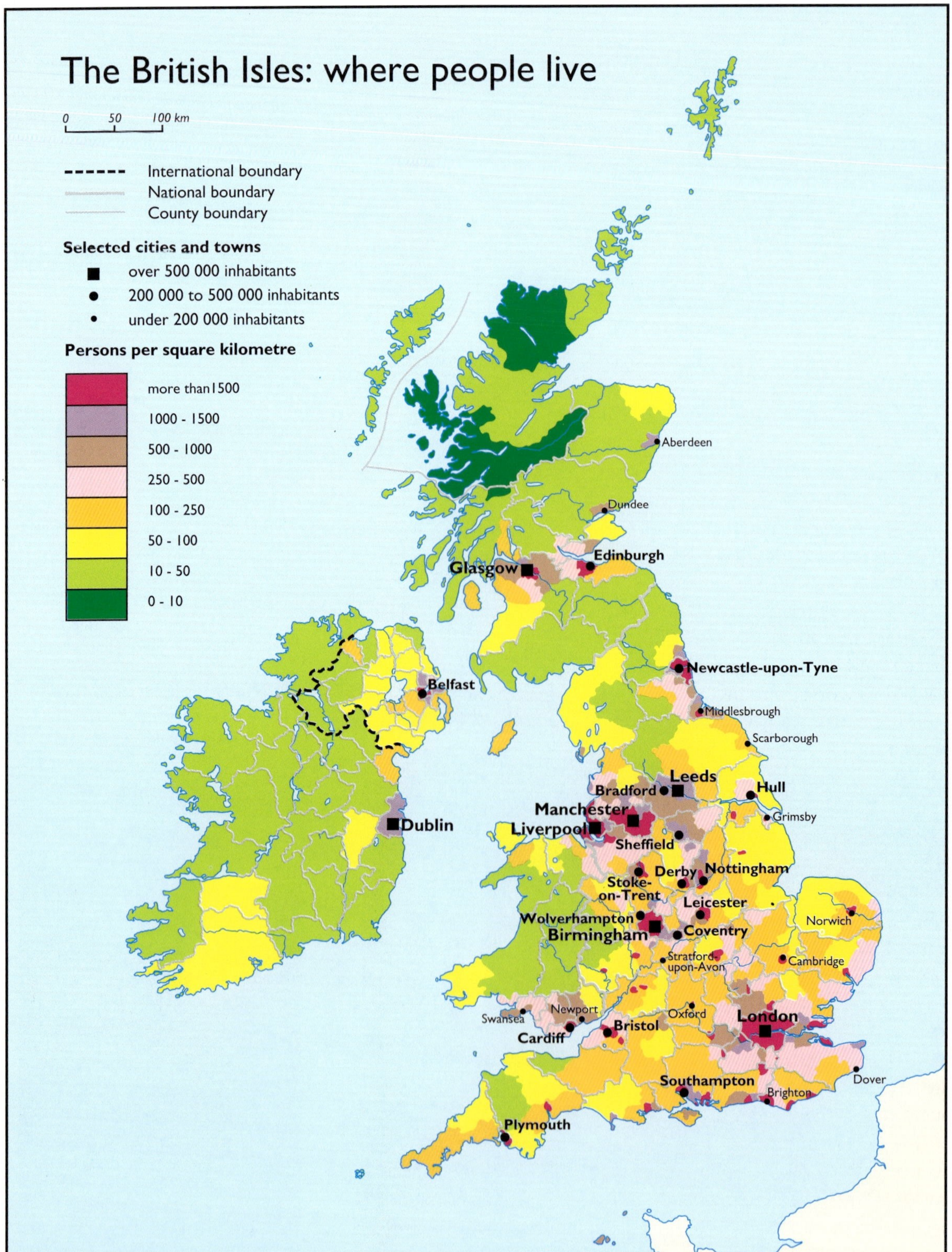
The British Isles: where people live
0 50 100 km
International boundary
National boundary
County boundary
Selected cities and towns
over 500 000 inhabitants
200 000 to 500 000 inhabitants
under 200 000 inhabitants
Persons per square kilometre
more than 1500
1000 - 1500
500 - 1000
250 - 500
100 - 250
50 - 100
10 - 50
0 - 10
Aberdeen
Dundee
Edinburgh
Glasgow
Belfast
Newcastle-upon-Tyne
Middlesbrough
Scarborough
Leeds
Bradford
Hull
Manchester
Grimsby
Dublin
Liverpool
Sheffield
Derby
Nottingham
Stoke-on-Trent
Leicester
Wolverhampton
Norwich
Birmingham
Coventry
Stratford-upon-Avon
Cambridge
Newport
Oxford
London
Swansea
Bristol
Cardiff
Dover
Southampton
Brighton
Plymouth

Much of the land is used for human habitation. This is not just because Britain is densely populated (▷ *The British Isles: where people live*). Partly because of their desire for privacy and their love of the countryside (see chapter 5), the English and the Welsh don't like living in blocks of flats in city centres and the proportion of people who do so is lower than in other European countries. As a result, cities in England and Wales have, wherever possible, been built outwards rather than upwards (although this is not so much the case in Scottish cities). For example, Greater London has about three times the population of greater Athens but it occupies ten times the area of land.

However, because most people (about 75%) live in towns or cities rather than in villages or in the countryside, this habit of building outwards does not mean that you see buildings wherever you go in Britain. There are areas of completely open countryside everywhere and some of the mountainous areas remain virtually untouched.

The environment and pollution

It was in Britain that the word 'smog' was first used (to describe a mixture of smoke and fog). As the world's first industrialized country, its cities were the first to suffer this atmospheric condition. In the nineteenth century London's 'pea-soupers' (thick smogs) became famous through descriptions of them in the works of Charles Dickens and in the Sherlock Holmes stories. The situation in London reached its worst point in 1952. At the end of that year a particularly bad smog, which lasted for several days, was estimated to have caused between 4,000 and 8,000 deaths.

Water pollution was also a problem. In the nineteenth century it was once suggested that the Houses of Parliament should be wrapped in enormous wet sheets to protect those inside from the awful smell of the River Thames. Until the 1960s, the first thing that happened to people who fell into the Thames was that they were rushed to hospital to have their stomachs pumped out!

Then, during the 1960s and 1970s, laws were passed which forbade the heating of homes with open coal fires in city areas and which stopped much of the pollution from factories. At one time, a scene of fog in a Hollywood film was all that was necessary to symbolize London. This image is now out of date, and by the end of the 1970s it was said to be possible to catch fish in the Thames outside Parliament.

However, as in the rest of western Europe, the great increase in the use of the motor car in the last quarter of the twentieth century caused an increase in a new kind of air pollution. This problem has become so serious that the television weather forecast now regularly issues warnings of 'poor air quality'. On some occasions it is bad enough to prompt official advice that certain people (such as asthma sufferers) should not even leave their houses, and that nobody should take any vigorous exercise, such as jogging, out of doors.

London

London (the largest city in Europe) dominates Britain. It is home for the headquarters of all government departments, Parliament, the major legal institutions and the monarch. It is the country's business and banking centre and the centre of its transport network. It contains the headquarters of the national television networks and of all the national newspapers. It is about seven times larger than any other city in the country. About a fifth of the total population of the UK lives in the Greater London area.

The original walled city of London was quite small. (It is known colloquially today as 'the square mile'.) It did not contain Parliament or the royal court, since this would have interfered with the autonomy of the merchants and traders who lived and worked there. It was in Westminster, another 'city' outside London's walls, that these national institutions met. Today, both 'cities' are just two areas of central London. The square mile is home to the country's main financial organizations, the territory of the stereotypical English 'city gent'. During the daytime, nearly a million people work there, but less than 8,000 people actually live there.

Two other well-known areas of London are the West End and the East End. The former is known for its many theatres, cinemas and expensive shops. The latter is known as the poorer residential area of central London. It is the home of the Cockney (see chapter 4) and in the twentieth century large numbers of immigrants settled there.

There are many other parts of central London which have their own distinctive characters, and central London itself makes up only a very small part of Greater London. In common with many other European cities, the population in the central area has decreased in the second half of the twentieth century. The majority of 'Londoners' live in its suburbs, millions of them travelling into the centre each day to work. These suburbs cover a vast area of land.

Like many large cities, London is in some ways untypical of the rest of the country in that it is so cosmopolitan. Although all of Britain's cities have some degree of cultural and racial variety, the variety is by far the greatest in London. A survey carried out in the 1980s found that 137 different languages were spoken in the homes of just one district.

In recent years it has been claimed that London is in decline. It is losing its place as one of the world's biggest financial centres and, in comparison with many other western European cities, it looks rather dirty and neglected. Nevertheless, its popularity as a tourist destination is still growing. And it is not only tourists who like visiting London – the readers of *Business Traveller* magazine often vote it their favourite city in the world in which to do business. This popularity is probably the result of its combination of apparently infinite cultural variety and a long history which has left many visible signs of its richness and drama.

Southern England

The area surrounding the outer suburbs of London has the reputation of being 'commuter land'. This is the most densely populated area in the UK which does not include a large city, and millions of its inhabitants travel into London to work every day.

Further out from London the region has more of its own distinctive character. The county of Kent, which you pass through when travelling from Dover or the Channel tunnel to London, is known as 'the garden of England' because of the many kinds of fruit and vegetables grown there. The Downs, a series of hills in a horseshoe shape to the south of London, are used for sheep farming (though not as intensively as they used to be). The southern side of the Downs reaches the sea in many places and forms the white cliffs of the south coast. Many retired people live along this coast. Employment in the south-east of England is mainly in trade, the provision of services and light manufacturing. There is little heavy industry. It has therefore not suffered the slow economic decline of many other parts of England.

The region known as 'the West Country' has an attractive image of rural beauty in British people's minds – notice the use of the word 'country' in its name. There is some industry and one large city (Bristol was once Britain's most important port after London), but farming is more widespread than it is in most other regions. Some parts of the west country are well-known for their dairy produce, such as Devonshire cream, and fruit. The south-west peninsula, with its rocky coast, numerous small bays (once noted for smuggling activities) and wild moorlands such as Exmoor and Dartmoor, is the most popular holiday area in Britain. The winters are so mild in some low-lying parts that it is even possible to grow palm trees, and the tourist industry has coined the phrase 'the English Riviera'.

East Anglia, to the north-east of London, is also comparatively rural. It is the only region in Britain where there are large expanses of uniformly flat land. This flatness, together with the comparatively dry climate, has made it the main area in the country for the growing of wheat and other arable crops. Part of this region, the area known as the Fens, has been reclaimed from the sea, and much of it still has a very watery, misty feel to it. The Norfolk Broads, for example, are criss-crossed by hundreds of waterways but there are no towns here, so this is a popular area for boating holidays.

Farmland in southeast England

Land's End, the extreme southwest point of England

The Midlands

Birmingham is Britain's second largest city. During the Industrial Revolution (see chapter 2), Birmingham, and the surrounding area of the West Midlands (sometimes known as the Black Country) developed into the country's major engineering centre. Despite the decline of heavy industry in modern times, factories in this area still convert iron and steel into a vast variety of goods.

▶ The north-south divide

There are many aspects of life in Britain which illustrate the so-called 'north-south divide'. This is a well-known fact of British life, although there is no actual geographical boundary. Basically, the south has almost always been more prosperous than the north, with lower rates of unemployment and more expensive houses. This is especially true of the south-eastern area surrounding London. This area is often referred to as the 'Home Counties'. The word 'home' in this context highlights the importance attached to London and its domination of public life.

An industrial town in northern England

There are other industrial areas in the Midlands, notably the towns between the Black Country and Manchester known as The Potteries (famous for producing china such as that made at the factories of Wedgewood, Spode and Minton), and several towns in the East Midlands, such as Derby, Leicester and Nottingham. On the east coast, Grimsby, although a comparatively small town, is one of Britain's most important fishing ports.

Although the midlands do not have many positive associations in the minds of British people, tourism has flourished in 'Shakespeare country' (centred on Stratford-upon-Avon, Shakespeare's birthplace), and Nottingham has successfully capitalized on the legend of Robin Hood (see chapter 2).

Northern England

The Pennine mountains run up the middle of northern England like a spine. On either side, the large deposits of coal (used to provide power) and iron ore (used to make machinery) enabled these areas to lead the Industrial Revolution in the eighteenth century. On the western side, the Manchester area (connected to the port of Liverpool by canal) became, in the nineteenth century, the world's leading producer of cotton goods; on the eastern side, towns such as Bradford and Leeds became the world's leading producers of woollen goods. Many other towns sprang up on both sides of the Pennines at this time, as a result of the growth of certain auxiliary industries and of coal mining. Further south, Sheffield became a centre for the production of steel goods. Further north, around Newcastle, shipbuilding was the major industry.

In the minds of British people the prototype of the noisy, dirty factory that symbolizes the Industrial Revolution is found in the industrial north. But the achievements of these new industrial towns also induced a feeling of civic pride in their inhabitants and an energetic realism, epitomized by the clichéd saying 'where there's muck there's brass' (wherever there is dirt, there is money to be made).

The decline in heavy industry in Europe in the second half of the twentieth century hit the industrial north of England hard. For a long time, the region as a whole has had a level of unemployment significantly above the national average.

The towns on either side of the Pennines are flanked by steep slopes on which it is difficult to build and are surrounded by land most of which is unsuitable for any agriculture other than sheep farming. Therefore, the pattern of settlement in the north of England is often different from that in the south. Open and uninhabited countryside is never far away from its cities and towns. The typically industrial and the very rural interlock. The wild, windswept moors which are the setting for Emily Brontë's famous novel *Wuthering Heights* seem a world away from the smoke and grime of urban life – in fact, they are just up the road (about 15 kilometres) from Bradford!

Further away from the main industrial areas, the north of England is sparsely populated. In the north-western corner of the country is the Lake District. The Romantic poets of the nineteenth century, Wordsworth, Coleridge and Southey (the 'Lake Poets'), lived here and wrote about its beauty. It is the favourite destination of people who enjoy walking holidays and the whole area is classified as a National Park (the largest in England).

Scotland

Scotland has three fairly clearly-marked regions. Just north of the border with England are the southern uplands, an area of small towns, quite far apart from each other, whose economy depends to a large extent on sheep farming. Further north, there is the central plain. Finally, there are the highlands, consisting of mountains and deep valleys and including numerous small islands off the west coast. This area of spectacular natural beauty occupies the same land area as southern England but fewer than a million people live there. Tourism is important in the local economy, and so is the production of whisky.

It is in the central plain and the strip of east coast extending northwards from it that more than 80% of the population of Scotland lives. In recent times, this region has had many of the same difficulties as the industrial north of England, although the North Sea oil industry has helped to keep unemployment down.

Scotland's two major cities have very different reputations. Glasgow is the third largest city in Britain. It is associated with heavy industry and some of the worst housing conditions in Britain (the district called the Gorbals, although now rebuilt, was famous in this respect). However, this image is one-sided. Glasgow has a strong artistic heritage. A hundred years ago the work of the Glasgow School (led by Mackintosh) put the city at the forefront of European design and architecture. In 1990, it was the European City of Culture. Over the centuries, Glasgow has received many immigrants from Ireland and in some ways it reflects the divisions in the community that exist in Northern Ireland (see chapter 4). For example, of its two rival football teams, one is Catholic (Celtic) and the other is Protestant (Rangers).

Edinburgh, which is half the size of Glasgow, has a comparatively middle-class image (although class differences between the two cities are not really very great). It is the capital of Scotland and is associated with scholarship, the law and administration. This reputation, together with its many fine historic buildings, and also perhaps its topography (there is a rock in the middle of the city on which stands the castle) has led to its being called 'the Athens of the north'. The annual Edinburgh Festival of the arts is internationally famous (see chapter 22).

Part of Snowdonia National Park

Wales

As in Scotland, most people in Wales live in one small part of it. In the Welsh case, it is the south-east of the country that is most heavily populated. Coal has been mined in many parts of Britain, but just as British people would locate the prototype factory of the industrial revolution in the north of England, so they would locate its prototype coal mine in south Wales. Despite its industry, no really large cities have grown up in this area (Cardiff, the capital of Wales, has a population of about a quarter of a million). It is the only part of Britain with a high proportion of industrial villages. Coal mining in south Wales has now ceased and, as elsewhere, the transition to other forms of employment has been slow and painful.

Most of the rest of Wales is mountainous. Because of this, communication between south and north is very difficult. As a result, each part of Wales has closer contact with its neighbouring part of England than it does with other parts of Wales: the north with Liverpool, and mid-Wales with the English west midlands. The area around Mount Snowdon in the north-west of the country is very beautiful and is the largest National Park in Britain.

Northern Ireland

With the exception of Belfast, which is famous for the manufacture of linen (and which is still a shipbuilding city), this region is, like the rest of Ireland, largely agricultural. It has several areas of spectacular natural beauty. One of these is the Giant's Causeway on its north coast, so-called because the rocks in the area form what look like enormous stepping stones.

QUESTIONS

1 Bearing in mind its climate and general character, which part of Britain would you choose to live in? Why? Is this the same part that you would like to visit for a holiday? Why (not)?
2 How is the pattern of human settlement in your country different from that in Britain?
3 Does the capital city of your country stand in the same relation to the rest of the country as London does to Britain?
4 The two big television news organizations in Britain, the BBC and ITN, both have 'North of England' correspondents. But neither has a 'South of England' correspondent. Why do you think this is? What is it an example of?
5 In the short 'tour' of the regions of Britain in this chapter, some sections are longer than others. This is partly because some regions have 'higher profiles' than others – that is, more is known or imagined about them than others. Which are the regions in Britain that seem to have the higher profiles? What do their reputations consist of?

SUGGESTIONS

- *Spotlight on Britain* by Sheerin, Seath and White (Oxford University Press) is a book written for the non-native student of Britain using a geographical approach.
- If you enjoy travel writing, there are several books which offer accounts of journeys through or around Britain. *The Kingdom by the Sea* by the respected novelist Paul Theroux (Penguin) is an example.
- There are many nineteenth century English novels which invoke a sense of place. The action in Thomas Hardy's novels, such as *Return of the Native* and *Tess of the D'Urbervilles*, usually takes place in the south west of England (mainly the county of Dorset), in an area which Hardy called Wessex. *Wuthering Heights* by Emily Brontë has the Yorkshire moors as its setting. More recently, Graham Swift's novel *Waterland* (Picador), as its title suggests, takes account of the effect of the landscape of the fens in East Anglia on the actions of the people who live there.

4
Identity

How do British people identify themselves? Who do they feel they are? Everybody has an image of themselves, but the things that make up this image can vary. For example, in some parts of the world, it is very important that you are a member of a particular family; in other parts of the world, it might be more important that you come from a particular place; in others, that you belong to a certain social class. This chapter explores the loyalties and senses of identity most typically felt by British people.

Ethnic identity: the native British

National ('ethnic') loyalties can be strong among the people in Britain whose ancestors were not English (see chapter 1). For some people living in England who call themselves Scottish, Welsh or Irish, this loyalty is little more than a matter of emotional attachment. But for others, it goes a bit further and they may even join one of the sporting and social clubs for 'exiles' from these nations. These clubs promote national folk music, organize parties on special national days and foster a consciousness of doing things differently from the English. For people living in Scotland, Wales and Northern Ireland, the way that ethnic identity commonly expresses itself varies. People in Scotland have constant reminders of their distinctiveness. First, several important aspects of public life are organized separately, and differently, from the rest of Britain – notably, education, law and religion. Second, the Scottish way of speaking English is very distinctive. A modern form of the dialect known as Scots (see chapter 2) is spoken in everyday life by most of the working classes in the lowlands. It has many features which are different from other forms of English and cannot usually be understood by people who are not Scottish. Third, there are many symbols of Scottishness which are well-known throughout Britain (see chapter 1).

However, the feeling of being Scottish is not that simple (▷ *What does it mean to be Scottish?*). This is partly because of the historical cultural split between highland and lowland Scotland (see chapter 2). A genuinely Scottish Gaelic sense of cultural identity is, in modern times, felt only by a few tens of thousands of people in some of the western isles of Scotland and the adjoining mainland. These people speak Scottish Gaelic (which they call 'Gallic') as a first language.

What does it mean to be Scottish?

On 25 January every year, many Scottish people attend 'Burns' suppers'. At these parties they read from the work of the eighteenth century poet Robert Burns (regarded as Scotland's national poet), wear kilts, sing traditional songs, dance traditional dances (called 'reels') and eat haggis (made from sheep's heart, lungs and liver).

Here are two opposing views of this way of celebrating Scottishness.

The ceremonial cutting of the haggis at a Burns' supper

The sentimental nationalist

That national pride that ties knots in your stomach when you see your country's flag somewhere unexpected is particularly strong among the Scots. On Burns' Night, people all over the world fight their way through haggis and Tam o'Shanter[1], not really liking either. They do it because they feel allegiance to a small, wet, under-populated, bullied country stuck on the edge of Europe.

Many Scottish Scots hate the romantic, sentimental view of their country; the kilts, the pipes, the haggis, Bonnie Prince Charlie. The sight of a man in a skirt, or a Dundee cake[2], makes them furious. To them, this is a tourist view of Scotland invented by the English. But I adore the fierce romantic, tartan, sentimental Scotland. The dour McStalinists are missing the point – and the fun.

In the eighteenth century, the English practically destroyed Highland Scotland. The normalizing of relations between the two countries was accomplished by a novelist, Sir Walter Scott, whose stories and legends intrigued and excited the English. Under his direction, the whole country reinvented itself. Everyone who could get hold of a bit of tartan wore a kilt, ancient ceremonies were invented. In a few months, a wasteland of dangerous beggarly savages became a nation of noble, brave, exotic warriors. Scott did the best public relations job in history.

The realpolitik[3] Scot doesn't see it like that. He only relates to heavy industry, 1966 trade unionism and a supposed class system that puts Englishmen at the top of the heap and Scottish workers at the bottom. His heart is in the Gorbals, not the Highlands. But I feel moved by the pipes, the old songs, the poems, the romantic stories, and the tearful, sentimental nationalism of it all.

A A Gill, *The Sunday Times*,
23 January 1994 (adapted)

1 the title of a poem by Burns, and also the name for the traditional cap of highland dress
2 a rich fruit cake, supposedly originating from the town of Dundee
3 an approach to politics based on realities and material needs

The realist

When I assure English acquaintances that I would rather sing a chorus of Land of Hope and Glory[1] than attend a Burns' supper, their eyebrows rise. Who could possibly object to such a fun night out?

In fact, only a few Scots are prepared to suffer the boredom of these occasions. The people who are really keen on them aren't Scottish at all. They *think* they are, especially on 25 January or Saint Andrew's Day or at international matches at Murrayfield[2], when they all make a great business of wearing kilts, dancing reels, reciting their Tam o'Shanters and trying to say 'loch'[3] properly without coughing up phlegm. But these pseudo-Scots have English accents because they went to posh public schools. They are Scottish only in the sense that their families have, for generations, owned large parts of Scotland – while living in London.

This use of Scottish symbols by pseudo-Scots makes it very awkward for the rest of us Scots. It means that we can't be sure which bits of our heritage are pure. Tartan? Dunno[4]. Gay Gordons?[5] Don't care. Whisky? No way, that's ours. Kilts worn with frilly shirts? Pseudo-Scottish. Lions rampant? Ours, as any Hampden[6] crowd will prove. And Burns' suppers? The Farquhar-Seaton-Bethune-Buccleuchs[7] can keep them. And I hope they all choke on their haggis.

Harry Ritchie, *The Sunday Times*,
23 January 1994 (adapted)

1 a patriotic British song which refers to the 'rebellious Scots'
2 the Scottish national rugby stadium
3 'loch' is Gaelic for 'lake'
4 i.e. 'I don't know'
5 the name of a particular reel
6 the Scottish national football stadium
7 ▷*What's in a name?*

A sign in Welsh and English

The people of Wales do not have as many reminders of their Welshness in everyday life. The organization of public life is similar to that in England. Nor are there as many well-known symbols of Welshness. In addition, a large minority of the people in Wales probably do not consider themselves to be especially Welsh at all. In the nineteenth century large numbers of Scottish, Irish and English people went to find work there, and today many English people still make their homes in Wales or have holiday houses there. As a result, a feeling of loyalty to Wales is often similar in nature to the fairly weak loyalties to particular geographical areas found throughout England (see below) – it is regional rather than nationalistic.

However, there is one single highly-important symbol of Welsh identity – the Welsh language. Everybody in Wales can speak English, but it is not everybody's first language. For about 20% of the population (that's more than half a million people), the mother-tongue is Welsh. For these people Welsh identity obviously means more than just living in the region known as Wales. Moreover, in comparison to the other small minority languages of Europe, Welsh shows signs of continued vitality. Thanks to successive campaigns, the language receives a lot of public support. All children in Wales learn it at school, there are many local newspapers in Welsh, there is a Welsh television channel and nearly all public notices and signs are written in both Welsh and English.

▶ **Meibion Glyndwr**

Most of the Welsh-speaking Welsh feel a certain hostility to the English cultural invasion of their country. Usually, this feeling is not personal. But sometimes it can be, and there are extremist groups who use violence to achieve their aims. This newspaper article describes the actions of one such group.

Trouble at Llangybi

Every morning, Ray and Jan Sutton check their mail and car for bombs. Targeted last week by arsonists, the defiant English couple are deaf to the abuse hurled from passing vehicles at their village shop.

The Suttons are holding out against an ultimatum to leave Wales by St David's day next year or be burnt out of the village store they have run for seven years at Llangybi.

They are on a hit list issued by the mysterious group Meibion Glyndwr, or Sons of Glendower[1]. Over the past thirteen years the Sons of Glendower have left a fiery trail of destruction across north and west Wales, claiming responsibility for attacks on English holiday homes, estate agents, boatyards and shops.

Last year, Ray Sutton refused to put up a poster in Welsh. The shop's policy for the past twenty-six years had been to accept only bilingual posters, he said. The warning letter he received read 'You are an English colonist, you are racist and anti-Welsh. You are on Meibion Glyndwr's blacklist. You must leave Wales by the first of March 1993.'

Julian Cayo-Evans, a local businessman and former 'supreme commandant' of the Free Wales Army, denied having links with the terrorist group but said, 'They have a point. Young Welsh people are forced to emigrate whereas these crooks from Birmingham buy second homes and live in them for three weeks of the year.'

Stuart Wavell, *The Sunday Times*, 15 November 1992

[1] Owen Glendower fought against the English in medieval times.

The question of identity in Northern Ireland is a much more complex issue and is dealt with at the end of this chapter.

As for English identity, most people who describe themselves as English usually make no distinction in their minds between 'English' and 'British'. There is plenty of evidence of this. For example, at international football or rugby matches, when the players stand to attention to hear their national anthems, the Scottish, Irish and Welsh have their own songs, while the English one is just 'God Save the Queen' – the same as the British national anthem.

Ethnic identity: the non-native British

The long centuries of contact between the peoples of the four nations of the British Isles means that there is a limit to their significant differences. With minor variations, they look the same, speak the same language, eat the same food, have the same religious heritage (Christianity) and have the same attitudes to the roles of men and women.

The situation for the several million people in Britain whose family roots lie in the Caribbean or in south Asia or elsewhere in the world is different. For them, ethnic identity is more than a question of deciding which sports team to support. Non-whites (about 6% of the total British population) cannot, as white non-English groups can, *choose* when to advertise their ethnic identity and when not to.

Most non-whites, although themselves born in Britain, have parents who were born outside it. The great wave of immigration from the Caribbean and south Asia took place between 1950 and 1965. These immigrants, especially those from south Asia, brought with them different languages, different religions (Hindu and Muslim) and everyday habits and attitudes that were sometimes radically different from traditional British ones. As they usually married among themselves, these habits and customs have, to some extent, been preserved. For some young people brought up in Britain, this mixed cultural background can create problems. For example, many young Asians resent the fact that their parents expect to have more control over them than most black or white parents expect to have over their children. Nevertheless, they cannot avoid these experiences, which therefore make up part of their identity.

As well as this 'given' identity, non-white people in Britain often take pride in their cultural roots. This pride seems to be *increasing* as their cultural practices, their everyday habits and attitudes, gradually become *less* distinctive. Most of the country's non-whites are British citizens. Partly because of this, they are on the way to developing the same kind of division of loyalties and identity that exists for many Irish, Scottish and Welsh people. Pride can increase as a defensive reaction to racial discrimination. There is quite a lot of this in Britain. There are tens of thousands of racially motivated attacks on people every year, including one or two murders. All in all, however, overt racism is not as common as it is in many other parts of Europe.

▶ **Children born outside marriage in Britain**

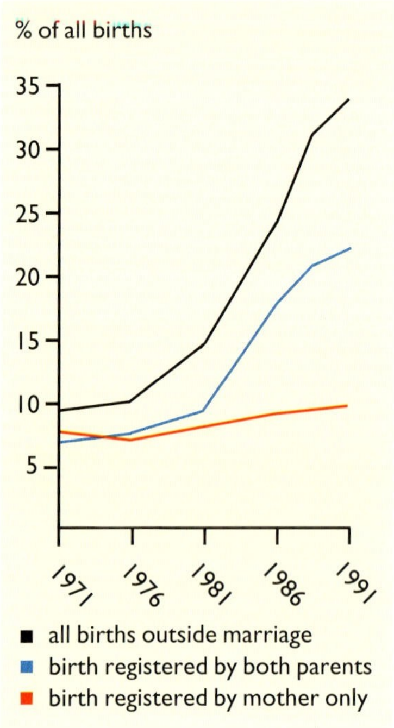

Source: Key Data

The family

In comparison with most other places in the world, family identity is rather weak in Britain, especially in England. Of course, the family unit is still the basic living arrangement for most people. But in Britain this definitely means the nuclear family. There is little sense of extended family identity, except among some racial minorities. This is reflected in the size and composition of households. It is unusual for adults of different generations within the family to live together. The average number of people living in each household in Britain is lower than in most other European countries. The proportion of elderly people living alone is similarly high (▷ *Family size*).

Significant family events such as weddings, births and funerals are not automatically accompanied by large gatherings of people. It is still common to appoint people to certain roles on such occasions, such as 'best man' at a wedding, or godmother and godfather when a child is born. But for most people these appointments are of sentimental significance only. They do not imply lifelong responsibility. In fact, family gatherings of any kind beyond the household unit are rare. For most people, they are confined to the Christmas period.

Even the stereotyped nuclear family of father, mother and children is becoming less common. Britain has a higher rate of divorce than anywhere else in Europe except Denmark and the proportion of children born outside marriage has risen dramatically and is also one of the highest (about a third of all births) (▷ *Children born outside marriage in Britain*). However, these trends do not necessarily mean that the nuclear family is disappearing. Divorces have increased, but the majority of marriages in Britain (about 55%) do not break down. In addition, it is notable that about three-quarters of all births outside marriage are officially registered by both parents and more than half of the children concerned are born to parents who are living together at the time.

▶ **Family size**

Source: Europe in Figures

Geographical identity

A sense of identity based on place of birth is, like family identity, not very common or strong in most parts of Britain – and perhaps for the same reason. People are just too mobile and very few live in the same place all their lives. There is quite a lot of local pride, and people find many opportunities to express it. This pride, however, arises because people are happy to live in what they consider to be a nice place and often when they are fighting to preserve it. It does not usually mean that the people of a locality feel strongly that they *belong* to that place.

A sense of identity with a larger geographical area is a bit stronger. Nearly everybody has a spoken accent that identifies them as coming from a particular large city or region. In some cases there is quite a strong sense of identification. Liverpudlians (from Liverpool), Mancunians (from Manchester), Geordies (from the Newcastle area) and Cockneys (from London) are often proud to be known by these names (▷ *What is a Cockney?*). In other cases, identity is associated with a county. These are the most ancient divisions of England. Although their boundaries and names do not always conform to the modern arrangement of local government (see chapter 6), they still claim the allegiance of some people. Yorkshire, in the north of England, is a notable example. Another is Cornwall, in the south-west corner of England. Even today, some Cornish people still talk about 'going to England' when they cross the county border – a testament to its ethnic Celtic history.

Many English people see themselves as either 'northerners' or 'southerners'. The fact that the south is on the whole richer than the north, and the domination of the media by the affairs of London and the south-east, leads to resentment in the north. This reinforces the pride in their northern roots felt by many northerners, who, stereotypically, see themselves as tougher, more honest and warmer-hearted than the soft, hypocritical and unfriendly southerners. To people in the south, the stereotypical northerner (who is usually male) is rather ignorant and uncultured and interested only in sport and beer-drinking.

Regional identity is often felt strongly at sporting events such as football matches

▶ What is a Cockney?

Traditionally, a true Cockney is anybody born within the sound of Bow bells (the bells of the church of St Mary-le-Bow in the East End of London). In fact, the term is commonly used to denote people who come from a wider area of the inner-most eastern suburbs of London and also an adjoining area south of the Thames.

'Cockney' is also used to describe a strong London accent and, like any such local accent, is associated with working-class origins.

A feature of Cockney speech is rhyming slang, in which, for example, 'wife' is referred to as 'trouble and strife', and 'stairs' as 'apples and pears' (usually shortened to 'apples'). Some rhyming slang has passed into general informal British usage; some examples are 'use your loaf', which means 'think' (from 'loaf of bread' = 'head') and 'have a butcher's', which means 'have a look' (from 'butcher's hook' = 'look').

▶ What's in a name?

In England, the notion of the honour of the family name is almost non-existent (though it exists to some degree in the upper classes, in the other three British nations and among ethnic minorities). In fact, it is very easy to change your family name – and you can choose any name you like. In the 1980s one person changed his surname to Oddsocks McWeirdo El Tutti Frutti Hello Hippopotamus Bum.

There are no laws in Britain about what surname a wife or child must have. Because of this freedom, names can be useful pointers to social trends. The case of double-barrelled names is an example. These are surnames with two parts separated by a hyphen; for example, Barclay-Finch. For centuries they have been a symbol of upper-class status (originating in the desire to preserve an aristocratic name when there was no male heir). Until recently, most people in Britain have avoided giving themselves double-barrelled names – they would have been laughed at for their pretensions. In 1962, only one in every 300 surnames was double-barrelled.

By 1992, however, one person in fifty had such a name. Why the change? One reason is feminism. Although an increasing number of women now keep their maiden name when they marry, it is still normal to take the husband's name. Independent-minded women are now finding a compromise by doing both at the same time – and then passing this new double-barrelled name onto their children. Another motive is the desire of parents from different cultural and racial backgrounds for their children to have a sense of both of their heritages.

The same lack of rigid tradition applies with regard to the first names that can be given to children. This is usually simply a matter of taste. Moreover, the concept of celebrating name-days is virtually unknown.

Class

Historians say that the class system has survived in Britain because of its flexibility. It has always been possible to buy or marry or even work your way up, so that your children (and their children) belong to a higher social class than you do. As a result, the class system has never been swept away by a revolution and an awareness of class forms a major part of most people's sense of identity.

People in modern Britain are very conscious of class differences. They regard it as difficult to become friends with somebody from a different class. This feeling has little to do with conscious loyalty, and nothing to do with a positive belief in the class system itself. Most people say they do not approve of class divisions. Nor does it have very much to do with political or religious affiliations. It results from the fact that the different classes have different sets of attitudes and daily habits. Typically, they tend to eat different food at different times of day (and call the meals by different names – see chapter 20), they like to talk about different topics using different styles and accents of English, they enjoy different pastimes and sports (see chapter 21), they have different values about what things in life are most important and different ideas about the correct way to behave. Stereotypically, they go to different kinds of school (see chapter 14).

An interesting feature of the class structure in Britain is that it is not just, or even mainly, relative wealth or the appearance of it which determines someone's class. Of course, wealth is part of it – if you become wealthy, you can provide the conditions to enable your children to belong to a higher class than you do. But it is not always possible to guess reliably the class to which a person belongs by looking at his or her clothes, car or bank balance. The most obvious and immediate sign comes when a person opens his or her mouth, giving the listener clues to the speaker's attitudes and interests, both of which are indicative of class.

But even more indicative than *what* the speaker says is the *way* that he or she says it. The English grammar and vocabulary which is used in public speaking, radio and television news broadcasts, books and newspapers (and also – unless the lessons are run by Americans – as a model for learners of English as a foreign language) is known as 'standard British English'. Most working-class people, however, use lots of words and grammatical forms in their everyday speech which are regarded as 'non-standard'.

Nevertheless, nearly everybody in the country is capable of using standard English (or something very close to it) when they judge that the situation demands it. They are taught to do so at school. Therefore, the clearest indication of a person's class is often his or her accent. Most people cannot change this convincingly to suit the situation. The most prestigious accent in Britain is known as 'Received Pronunciation' (RP). It is the combination of standard English spoken with an RP accent that is usually meant when people

Scene: Night has just fallen. The ex-queen and her husband arrive with a driver in a furniture van (with all their belongings in it), ready to move in to the house which they have been allotted. Their new neighbours, Tony and Beverly Threadgold, are standing at the front door of their house.

The Threadgolds watched as a shadowy figure ordered a tall man out of the van. Was she a foreigner? It wasn't English she was talking was it? But as their ears became more accustomed they realized it was English, but posh English, *really* posh.

'Tone, why they moved a posho in Hell Close?' asked Beverly.

'Dunno,' replied Tony, peering into the gloom, 'Christ, just our bleedin'[1] luck to have poshos nex' door.'[2]

A few minutes later, the Queen addressed them. 'Excuse me, but would you have an axe I could borrow?'

'An *ix*?' repeated Tony.

'Yes, an axe.' The Queen came to their front gate.

'An *ix*?' puzzled Beverly.

'Yes.'

'I dunno what an "ix" is,' Tony said.

'You don't know what an axe is?'

'No.'

'One uses it for chopping wood.' The Queen was growing impatient. She had made a simple request; her new neighbours were obviously morons. She was aware that educational standards had fallen, but not to know what an *axe* was . . . It was a scandal.

'I need an implement of some kind to gain access to my house.'

'Arse?'

'*House!*'

The driver volunteered his services as translator. His hours talking to the Queen on the motorway had given him confidence.

'This lady wants to know if you've got an *axe*.'

Just then, the Queen came down the garden path towards the Threadgolds and the light from their hall illuminated her face. Beverly gasped. Tony clutched the front-door frame for support before saying, 'It's out the back, I'll geddit.'

Left alone, Beverly burst into tears.

'I mean, who would believe it?' she said later, as she and Tony lay in bed unable to sleep. 'I still don't believe it, Tone.'

'Nor do I, Bev. I mean, the Queen next door. We'll put in for a transfer, eh?'[3]

Slightly comforted, Beverly went to sleep.

From *The Queen and I* by Sue Townsend

[1] a fairly strong swear word

[2] i.e. he is automatically unhappy about somebody from a different class moving in next door

[3] i.e. they will ask the local council to move them to another house

Poshos

The extract on the left illustrates how people from different classes do not like to mix and how language is an important aspect of class. It is taken from a fantasy novel in which a republican government is elected in Britain and the royal family are sent to live on a working-class housing estate, in a road known to its inhabitants as 'Hell Close'.

talk about 'BBC English' or 'Oxford English' (referring to the university, not the town) or 'the Queen's English'.

RP is not associated with any particular part of the country. The vast majority of people, however, speak with an accent which is geographically limited. In England and Wales, anyone who speaks with a strong regional accent is automatically assumed to be working class. Conversely, anyone with an RP accent is assumed to be upper or upper-middle class. (In Scotland and Northern Ireland, the situation is slightly different; in these places, some forms of regional accent are almost as prestigious as RP.)

During the last quarter of the twentieth century, the way that people wish to identify themselves seems to have changed. In Britain, as anywhere else where there are recognized social classes, a certain amount of 'social climbing' goes on; that is, people try to appear as if they belong to as high a class as possible. These days, however, nobody wants to be thought of as snobbish. The word 'posh' illustrates this tendency. It is used by people from all classes to mean 'of a class higher than the one I (the speaker) belong to' and it is normally used with negative connotations. To accuse someone of being posh is to accuse them of being pretentious.

Working-class people in particular are traditionally proud of their class membership and would not usually wish to be thought of as belonging to any other class. Interestingly, a survey conducted in the early 1990s showed that the proportion of people who describe themselves as working class is actually greater than the proportion whom sociologists would classify as such! This is one manifestation of a phenomenon known as 'inverted snobbery', whereby middle-class people try to adopt working-class values and habits. They do this in the belief that the working classes are in some way 'better' (for example, more honest) than the middle classes.

In this egalitarian climate, the unofficial segregation of the classes in Britain has become less rigid than it was. A person whose accent shows that he or she is working class is no longer prohibited from most high-status jobs for that reason alone. Nobody takes elocution lessons any more in order to sound more upper class. It is now acceptable for radio and television presenters to speak with 'an accent' (i.e. not to use strict RP). It is also notable that, at the time of writing, only one of the last six British Prime Ministers went to an élitist school for upper-class children, while almost every previous Prime Minister in history did.

In general, the different classes mix more readily and easily with each other than they used to. There has been a great increase in the number of people from working-class origins who are houseowners (see chapter 19) and who do traditionally middle-class jobs (see chapter 15). The lower and middle classes have drawn closer to each other in their attitudes.

▶ The three classes

A stereotyped view of the upper, middle and working classes (left to right), as seen in a satirical television programme, *Frost over England*, in 1967. This view is now quite a long way from the reality, but still lives on in people's minds.

A stereotyped representation of the three classes

Men and women

Generally speaking, British people invest about the same amount of their identity in their gender as people in other parts of northern Europe do. On the one hand, society no longer overtly endorses differences in the public and social roles of men and women, and it is illegal to discriminate on the basis of sex. On the other hand, people still (often unconsciously) expect a fairly large number of differences in everyday behaviour and domestic roles.

In terms of everyday habits and mannerisms, British society probably expects a sharper difference between the sexes than most other European societies do. For example, it is still far more acceptable for a man to look untidy and scruffy than it is for a woman; and it is still far more acceptable for a woman to display emotions and be demonstrably friendly than it is for a man to do so.

As far as roles are concerned, most people assume that a family's financial situation is not just the responsibility of the man. On the other hand, they would still normally complement the woman, not the man, on a beautifully decorated or well-kept house. Everyday care of the children is still seen as mainly the woman's responsibility. Although almost as many women have jobs as men, nearly half of the jobs done by women are part-time. In fact, the majority of mothers with children under the age of twelve either have no job or work only during school hours. Men certainly take a more active domestic role than they did forty years ago. Some things, however, never seem to change. A comparison of child-rearing habits of the 1950s and the 1980s showed that the proportion of men who never changed a baby's nappy had remained the same (40%)!

In general, the sharpest distinction between the expected roles and behaviour of the two sexes is found in the lower and upper classes. The distinction is far less clear among the middle classes, but it is still there.

At the public level there are contradictions. Britain was one of the first European countries to have a woman Prime Minister and a woman chairperson of debate in its Parliament. However, in the early nineties, only about 5% of MPs were women, only 20% of lawyers in Britain were women, less than 10% of accountants were women and there was one female consultant brain surgeon in the whole country (see also chapter 15).

At the 1997 election the proportion of women MPs increased sharply (to 18%) and nearly every institution in the country has opened its doors to women now. One of the last to do so was the Anglican Church, which, after much debate, decided in favour of the ordination of women priests in 1993. However, there are a few institutions which, at the time of writing, still don't accept female members – for example, the Oxford and Cambridge Club in London, an association for graduates of these two universities.

Religious and political identity

In comparison with some other European countries, and with the one notable exception of Northern Ireland (see below), neither religion nor politics is an important part of people's social identity in modern Britain. This is partly because the two do not, as they do in some other countries, go together in any significant way.

Of course, there are many people who regard themselves as belonging to this or that church or party. Some people among the minority who are regular churchgoers and the very small minority who are active members of political parties feel this sense of belonging strongly and deeply. It may form a very important part of their own idea of themselves as individuals. But even for these people it plays little part in determining other aspects of their lives such as where they work, which trade union they belong to, who their friends are or who they would like their neighbours to be. For the vast majority of parents in the country (some ethnic groups excepted), the religion or voting habits of their future son-in-law's or daughter-in-law's family are of only passing interest and rarely the major cause of objection to the proposed marriage.

Social and everyday contacts

British people give a relatively high value to the everyday personal contacts that they make. Some writers on Britain have talked about the British desire to 'belong', and it is certainly true that the pub, or the working man's club, or the numerous other clubs devoted to various sports and pastimes play a very important part in many people's lives. In these places people forge contacts with other people who share some of the same interests and attitudes. For many people these contacts are an important part of their social identity. Another factor is work. Many people make their social contacts through work and, partly as a result of this, the profession or skill which they practise is also an important aspect of their sense of identity. However, since British people do not spend more of their free time out of the house than most other Europeans do, these means of self-identification should not be over-emphasized.

Identity in Northern Ireland

In this part of the UK, the pattern of identity and loyalty outlined above does not apply. Here, ethnicity, family, politics and religion are all inter-related, and social class has a comparatively minor role in establishing identity. Northern Ireland is a polarized society where most people are born into, and stay in, one or other of the two communities for the whole of their lives.

On one side of the divide are people whose ancestors came from lowland Scotland or England. They are self-consciously Protestant and want Northern Ireland to remain in the UK. On the other side

A divided community

This is the wall, built in 1984, which separates the Catholic Falls Road from the Protestant Shankhill Road – a vivid sign of segregation in Belfast.

are people whose ancestors were native Irish. They are self-consciously Catholic and would like Northern Ireland to become part of the Irish Republic.

Although the two communities live side-by-side, their lives are almost entirely segregated. They live in different housing estates, listen to different radio and television programmes, register with different doctors, have prescriptions made up by chemists of their own denominations, march to commemorate different anniversaries and read different newspapers. Their children go to different schools, so that those who go on to university often find themselves mixing with people from the 'other' community for the first time in their lives. For the majority who do not go to university, merely talking to somebody from the other community is a rare event.

In this atmosphere, marrying a member of the other community is traditionally regarded with horror, and has sometimes even resulted in the deaths of the Romeos and Juliets concerned (as punishment for the 'betrayal' of their people). The extremes of these hard-line attitudes are gradually softening. It should also be noted that they apply to a much lesser extent among the middle-classes. It is illustrative of this that while in football, a mainly working-class sport, Northern Ireland and the Republic have separate teams, in rugby, a more middle-class sport, there is only one team for the whole of Ireland, in which Protestants from the north play alongside Catholics from the south with no sign of disharmony whatsoever.

Being British

Last of all, a few words about *British* identity and loyalty. How important is it to British people that they are British? Do they feel they 'belong' to Britain?

Perhaps because of the long tradition of a clear separation between the individual and the state, British people, although many of them feel proud to be British, are not normally actively patriotic. They often feel uncomfortable if, in conversation with somebody from another country, that person refers to 'you' where 'you' means Britain or the British government. They are individualistic and do not like to feel that they are personally representing their country.

During the last quarter of the twentieth century there was a dramatic and severe loss of confidence in British public institutions (see chapter 6). Nearly one third of the people questioned in an opinion poll in the early 1990s said that they could think of nothing about Britain to be proud of. In addition, almost half said that they would emigrate if they could – suggesting a low degree of attachment to the country. This decrease in confidence was accompanied by a change in the previous rather patronizing attitude to foreigners and foreign ways. In the days of empire, foreigners were often considered amusing, even interesting, but not really to be taken seriously. These days, many foreign ways of doing things are admired (although perhaps a bit resentfully) and there is a greater openness to foreign influences.

Along with this openness, however, goes a sense of vulnerability, so that patriotism often takes a rather defensive form. For instance, there are worries about the loss of British identity in the European Union (see chapter 12). This is perhaps why the British cling so obstinately to certain distinctive ways of doing things, such as driving on the left and using different systems of measurement (see chapter 5).

It is in this climate of opinion that the dramatic increase in support for the government during the Falklands/Malvinas War in 1982 must be interpreted (see chapter 12). Here was a rare modern occasion for the British people to be actively patriotic. Many of them felt that here, for once, Britain was doing something right and doing it effectively!

The modern British are not really chauvinistic. Open hostility to people from other countries is very rare. If there is any chauvinism at all, it expresses itself through ignorance. Most British people know remarkably little about Europe and who lives there. The popular image of Europe seems to be that it is something to do with the French. An entry in the *Radio Times* can serve as an example. This is a very popular magazine which gives details of all the week's radio and television programmes. In April 1994 it subtitled its introduction to a programme which previewed that year's entries for the Eurovision Song Contest as 'tips for le top'. Notice the 'le'. It is an indication of the apparently widespread assumption that Europe is a place where everybody speaks French.

The British continue to be very bad about learning other peoples' languages. Fluency in any European language other than English is generally regarded as exotic. But there is nothing defensive or deliberate about this attitude. The British do not refuse to speak other languages. They are just lazy.

QUESTIONS

1. In the early years of the twentieth century, the playwright and social commentator George Bernard Shaw remarked that an Englishman only had to open his mouth to make some other Englishman despise him. What was he talking about? Would he say the same thing today?
2. In the 1930s people in middle-class neighbourhoods often reacted angrily to the building of housing estates for the working class nearby. In one area they even built a wall to separate the two neighbourhoods! This could never happen today. Why not? What has changed?
3. Standard English is used 'naturally' in everyday speech by between 15% and 30% of the population in Britain (it depends how you define it). Received pronunciation (RP), again depending on how you define it, is used in everyday speech by only 3% to 12% of the population. So why is standard English with an RP accent the usual model for people learning British English as a foreign language? What justification can you find for this practice?
4. Do the social classes in your country differentiate themselves in the same ways as they do in Britain? Do language, accent, clothes, money, habits and attitudes play the same roles in your country?
5. This chapter considers several factors that can go towards creating a person's sense of identity. Some of these are more important in Britain and some are less important. Are the same factors the important ones in your country?

SUGGESTIONS

- Many BBC television comedy programmes depend for much of their humour on habits and values determined by social class. Recent examples (which you may be able to get on video) include *Only Fools and Horses* and *Birds of a Feather*, both of which portray Cockney values, and *Keeping Up Appearances*, which makes fun of the pretentiousness of some middle-class people.
- If you are interested in accents and dialects, *English Accents and Dialects* by Hughes and Trudgill (Edward Arnold) is an academic book with long texts exemplifying the main types of English spoken in Britain. There is an accompanying cassette.
- *The Queen and I* by Sue Townsend (Mandarin) is fun to read and portrays working class characters humorously contrasted with members of the upper classes (the royal family).

5
Attitudes

The British, like the people of every country, tend to be attributed with certain characteristics which are supposedly typical. However, it is best to be cautious about accepting such characterizations too easily, and in the case of Britain there are three particular reasons to be cautious. The first three sections of this chapter deal with them in turn and comment on several stereotyped images of the British.

Stereotypes and change

Societies change over time while their reputations lag behind. Many things which are often regarded as typically British derive from books, songs or plays which were written a long time ago and which are no longer representative of modern life. One example of this is the popular belief that Britain is a 'land of tradition'. This is what most tourist brochures claim (▷ *Land of tradition*). The claim is based on what can be seen in public life and on centuries of political continuity. And at this level – the level of *public* life – it is undoubtedly true. The annual ceremony of the state opening of Parliament, for instance, carefully follows customs which are centuries old (see chapter 9). So does the military ceremony of 'trooping the colour'. Likewise, the changing of the guard outside Buckingham Palace never changes.

However, in their private everyday lives, the British as individuals are probably less inclined to follow tradition than are the people of most other countries. There are very few ancient customs that are followed by the majority of families on special occasions. The country has fewer local parades or processions with genuine folk roots than most other countries have. The English language has fewer sayings or proverbs that are in common everyday use than many other languages do. The British are too individualistic for these things. In addition, it should be noted that they are the most enthusiastic video-watching people in the world – the very opposite of a traditional pastime!

There are many examples of supposedly typical British habits which are simply not typical any more. For example, the stereotyped image of the London 'city gent' includes the wearing of a bowler hat. In fact, this type of hat has not been commonly worn for a long time. Food and drink provide other examples. The traditional 'British' (or

▶ Land of tradition

A reputation for tradition can lead to its artificial preservation – or even its re-introduction. A notable example is the Asquith taxi. This was introduced onto the streets of London in 1994. It is an exact replica of London taxis of the 1930s (except, of course, that it has modern facilities – and a modern meter!). It is deliberately designed that way to appeal to tourists, who equate London with tradition.

Similarly, when London's famous red buses were privatized (sold to private companies) in the early 1990s, the different bus companies wanted to paint their buses in their company colours. The government ruled that all buses had to stay red because that is what the people of London wanted, and that is what the government believed would help the tourist trade.

An Asquith taxi

'English') breakfast is a large 'fry-up' (see chapter 20) preceded by cereal with milk and followed by toast, butter and marmalade, all washed down with lots of tea. In fact, only about 10% of the people in Britain actually have this sort of breakfast. Two-thirds have cut out the fry-up and just have the cereal, tea and toast. The rest have even less. What the vast majority of British people have in the mornings is therefore much closer to what they call a 'continental' (i.e. European) breakfast than it is to a 'British' one. The image of the British as a nation of tea-drinkers is another stereotype which is somewhat out of date. It is true that it is still prepared in a distinctive way (strong and with milk), but more coffee than tea is now bought in the country's shops. As for the tradition of afternoon tea with biscuits, scones, sandwiches or cake, this is a minority activity, largely confined to retired people and the leisured upper-middle class (although preserved in tea shops in tourist resorts).

Even when a British habit conforms to the stereotype, the wrong conclusions can sometimes be drawn from it. The supposed British love of queuing is an example. Yes, British people do form queues whenever they are waiting for something, but this does not mean that they enjoy it. In 1992, a survey found that the average wait to pay in a British supermarket was three minutes and twenty-three seconds, and that the average wait to be served in a bank was two minutes and thirty-three seconds. You might think that these times sound very reasonable. But *The Sunday Times* newspaper did not think so. It referred to these figures as a 'problem'. Some banks now promise to serve their customers 'within two minutes'. It would therefore seem wrong to conclude that their habit of queuing shows that the British are a patient people. Apparently, the British hate having to wait and have less patience than people in many other countries.

English versus British

Because English culture dominates the cultures of the other three nations of the British Isles (see chapter 1), everyday habits, attitudes and values among the peoples of the four nations are very similar. However, they are not identical, and what is often regarded as typically British may in fact be only typically English. This is especially true with regard to one notable characteristic – anti-intellectualism.

Among many people in Britain, there exists a suspicion of intelligence, education and 'high culture'. Teachers and academic staff, although respected, do not have as high a status as they do in most other countries. Nobody normally proclaims their academic qualifications or title to the world at large. No professor would expect, or want, to be addressed as 'Professor' on any but the most formal occasion. There are large sections of both the upper and working class in Britain who, traditionally at least, have not encouraged their children to go to university (see chapter 14). This lack of enthusiasm for education is certainly decreasing. Nevertheless, it is still unusual for

▶ Swots

The slang word 'swot' was first used in public schools (see chapter 14). It describes someone who works hard and does well academically. It is a term of abuse. Swots are not very popular. In the English mind, scholarship is something rather strange and exotic, so much so that the sight of the manager of a football team simply writing something down during a match is considered worthy of comment. During the 1990 English football Cup Final, when he saw this happening, the BBC commentator said (without apparent irony), 'And you can see Steve Coppell's been to university – he's taking notes!'

parents to arrange extra private tuition for their children, even among those who can easily afford it.

Anti-intellectual attitudes are held consciously only by a small proportion of the population, but an indication of how deep they run in society is that they are reflected in the English language. To refer to a person as somebody who 'gets all their ideas from books' is to speak of them negatively. The word 'clever' often has negative connotations. It suggests someone who uses trickery, a person who cannot quite be trusted (as in the expression 'too clever by half') (▷ *Swots*).

Evidence of this attitude can be found in all four nations of the British Isles. However, it is probably better seen as a specifically English characteristic and not a British one. The Scottish have always placed a high value on education for all classes. The Irish of all classes place a high value on being quick, ready and able with words. The Welsh are famous for exporting teachers to other parts of Britain and beyond.

Multiculturalism

The third reason for caution about generalizations relates to the large-scale immigration to Britain from places outside the British Isles in the twentieth century (see chapter 4). In its cities at least, Britain is a multicultural society. There are areas of London, for example, in which a distinctively Indian way of life predominates, with Indian shops, Indian clothes, Indian languages. Because in the local schools up to 90% of the pupils may be Indian, a distinctively Indian style of learning tends to take place.

These 'new British' people have brought widely differing sets of attitudes with them. For example, while some seem to care no more about education for their children than people in traditional English culture, others seem to care about it a great deal more.

However, the divergence from indigenous British attitudes in new British communities is constantly narrowing. These communities sometimes have their own newspapers but none have their own TV stations as they do in the United States. There, the numbers in such communities are larger and the physical space between them and other communities is greater, so that it is possible for people to live their whole lives in such communities without ever really learning English. This hardly ever happens in Britain.

It is therefore still possible to talk about British characteristics in general (as the rest of this chapter does). In fact, the new British have made their own contribution to British life and attitudes. They have probably helped to make people more informal (see below); they have changed the nature of the 'corner shop' (see chapter 15); the most popular, well-attended festival in the whole of Britain is the annual Notting Hill Carnival in London at the end of August, which is of Caribbean inspiration and origin.

Conservatism

The British have few living folk traditions and are too individualistic to have the same everyday habits as each other. However, this does not mean that they like change. They don't. They may not behave in traditional ways, but they like symbols of tradition and stability. For example, there are some very *untraditional* attitudes and habits with regard to the family in modern Britain (see chapter 4). Nevertheless, politicians often cite their enthusiasm for 'traditional family values' (both parents married and living together, parents as the main source of authority for children etc) as a way of winning support.

In general, the British value continuity over modernity for its own sake. They do not consider it especially smart to live in a new house and, in fact, there is prestige in living in an obviously old one (see chapter 19). They have a general sentimental attachment to older, supposedly safer, times. Their Christmas cards usually depict scenes from past centuries (see chapter 23); they like their pubs to look old (see chapter 20); they were reluctant to change their system of currency (see chapter 15).

Moreover, a look at children's reading habits suggests that this attitude is not going to change. Publishers try hard to make their books for children up-to-date. But perhaps they needn't try so hard. In 1992 the two most popular children's writers were noticeably un-modern (they were both, in fact, dead). The most popular of all was Roald Dahl, whose fantasy stories are set in a rather old-fashioned world. The second most popular writer was Enid Blyton, whose stories take place in a comfortable white middle-class world before the 1960s. They contain no references to other races or classes and mention nothing more modern than a radio. In other words, they are mostly irrelevant to modern life (▷ *Lord Snooty*).

▶ Lord Snooty

Lord Snooty illustrates the enthusiasm of British children for characters from earlier times. He first appeared in the *Beano*, a children's comic, in 1938. He is a young English aristocrat aged about ten, who loves sneaking out of his castle to play with local village children. He has always worn the same clothes, typical of wealthy youngsters of an earlier age but by now out of date. Surely, the children of the 1990s would prefer a present-day hero with whom to identify? That is what the editors of the *Beano* thought. In 1992 they decided to give Lord Snooty a rest. But loud protest followed, and he quickly found a new job in *The Funday Times* (the children's comic which is issued with *The Sunday Times* newspaper), as well as making further appearances in the *Beano*.

Lord Snooty

Being different

The British can be particularly and stubbornly conservative about anything which is perceived as a token of Britishness. In these matters, their conservatism can combine with their individualism; they are rather proud of being different. It is, for example, very difficult to imagine that they will ever agree to change from driving on the left-hand side of the road to driving on the right. It doesn't matter that nobody can think of any intrinsic advantage in driving on the left. Why should they change just to be like everyone else? Indeed, as far as they are concerned, *not* being like everyone else is a good reason *not* to change.

Developments at European Union (EU) level which might cause a change in some everyday aspect of British life are usually greeted with suspicion and hostility. The case of double-decker buses (see chapter 17) is an example. Whenever an EU committee makes a recommendation about standardizing the size and shape of these, it provokes warnings from British bus builders about 'the end of the double-decker bus as we know it'. The British public is always ready to listen to such predictions of doom.

Systems of measurement are another example. The British government has been trying for years and years to promote the metric system and to get British people to use the same scales that are used nearly everywhere else in the world. But it has had only limited success. British manufacturers are obliged to give the weight of their tins and packets in kilos and grams. But everybody in Britain still shops in pounds and ounces (see chapter 15). The weather forecasters on the television use the Celsius scale of temperature. But nearly everybody still thinks in Fahrenheit (see chapter 3). British people continue to measure distances, amounts of liquid and themselves using scales of measurement that are not used anywhere else in Europe (▷ *How far? How big? How much?*). Even the use of the 24-hour clock is comparatively restricted.

British governments sometimes seem to promote this pride in being different. In 1993 the managers of a pub in Slough (west of London) started selling glasses of beer which they called 'swifts' (25 cl) and 'larges' (50 cl), smaller amounts than the traditional British equivalents of half a pint and a pint. You might think that the authorities would have been pleased at this voluntary effort to adopt European habits. But they were not. British law demands that draught beer be sold in pints and half-pints only. The pub was fined £3,100 by a court and was ordered to stop selling the 'continental' measures. British governments have so far resisted pressure from business people to adopt Central European Time, remaining stubbornly one hour behind, and they continue to start their financial year not, as other countries do, at the beginning of the calendar year but at the beginning of April!

▶ **How far? How big? How much?**

Distances on road signs in Britain are shown in miles, not kilometres, and people talk about yards, not metres. If you described yourself as being 163 tall and weighing 67 kilos a British person would not be able to imagine what you looked like. You would have to say you were 'five foot four' (5 feet and 4 inches tall) and weighed 'ten stone seven' or 'ten and a half stone' (10 stone and 7 pounds). British people think in pounds and ounces when buying their cheese, in pints when buying their milk and in gallons when buying their petrol. Americans also use this non-metric system of weights and measures.

Imperial	Metric
1 inch	2.54 centimetres
12 inches (1 foot)	30.48 centimetres
3 feet (1 yard)	0.92 metres
1760 yards (1 mile)	1.6 kilometres
1 ounce	28.35 grams
16 ounces (1 pound)	0.456 kilograms
14 pounds (1 stone)	6.38 kilograms
1 pint	0.58 litres
2 pints (1 quart)	1.16 litres
8 pints (1 gallon)	4.64 litres

The love of nature

Most of the British live in towns and cities. But they have an idealized vision of the countryside. To the British, the countryside has almost none of the negative associations which it has in some countries, such as poor facilities, lack of educational opportunities, unemployment and poverty. To them, the countryside means peace and quiet, beauty, good health and no crime. Most of them would live in a country village if they thought that they could find a way of earning a living there. Ideally, this village would consist of thatched cottages (see chapter 19) built around an area of grass known as a 'village green'. Nearby, there would be a pond with ducks on it. Nowadays such a village is not actually very common, but it is a stereotypical picture that is well-known to the British.

Some history connected with the building of the Channel tunnel (see chapter 17) provides an instructive example of the British attitude. While the 'chunnel' was being built, there were also plans to build new high-speed rail links on either side of it. But what route would these new railway lines take? On the French side of the channel, communities battled with each other to get the new line built through their towns. It would be good for local business. But on the English side, the opposite occurred. Nobody wanted the rail link near them! Communities battled with each other to get the new line built somewhere else. Never mind about business, they wanted to preserve their peace and quiet.

Perhaps this love of the countryside is another aspect of British conservatism. The countryside represents stability. Those who live in towns and cities take an active interest in country matters and the British regard it as both a right and a privilege to be able to go 'into the country' whenever they want to. Large areas of the country are official 'national parks' where almost no building is allowed. There is an organization to which thousands of enthusiastic country walkers belong, the Ramblers' Association. It is in constant battle with landowners to keep open the public 'rights of way' across their lands. Maps can be bought which mark, in great detail, the routes of all the public footpaths in the country. Walkers often stay at youth hostels. The Youth Hostels Association is a charity whose aim is 'to help all, especially young people of limited means, to a greater knowledge, love and care of the countryside'. Their hostels are cheap and rather self-consciously bare and simple. There are more than 300 of them around the country, most of them in the middle of nowhere!

Even if they cannot get into the countryside, many British people still spend a lot of their time with 'nature'. They grow plants. Gardening is one of the most popular hobbies in the country. Even those unlucky people who do not have a garden can participate. Each local authority owns several areas of land which it rents very cheaply to these people in small parcels. On these 'allotments', people grow mainly vegetables.

Allotments in London

The National Trust

A notable indication of the British reverence for both the countryside and the past is the strength of the National Trust. This is an officially recognized charity whose aim is to preserve as much of Britain's countryside and as many of its historic buildings as possible by acquiring them 'for the nation'. With more than one-and-a-half million members, it is the largest conservation organization in the world. It is actually the third largest landowner in Britain (after the Crown and the Forestry Commission). It owns more than 500 miles of the coastline. The importance of its work has been supported by several laws, among which is one which does not allow even the government to take over any of its land without the approval of Parliament.

Polesden Lacey, built in the 1820s and now owned by the National Trust

▶ The railway cats

It is said that the British often treat their animals as if they were people. Well, this is true. One of the most common things that people do is to be employed. And so, on British railways, are cats. The names of Olive, Katie, Pickles and around 200 others appear on the company payroll, officially recognized as employees. Their job is to catch rats and other vermin. There is usually one cat per station. Their pay (tax free) is food, and they also get free medical treatment (without deductions from their salary). They are very popular with the human BR staff, who admit that their 'productivity rate' is not always very high (in other words, they don't catch many rats) but claim that they are good for morale.

▶ The RSPCA

The desire for animal welfare has official recognition. Cruelty to animals of any kind is a criminal offence. Such offences are investigated and acted upon by a well-known charity, the Royal Society for the Prevention of Cruelty to Animals (RSPCA).

The love of animals

Rossendale Pet Cemetery in Lancashire is just one example of an animal graveyard in Britain. It was started by a local farmer who ran over his dog with a tractor. He was so upset that he put up a headstone in memory of his dog. Now, Rossendale has thousands of graves and plots for caskets of ashes, with facilities for every kind of animal, from a budgie to a lioness. Many people are prepared to pay quite large sums of money to give their pets a decent burial (a trait they share with many Americans). As this example shows, the British tend to have a sentimental attitude to animals. Nearly half of the households in Britain keep at least one domestic pet. Most of them do not bother with such grand arrangements when their pets die, but there are millions of informal graves in people's back gardens. Moreover, the status of pets is taken seriously. It is, for example, illegal to run over a dog in your car and then keep on driving. You have to stop and inform the owner.

But the love of animals goes beyond sentimental attachment to domestic pets. Wildlife programmes are by far the most popular kind of television documentary. Millions of families have 'bird-tables' in their gardens. These are raised platforms on which birds can feed, safe from local cats, during the winter months. There is even a special hospital (St Tiggywinkles) which treats injured wild animals.

Perhaps this overall concern for animals is part of the British love of nature. Studies indicating that some wild species of bird or mammal is decreasing in numbers become prominent articles in the national press. Thousands of people are enthusiastic bird-watchers. This peculiarly British pastime often involves spending hours lying in wet and cold undergrowth, trying to get a glimpse of some rare species.

Formality and informality

The tourist view of Britain involves lots of formal ceremonies. Some people have drawn the conclusion from this that the British are rather formal in their general behaviour. This is not true. There is a difference between observing formalities and being formal in everyday life. Attitudes towards clothes are a good indication of this difference. It all depends on whether a person is playing a public role or a private role. When people are 'on duty', they have to obey some quite rigid rules. A male bank employee, for example, is expected to wear a suit with a tie, even if he cannot afford a very smart one. So are politicians. There was once a mild scandal during the 1980s because the Leader of the Opposition (see chapter 8) wore clothes on a public occasion which were considered too informal.

On the other hand, when people are not playing a public role – when they are just being themselves – there seem to be no rules at all. The British are probably more tolerant of 'strange' clothing than people in most other countries. You may find, for example, the same bank employee, on his lunch break in hot weather, walking through the streets with his tie round his waist and his collar unbuttoned. He is no longer 'at work' and for his employers to criticize him for his appearance would be seen as a gross breach of privacy. Perhaps because of the clothing formalities that many people have to follow during the week, the British, unlike the people of many other countries, like to 'dress down' on Sundays. They can't wait to take off their respectable working clothes and slip into something really scruffy. Lots of men who wear suits during the week can then be seen in old sweaters and jeans, sometimes with holes in them. And male politicians are keen to get themselves photographed *not* wearing a tie when 'officially' on holiday, to show that they are really ordinary people.

This difference between formalities and formality is the key to what people from other countries sometimes experience as a coldness among the British. The key is this: being friendly in Britain often involves showing that you are not bothering with the formalities. This means *not* addressing someone by his or her title (Mr, Mrs, Professor etc), *not* dressing smartly when entertaining guests, *not* shaking hands when meeting and *not* saying 'please' when making a request. When they avoid doing these things with you, the British are not being unfriendly or disrespectful, they are implying that you are in the category 'friend', and so all the rules can be ignored. To address someone by his or her title or to say 'please' is to observe formalities and therefore to put a distance between the people involved. The same is true of shaking hands. Although this sometimes has the reputation of being a very British thing to do, it is actually rather rare. Most people would do it only when being introduced to a stranger or when meeting an acquaintance (but not a friend) after a long time. Similarly, most British people do not feel welcomed if, on being invited to somebody's house, they find the hosts in smart clothes and a grand table set for them. They do not feel flattered by this, they feel intimidated. It makes them feel they can't relax.

It is probably true that the British, especially the English, are more reserved than the people of many other countries. They find it comparatively difficult to indicate friendship by open displays of affection. For example, it is not the convention to kiss when meeting a friend. Instead, friendship is symbolized by behaving as casually as possible. If you are in a British person's house, and you are told to 'help yourself' to something, your host is not being rude or suggesting that you are of no importance – he or she is showing that you are completely accepted and just like 'one of the family'.

In the last decades of the twentieth century, the general amount of informality increased. Buffet-type meals, at which people do not sit down at a table to eat, are now a common form of hospitality.
At the same time, the traditional reserve has also been breaking down. More groups in society now kiss when meeting each other (women and women, and men and women, but still never men and men!).

▶ The scruffy British

The British are comparatively uninterested in clothes. They spend a lower proportion of their income on clothing than people in most other European countries do. Many people buy second-hand clothes and are not at all embarrassed to admit this. If you are somewhere in a Mediterranean holiday area it is usually possible to identify the British tourist – he or she is the one who looks so badly dressed!

Public spiritedness and amateurism

In public life Britain has traditionally followed what might be called 'the cult of the talented amateur', in which being too professionally dedicated is looked at with suspicion. 'Only doing your job' has never been accepted as a justification for actions. There is a common assumption that society is best served by everybody 'chipping in' – that is, by lots of people giving a little bit of their free time to help in a variety of ways. This can be seen in the structure of the civil service (see chapter 8), in the circumstances under which Members of Parliament do their work (see chapter 9), in the use of unpaid non-lawyers to run much of the legal system (see chapter 11), in some aspects of the education system (see chapter 14), and in the fact that, until recently, many of the most popular sports in the country were officially amateur even at top level (see chapter 21).

This characteristic, however, is on the decline. In all the areas mentioned above, 'professionalism' has changed from having a negative connotation to having a positive one. Nevertheless, some new areas of amateur participation in public life have developed in the last decade, such as neighbourhood watch schemes (see chapter 11). Moreover, tens of thousands of 'amateurs' are still actively involved in charity work (see chapter 18). As well as giving direct help to those in need, they raise money by organizing jumble sales, fêtes and flag days (on which they stand in the street collecting money). This voluntary activity is a basic part of British life. It has often been so effective that whole countrywide networks have been set up without any government help at all (▷ *Self-help*). It is no accident that many of the world's largest and most well-known charities (for example, Oxfam, Amnesty International and the Save the Children Fund) began in Britain. Note also that, each year, the country's blood transfusion service collects over two million donations of blood from unpaid volunteers.

Volunteers ready to collect money for the RSPCA

▶ Self-help

The National Trust is one example of a charity which became very important without any government involvement. Another is the Family Planning Association. By 1938, this organization ran 935 clinics around Britain which gave advice and help regarding birth control to anybody who wanted it. Not until ten years later, with the establishment of the National Health Service (see chapter 18), did the British government involve itself in such matters.

A further example of 'self-help' is the Consumers' Association. In 1957, a small group of people working from an abandoned garage started *Which?*, a magazine exposing abuses in the marketplace, investigating trickery by manufacturers and comparing different companies' brands of the same product. Thirty years later, 900,000 people regularly bought this magazine and the Consumer's Association was making a £10 million surplus (not a 'profit' because it is a registered charity). By then it had successfully campaigned for many new laws protecting consumers and *Which?* had become the British consumer's bible.

▶ Supporting the underdog

Some customs of road use illustrate the British tendency to be on the side of 'the underdog' (i.e. the weaker side in any competition). On the roads the underdog is the pedestrian. The law states that if a person has just one foot on a zebra crossing then vehicles must stop. And they usually do. Conversely, British pedestrians interpret the colour of the human figure at traffic lights as advice, not as an instruction. If the figure is red but no cars are approaching, they feel perfectly entitled to cross the road immediately. In Britain, jay-walking (crossing the road by dodging in between cars) has never been illegal.

Privacy and sex

Respect for privacy underlies many aspects of British life. It is not just privacy in your own home which is important (see chapter 19). Just as important is the individual's right to keep information about himself or herself private. Despite the increase in informality, it is still seen as rude to ask people what are called 'personal' questions (for example, about how much money they earn or about their family or sex life) unless you know them very well. Notice that the conventional formula on being introduced to someone in Britain, 'how do you do?', is not interpreted as a real request for information at all; the conventional reply is not to 'answer the question' but to reply by saying 'how do you do?' too.

The modern British attitude to sex is an example of how, while moral attitudes have changed, the habit of keeping things private is still deeply ingrained. British (like American) public life has a reputation for demanding puritanical standards of behaviour. Revelations about extra-marital affairs or other deviations from what is considered normal in private life have, in the past, ruined the careers of many public figures. This would seem to indicate a lack of respect for privacy and that the British do not allow their politicians a private life. However, appearances in this matter can be misleading. In most of these cases, the disgrace of the politician concerned has not been because of his sexual activity. It has happened because this activity was mixed up with a matter of national security, or involved breaking the law or indicated hypocrisy (in acting against the stated policy of the politician's party). In other words, the private sexual activity had a direct relevance to the politician's public role. The scandal was that in these cases, the politicians had not kept their private lives and public roles separate enough. When no such connections are involved, there are no negative consequences for the politicians. In fact when, in 1992, a leading politician announced that five years previously he had had an affair with his secretary, his popularity actually increased!

In 1992 a million copies of very explicit and realistic videos with titles such as *Super Virility, Better Sex, The Gay Man's Guide to Safer Sex* and *The Lovers' Guide* were sold in Britain. There was some debate about whether they should be banned. However, an opinion poll showed that the British public agreed that they were not 'pornographic' but 'educational'. Three out of four of those asked were happy for the videos to be freely on sale. Examples such as this suggest that modern Britons have a positive and open attitude to sex. However, they continue to regard it as an absolutely private matter. Sex may no longer be 'bad', but it is still embarrassing. Take the example of sex education in schools. Partly because of worries about AIDS, this is now seen as a vital part of the school curriculum. It is the legal responsibility of schools to teach it. However, research in the early 1990s suggested that little or no sex education was taking place in

▶ Lovely weather we're having

The British are always talking about the weather. Unlike many others, this stereotype is actually true to life. But constant remarks about the weather at chance meetings are not the result of polite conventions. They are not obligatory. Rather, they are the result of the fact that, on the one hand, to ask personal questions would be rude while, at the same time, silence would also be rude. The weather is a very convenient topic with which to 'fill the gap'.

▶ Blind Date

Blind Date is a very popular television programme. In it, a member of one sex asks three members of the opposite sex (whom he or she cannot see) questions and then chooses which one to go out with. The questions and answers are always full of sexual innuendo. The audience loves it.

On one show in 1993, one of the possible blind dates was a German girl. In conversation with the show's host, her knowledge of languages came up. The girl said, 'My teacher told me that the quickest way to learn a foreign language is to have sex with a native speaker. And you know, it really works!' Uproar! This remark caused the loudest audience reaction, the most hysterical laughs, which the show had ever known. The show's popularity is precisely because sex is possibly on the agenda, but this was the first time that anyone on the programme had actually admitted to having sex. Very un-British!

The television programme 'Blind Date'

▶ Carry on laughing

In the history of British comedy, there is a special place for the *Carry On* series of films. Starting in the late 1950s and continuing into the mid 1970s, there were twenty-nine *Carry On* films. All of them used the same formula (and always with more or less the same set of actors): a well-known situation or place (a hospital, the army, the British empire in India) peopled with absurd characters whose dialogue consists of almost nothing but puns relating to sex or toilets.

Nevertheless, they became, over the years, an essential part of British culture. Anybody who went to see a *Carry On* film knew exactly what sort of thing to expect. This predictability, in fact, was part of the enjoyment. The jokes, so obvious and continuous, could often be spotted by the audience before they came.

nearly half of the schools in the country. Why? The most common reason was that teachers simply felt too embarrassed to tackle the subject. Similarly, public references to sex in popular entertainment are very common, but they typically take the form of joking innuendo and clumsy double-entendre (▷ *Carry on laughing* and see chapter 23).

The same mixture of tolerance and embarrassment can be seen in the official attitude to prostitution in Britain. It is not illegal to *be* a prostitute in Britain, but it is illegal to publicly behave like one. It is against the law to 'solicit' – that is, to do anything in public to find customers.

A poster advertising a 'Carry On' film

QUESTIONS

1. Frequent mention is made in this chapter of British individualism. How many examples of this can you find? Can you think of any others?
2. It has been said that the British are suspicious of things in public life which are logical or systematic. Can you find examples in this chapter which could be used to support this opinion?
3. Imagine this situation: you are at home, just about to have lunch, when there is a knock at the door. It is a British friend of yours, not a very close friend, but closer than a mere acquaintance. He or she has come to pay you an unexpected visit. You suggest that your friend comes in and stays for lunch. But your friend is embarrassed to find that he or she has called at a mealtime and refuses the invitation. You want to persuade your friend to change his or her mind. Here are two possible ways of doing this:
   A *Please stay. We don't have much, I'm afraid, but we'd be honoured. Whatever we have is yours.*
   B *It's no trouble at all. There's plenty of food. Don't think twice about it. We're used to people popping in.*
   Which of these two do you think would be a more successful way to persuade a British person? A or B? Why?
4. Which (if any) of the British characteristics described in this chapter would you regard as also characteristic of people in your country? To what extent?

SUGGESTIONS

- George Mikes' humorous books about the English, such as *How to be an Alien*, *How to be Inimitable* and *How to be Decadent* (all published by Penguin) are easy and fun to read. As they span thirty years, together they offer insights into changing attitudes in Britain.
- Read *Notes from a Small Island* by Bill Bryson, a humorous tour round Britain by an American who lived there for many years.

6
Political life

Look at the extract from a fictional diary on the next page (▷ *The killer instinct*). It is taken from the book of *Yes, Prime Minister*, a very popular radio and television comedy of the 1980s. Like all political satire, this programme could only have been popular because people believed that it was, at least partly, a true reflection of reality. It therefore illustrates the British attitude to politicians and politics.

The public attitude to politics

Politicians in Britain do not have a good reputation. To describe someone who is not a professional politician as 'a politician' is to criticize him or her, suggesting a lack of trustworthiness. It is not that people hate their politicians. They just regard them with a high degree of suspicion. They do not expect them to be corrupt or to use their position to amass personal wealth, but they do expect them to be frequently dishonest. People are not really shocked when the government is caught lying. On the other hand, they would be very shocked indeed if it was discovered that the government was doing anything actually illegal. A scandal such as the Watergate affair in the USA in the early 1970s would endanger the stability of the whole of political life.

At an earlier point in the 'diary', Jim Hacker is wondering why the Prime Minister has resigned. He does not believe the rumour that £1 million worth of diamonds have been found in the Prime Minister's house. This is partly, no doubt, because he does not think the Prime Minister could be so corrupt but it is also because 'it's never been officially denied . . . The first rule of politics is Never Believe Anything Until It's Been Officially Denied'. This is the basis of the joke in the two conversations in the extract. Duncan and Eric are only sure that Jim wants to be Prime Minister after he implies that he doesn't!

The lack of enthusiasm for politicians may be seen in the fact that surveys have shown a general ignorance of who they are. More than half of the adults in Britain do not know the name of their local Member of Parliament (MP), even though there is just one of these for each area, and quite a high proportion do not even know the names of the important government ministers or leaders of the major political parties.

▶The killer instinct

In this extract from *Yes, Prime Minister*, the Prime Minister has just resigned. There are two candidates to be the new Prime Minister, Eric Jeffries and Duncan Short, both of them ministers in the present government. Another minister, Jim Hacker, also wants the job. He has recently learnt some scandalous information about events in the pasts of the other two candidates, so now he has the opportunity to make them withdraw. Here is an extract from his diary.

I told Duncan that some information had come my way. Serious information. To do with his personal financial operations. I referred to the collapse of Continental and General.

He argued that there was nothing improper about that. I replied that technically there wasn't, but if you looked at it in conjunction with a similar case at Offshore Securities . . . I indicated that, if he stayed in the running for PM[1], I would be obliged to share my knowledge with senior members of the party, the Fraud Squad, and so forth. The Americans would also have to know. And Her Majesty . . .

He panicked. 'Hang on! Financial matters can be misinterpreted.'

I sipped my drink and waited. It didn't take long. He said that he didn't really want Number Ten[2] at all. He felt that the Foreign Office was a much better job in many ways. 'But I won't support Eric!' he insisted hotly.

'How would it be if you transferred all your support to someone else?' I suggested.

Duncan looked blank. 'Who?'

'Someone who recognized your qualities. Someone who'd want you to stay on as Foreign Secretary. Someone who would be discreet about Continental and General. Someone you trust.'

Gradually, I saw it dawning upon him. 'Do you mean – you?' he asked.

I pretended surprise. 'Me? I have absolutely no ambitions in that direction.'

'You *do* mean you,' he observed quietly. He knows the code.

*

I told Eric what I knew. He went pale. 'But you said you were going to help me get elected Prime Minister.'

I pointed out that my offer to help him was before my knowledge of the shady lady from Argentina. And others. 'Look, Eric, as party Chairman I have my duty. It would be a disaster for the party if you were PM and it came out. I mean, I wouldn't care to explain your private life to Her Majesty, would you?'

'I'll withdraw,' he muttered.

I told him reassuringly that I would say no more about it. To anyone.

He thanked me nastily and snarled that he supposed that bloody Duncan would now get Number Ten.

'Not if I can help it,' I told him.

'Who then?'

I raised my glass to him, smiled and said, 'Cheers.'

The penny dropped[3]. So did his lower jaw. 'You don't mean – you?'

Again I put on my surprised face. 'Me?' I said innocently. 'Our children are approaching the age when Annie and I are thinking of spending much more time with each other.'

He understood perfectly. 'You *do* mean you.'

Adapted from *Yes, Prime Minister* by Jonathan Lynn and Antony Jay.

1 PM is short for 'Prime Minister'.
2 Number Ten Downing Street is where the Prime Minister lives.
3 He finally understood (that Hacker intended to be PM).

The British were not always so unenthusiastic. In centuries past, it was a maxim of gentlemen's clubs that nobody should mention politics or religion in polite conversation. If anybody did, there was a danger that the conversation would become too heated, people would become bad-tempered and perhaps violent. However, there has been no real possibility of a revolution or even of a radical change in the style of government for almost two centuries now. This stability is now generally taken for granted. Most people rarely see any reason to become passionate about politics and nobody regards it as a 'dangerous' topic of conversation. They are more likely to regard it as a boring topic of conversation! However, this lack of enthusiasm is not the same as complete disenchantment. Three-quarters of the adult population are interested enough in politics to vote at national elections, even though voting is not compulsory. There is a general feeling of confidence in the stability and workability of the system.

Yes, Prime Minister is just one of many programmes and publications devoted to political satire. All of them are consistently and bitingly critical. Moreover, their criticism is typically not about particular policies but is directed at the attitudes of politicians, their alleged dishonesty and disloyalty, and at the general style of political life (▷ *Figures of fun*). Given this, you might think that people would be very angry, that there would be loud demands that the system be cleaned up, even public demonstrations. Not at all! The last demonstrations about such matters took place 150 years ago. You might also think that the politicians themselves would be worried about the negative picture that these satires paint of them. Far from it! On the back cover of the 1989 edition of *Yes, Prime Minister* there is a tribute from Margaret Thatcher, the real Prime Minister of the country throughout the 1980s. In it, she refers to the book's 'closely observed portrayal of what goes on in the corridors of power' (suggesting it is accurate) and how this portrayal has given her 'hours of pure joy'.

In Britain it is generally accepted that politics is a dirty business, a necessary evil. Therefore, politicians make sure that they do not appear too keen to do the job. They see themselves as being politicians out of a sense of public duty. That is why, in the extract, Jim Hacker does not admit that he actually *wants* to be Prime Minister. Eric and Duncan, and Jim himself, all know and accept that to be the Prime Minister is the ultimate goal of most politicians. But for Jim Hacker to admit this openly, even in private conversation, would make him seem dangerously keen on power for its own sake.

The style of democracy

The British are said to have a high respect for the law. Although they may not have much respect for the present institutions of the law (see chapter 11), this reputation is more or less true with respect to the *principle* of law. Of course, lots of crimes are committed, as in any other country, but there is little systematic law-breaking by large

▶ Collectors' items?

An indication of the poor reputation of politicians in Britain is the value of their signatures. Autographs can sometimes be worth quite a lot of money – but not those of most politicians. Even those of Prime Ministers are not very valuable. In 1992 the signature of Margaret Thatcher, Prime Minister throughout the 1980s, was worth £75 if accompanied by a photograph; the signature of John Major, Prime Minister at the time, was worth £20, those of other recent Prime Ministers were worth even less. The one exception was Winston Churchill. His signed photograph was said to be worth £1,000.

▶ Figures of fun

Spitting Image was an example of television satire. It was a programme which showed puppets of well-known public figures speaking in fictional situations in order to make fun of them. Note that the figures were not naturalistic. Instead, they were more like cartoons, grotesquely emphasizing certain features. The *Spitting Image* format was copied in other European countries.

The 'Spitting Image' puppet of Margaret Thatcher (Prime Minister 1979–91)

▶ Official secrets

In 1992 the existence of MI6, the British Secret Service, was publicly admitted by the government for the first time. Nobody was surprised. Everybody already knew that there was a secret service, and that its name was MI6. But the admission itself *was* a surprise. British governments do not like public revelations of their activities, even if these are no longer secret. (In this case, the reason for the new openness was that, with the cold war over, MI6 had to start justifying why it needed money from taxpayers.)

For years during the 1980s, for instance, the government successfully prevented the publication in Britain of the book *Spycatcher* (the memoirs of an MI6 agent) even though, by the end of the decade, it had already been published in several other countries and could therefore not contain any genuine secrets. Eventually, in 1991, the European Court ruled that publication should be allowed in Britain too.

sections of the population. For example, tax evasion is not the national pastime that it is said to be in some countries.

However, while 'the law' as a concept is largely respected, the British are comparatively unenthusiastic about making new laws. The general feeling is that, while you have to have laws sometimes, wherever possible it is best to do without them. In many aspects of life the country has comparatively few rules and regulations. This lack of regulation works both ways. Just as there are comparatively few rules telling the individual what he or she must or must not do, so there are comparatively few rules telling the government what it can or cannot do. Two unique aspects of British life will make this clear.

First, Britain is one of the very few European countries whose citizens do not have identity cards. Before the 1970s, when tourism to foreign countries became popular (and so the holding of passports became more common), most people in the country went through life without ever owning a document whose main purpose was to identify them. British people are not obliged to carry identification with them. You do not even have to have your driving licence with you in your car. If the police ask to see it, you have twenty-four hours to take it to them!

Second, and on the other hand, Britain (unlike some other countries in western Europe) does not have a Freedom of Information Act. There is no law which obliges a government authority or agency to show you what information it has collected about you. In fact, it goes further than that. There *is* a law (called the Official Secrets Act) which obliges many government employees *not* to tell anyone about the details of their work. It seems that in Britain, both your own identity and the information which the government has about your identity are regarded as, in a sense, private matters.

These two aspects are characteristic of the relationship in Britain between the individual and the state. To a large degree, the traditional assumption is that both should leave each other alone as much as possible. The duties of the individual towards the state are confined to not breaking the law and paying taxes. There is no national service (military or otherwise); people are not obliged to vote at elections if they can't be bothered; people do not have to register their change of address with any government authority when they move house.

Similarly, the government in Britain has a comparatively free hand. It would be correct to call the country 'a democracy' in the generally accepted sense of this word. But in Britain this democracy involves less participation by ordinary citizens in governing and lawmaking than it does in many other countries. There is no concept of these things being done 'by the people'. If the government wants to make an important change in the way that the country is run – to change, for example, the electoral system or the powers of the Prime Minister – it does not have to ask the people. It does not even have to have a special vote in Parliament with an especially high proportion of MPs in favour. It just needs to get Parliament to agree in the same way as for any new law (see chapter 9).

In many countries an important constitutional change cannot be made without a referendum in which everybody in the country has the chance to vote 'yes' or 'no'. In other countries, such as the USA, people often have the chance to vote on particular proposals for changing laws that directly affect their everyday life, on smoking in public places or the location of a new hospital, for example. Nothing like this happens in Britain. There has only been one countrywide referendum in British history (in 1975, on whether the country should stay in the European Community). In Britain democracy has never meant that the people have a hand in the running of the country; rather it means that the people choose who is to govern the country, and then let them get on with it!

The constitution

Britain is a constitutional monarchy. That means it is a country governed by a king or queen who accepts the advice of a parliament. It is also a parliamentary democracy. That is, it is a country whose government is controlled by a parliament which has been elected by the people. In other words, the basic system is not so different from anywhere else in Europe. The highest positions in the government are filled by members of the directly elected parliament. In Britain, as in many European countries, the official head of state, whether a monarch (as in Belgium, the Netherlands and Denmark) or a president (as in Germany, Greece and Italy) has little real power.

However, there are features of the British system of government which make it different from that in other countries and which are not 'modern' at all. The most notable of these is the question of the constitution. Britain is almost alone among modern states in that it does not have 'a constitution' at all. Of course, there are rules, regulations, principles and procedures for the running of the country – all the things that political scientists and legal experts study and which are known collectively as 'the constitution'. But there is no single written document which can be appealed to as the highest law of the land and the final arbiter in any matter of dispute. Nobody can refer to 'article 6' or 'the first amendment' or anything like that, because nothing like that exists.

Instead, the principles and procedures by which the country is governed and from which people's rights are derived come from a number of different sources. They have been built up, bit by bit, over the centuries. Some of them are written down in laws agreed by Parliament, some of them have been spoken and then written down (judgements made in a court) and some of them have never been written down at all. For example, there is no written law in Britain that says anything about who can be the Prime Minister or what the

▶The pairing system

The pairing system is an excellent example of the habit of co-operation among political parties in Britain. Under this system, an MP of one party is 'paired' with an MP of another party. When there is going to be a vote in the House of Commons, and the two MPs know that they would vote on opposite sides, neither of them bother to turn up for the vote. In this way, the difference in numbers between one side and the other is maintained, while the MPs are free to get on with other work. The system works very well. There is hardly ever any 'cheating'.

powers of the Prime Minister are, even though he or she is probably the most powerful person in the country. Similarly, there is no single written document which asserts people's rights. Some rights which are commonly accepted in modern democracies (for example, the rights not to be discriminated against on the basis of sex or race) have been formally recognized by Parliament through legislation; but others (for example, the rights not to be discriminated against on the basis of religion or political views) have not. Nevertheless, it is understood that these latter rights are also part of the constitution.

The style of politics

Despite recent changes such as the televising of Parliament, political life in Britain is still influenced by the traditional British respect for privacy and love of secrecy. It is also comparatively informal. In both Parliament and government there is a tendency for important decisions to be taken, not at official public meetings, or even at pre-arranged private meetings, but at lunch, or over drinks, or in chance encounters in the corridors of power. It used to be said that the House of Commons was 'the most exclusive club in London'. And indeed, there are many features of Parliament which cause its members (MPs) to feel special and to feel a special sense of belonging with each other, even among those who have radically opposed political philosophies. First, constitutional theory says that Parliament has absolute control over its own affairs and is, in fact, the highest power in the land. Second, there are the ancient traditions of procedure (see chapter 9). Many of these serve to remind MPs of a time when the main division in politics was not between this party and that party but rather between Parliament itself and the monarch. Even the architecture of the Palace of Westminster (the home of both Houses of Parliament) contributes to this feeling. It is so confusing that only 'insiders' can possibly find their way around it.

These features, together with the long years of political stability, have led to a genuine habit of co-operation among politicians of different parties. When you hear politicians arguing in the House of Commons or in a television studio, you might think that they hate each other. This is rarely the case. Often they are good friends. And even when it is the case, both normally see the practical advantage of co-operation. The advantage is that very little time is wasted fighting about how political business is to be conducted fairly. For example, the order of business in Parliament is arranged by representatives of the parties beforehand so that enough time is given for the various points of view to be expressed. Another example is television advertising. By agreement, political parties are not allowed to buy time on television. Instead, each party is given a strict amount of time, with the two biggest parties getting exactly equal amounts. A very notable example is the system of 'pairing' of MPs (▷ *The pairing system*).

A guide to British political parties

Conservative party

CONSERVATIVE

- *History*: developed from the group of MPs known as the Tories in the early nineteenth century (see chapter 2) and still often known informally by that name (especially in newspapers, because it takes up less space!).
- *Traditional outlook*: right of centre; stands for hierarchical authority and minimal government interference in the economy; likes to reduce income tax; gives high priority to national defence and internal law and order.
- *Since 1979*: aggressive reform of education, welfare, housing and many public services designed to increase consumer-choice and/or to introduce 'market economics' into their operation.
- *Organization*: leader has relatively great degree of freedom to direct policy.
- *Leader (December 1999)*: William Hague.
- *Voters*: the richer sections of society, plus a large minority of the working classes.
- *Money*: mostly donations from business people.

Labour party

Labour

- *History*: formed at the beginning of the twentieth century from an alliance of trade unionists and intellectuals. First government in 1923.
- *Traditional outlook*: left of centre; stands for equality, for the weaker people in society and for more government involvement in the economy; more concerned to provide full social services than to keep income tax low.
- *Since 1979*: opposition to Conservative reforms, although has accepted many of these by now; recently, emphasis on community ethics and looser links with trade unions (see chapter 15).
- *Organization*: in theory, policies have to be approved by annual conference; in practice, leader has more power than this implies.
- *Leader (December 1999)*: Tony Blair.
- *Voters*: working class, plus a small middle-class intelligentsia.
- *Money*: more than half from trade unions.

Liberal Democratic party

Liberal Democrats

- *History*: formed in the late 1980s from a union of the Liberals (who developed from the Whigs of the early nineteenth century) and the Social Democrats (a breakaway group of Labour politicians).
- *Policies*: regarded as in the centre or slightly left of centre; has always been strongly in favour of the EU; places more emphasis on the environment than other parties; believes in giving greater powers to local government and in reform of the electoral system (see chapter 10).
- *Leader (December 1999)*: Charles Kennedy.
- *Voters*: from all classes, but more from the middle class.
- *Money*: private donations (much poorer than the big two).

Nationalist parties

Both Plaid Cymru ('party of Wales' in the Welsh language) and the SNP (Scottish National Party) fight for devolution of governmental powers. They want separate parliaments for their countries and many of their members, especially in the SNP, are willing to consider total independence from the UK. Both parties have usually had a few MPs in the second half of the twentieth century, but well under half of the total number of MPs from their respective countries.

Parties in Northern Ireland

Parties here normally represent either the Protestant or the Catholic communities (see chapter 4)! There is one large comparatively moderate party on each side (the Protestant Ulster Unionists and the Catholic Social Democratic and Labour Party) and one or more other parties of more extreme views on each side (for example, the Protestant Democratic Unionists and the Catholic Sinn Fein). There is one party which asks for support from both communities – the Alliance party. It had not, by 1999, won any seats.

Other parties

There are numerous very small parties, such as the Green Party, which is supported by environmentalists. There is a small party which was formerly the Communist party, and a number of other left-wing parties, and also an extreme right-wing party which is fairly openly racist (by most definitions of that word). It was previously called the National Front but since the 1980s has been called the British National Party (BNP). At the time of writing, none of these parties had won a single seat in Parliament in the second half of the twentieth century. In 1993, however, the BNP briefly won a seat on a local council.

▶ Image matters

In the age of television, the importance of the personal image of a party's leader to its political success has increased greatly. Since 1960 a great change has taken place with regard to the families of top politicians. Before then, the British public did not even know the name of the Prime Minister's wife. These days, the wives of male party leaders are well-known to the media, and their children are often featured with them in photographs to show what loving, normal family men they are.

The British scene has not, at the time of writing, reached the level of absurdity that it has in the USA where, for example, the daughter of Jimmy Carter (President 1975–79) was such a celebrity that the press once thought it worthwhile to report that she had been twelve minutes late for school!

Tony Blair with his wife and children outside Number 10 Downing Street, the official residence of the Prime Minister

The party system

Britain is normally described as having a 'two-party system'. This is because, since 1945, one of the two big parties has, by itself, controlled the government, and members of these two parties have occupied more than 90% of all of the seats in the House of Commons. Moreover, this is not a peculiarly modern phenomenon. Basically the same situation existed throughout the nineteenth century, except that the Liberals, rather than Labour, were one of the two big parties. The Labour party was formed at the start of the twentieth century and within about thirty years had replaced the Liberals in this role.

One reason for the existence of this situation is the electoral system (see chapter 10). The other is the nature of the origin of British political parties. Britain is unlike most other countries in that its parties were first formed inside Parliament, and were only later extended to the public at large. During the eighteenth century Members of Parliament tended to divide themselves into two camps, those who usually supported the government of the time and those who usually did not. During the nineteenth century it gradually became the habit that the party which did not control the government presented itself as an alternative government. This idea of an alternative government has received legal recognition. The leader of the second biggest party in the House of Commons (or, more exactly, of the biggest party which is not in government) receives the title 'Leader of Her Majesty's Opposition' and even gets a salary to prove the importance of this role. He or she chooses a 'shadow cabinet', thereby presenting the image of a team ready to fill the shoes of the government at a moment's notice.

As a result of these origins, neither party existed solely to look after the interests of one particular group (although some groups in society were naturally more attracted to one of the two parties than the other). Furthermore, although they could be distinguished by certain broad differences in their outlooks on life, the two parties did not exist to promote single, coherent political philosophies. The main reason for their existence was to gain power by forming effective coalitions of interest-groups and individuals.

Although the Labour party *was* formed outside Parliament, and, as its name implies, *did* exist to promote the interests of a particular group (the working class), it soon fitted into the established framework. It is very difficult for smaller parties to challenge the dominance of the bigger ones. If any of them seem to have some good ideas, these ideas tend to be adopted by one of the three biggest parties, who all try to appeal to as large a section of the population as possible.

The fact that the party system originated inside Parliament has other consequences. Parties do not, as they do in many other countries, extend into every area of public and social life in the country. Universities, for example, each have their Conservative, Labour and

Liberal Democrat clubs, but when there is an election for officers of the student union, it is not normally fought according to national party divisions. The same is true of elections within trade unions (see chapter 15).

Another consequence is that it is usually a party's MPs who have the most control over party policy and the biggest influence on the choice of party leader. This does not mean that the parties are undemocratic. Their members who are not MPs can have an effect on policy in a number of ways. First, they can make their views known at the annual party conference. In the case of the three main parties, this takes place in the autumn and lasts about a week. Second, the local party has the power to decide who is going to be the party's candidate for MP in its area at the next election. However, these powers are limited by one important consideration – the appearance of unity. Party policies are always presented as potential government policies, and a party's leading MPs are always presented as potential ministers. If you want to look like a realistic potential government, you don't want to show the public your disagreements. Party conferences are always televised. As a result they sometimes tend to be showcases whose main purpose is not so much to debate important matters as to boost the spirits of party members and to show the public a dynamic, unified party. Similarly, if local party members decide not to re-select the present MP as their candidate in an election, it betrays disagreement and argument. Therefore, party members do not like this happening and most MPs can be sure that their local party will choose them again at the next election (see chapter 11).

The modern situation

During the last forty or so years, the traditional confidence in the British political system has weakened. In 1950, Britain, despite the hardships of the Second World War, could claim to be the richest and most stable large country in Europe. Collectively, its people seemed to know what they wanted and what they believed in. They seemed to be sure of themselves.

This is no longer true. Britain is often rated as one of the poorest large countries in Europe, the policies of its governments have pulled in several different directions, and its people tend to be pessimistic about the future (▷*A loss of confidence*). It is now commonplace for politicians and political commentators, when calling for a change in some matter, to compare the country unfavourably with some other European country.

In these circumstances, it is quite possible that some of the distinctive characteristics of British public life will change. The matter of identity cards is one area of possible change. The British have always been rather proud of not having them. This has been seen as proof of the British dedication to the rights of the individual. It has also helped to give British people a feeling of being different. But what

▶ A loss of confidence

In 1991, Prime Minister John Major remarked on his vision of Britain as 'a nation at ease with itself'. However, an opinion poll published in February 1992 suggested that his vision was not reality. Over a thousand adults were interviewed face-to-face in 100 areas throughout Britain and were asked about their attitudes to various aspects of life in the country. In one series of questions, interviewees were asked whether they were proud of certain institutions. Here are some of the results of the poll, compared with the results of similar surveys done 20–30 years before.

	% agreeing with statement	
	1960s	1992
The British monarch is something to be proud of	86	26
The British Parliament is something to be proud of	75	35
The British health service is something to be proud of	89	41
The British education system is something to be proud of	77	27

In the 1992 poll, only 5% of those asked said that their pride in Britain and British institutions had increased in recent years; 54% said that it had decreased.

is the good of being different if 'different' means 'worse'? There has been growing concern about increasing crime in the country, and this has resulted in much discussion about identity cards. Britain's fellow states in the European Union would like to see them introduced in the country. At the same time, there has been increasing pressure for a Freedom of Information Act.

Another possibility is that Britain will finally get a written constitution. An unwritten constitution works very well if everybody in the country shares the same attitudes and principles about what is most important in political life and about what people's rights and obligations are. In other words, it works very well in a society where everybody belongs to the same culture. However, in common with most other European countries today, Britain is now multicultural. This means that some sections of society can sometimes hold radically different ideas about these things. The case of Salman Rushdie is an excellent example of this situation (▷ *The Rushdie affair*). As long as everybody in a country feels the same way, at the same time, about a case such as this, there is no real need to worry about inconsistencies in the law. There is no need to question the existence of laws or to update them. They are just interpreted in changing ways to match the change in prevailing opinion. This is what, up to now, has happened in Britain. But the Rushdie case is an example of what can happen when radically opposing views on a matter prevail in different sections of society at the same time. In these circumstances the traditional *laissez-faire* attitude to the law can become dangerous.

▶The Rushdie affair

Salman Rushdie is a British citizen from a Muslim background, and a respected writer. In early 1989, his book *The Satanic Verses* was published. Many Muslims in Britain were extremely angry about the book's publication. They regarded it as a terrible insult to Islam. They therefore demanded that the book be banned and that its author be taken to court for blasphemy (using language to insult God).

To do either of these things would have been to go against the long-established tradition of free speech and freedom of religious views. In any case, there is nothing in British law to justify doing either. There are censorship laws, but they relate only to obscenity and national security. There is a law against blasphemy, but it refers only to the Christian religion. Moreover, the tendency from the second half of the twentieth century has been to apply both types of law as little as possible and to give priority to the principle of free speech.

QUESTIONS

1. In what sense could the British attitude to politics be described as 'happily cynical'? Are people equally cynical in your country? Are they as happy about it?
2. In most Parliaments in the western world, the place where representatives debate is in the form of a semi-circle. But in Britain, there are two sets of rows facing each other. Why is the British Parliament different in this respect?
3. How does the role of political parties in Britain differ from their role in your country?
4. Why does Britain not have a written constitution? Does it need one?

SUGGESTIONS

- Try to watch some of the *Yes, Prime Minister* programmes (available as a BBC video). There is a book of the same name published by BBC Books.

7
The monarchy

The appearance

The position of the monarch in Britain is a perfect illustration of the contradictory nature of the constitution. From the evidence of written law only, the Queen has almost absolute power, and it all seems very undemocratic. The American constitution talks about 'government of the people for the people by the people'. There is no law in Britain which says anything like that. In fact, there is no legal concept of 'the people' at all.

Every autumn, at the state opening of Parliament, Elizabeth II, who became Queen in 1952, makes a speech. In it, she says what 'my government' intends to do in the coming year. And indeed, it is her government, not the people's. As far as the law is concerned, she can choose anybody she likes to run the government for her. There are no restrictions on whom she picks as her Prime Minister. It does not have to be somebody who has been elected. She could choose me; she could even choose *you*. The same is true for her choices of people to fill some hundred or so other ministerial positions. And if she gets fed up with her ministers, she can just dismiss them. Officially speaking, they are all 'servants of the Crown' (not servants of anything like 'the country' or 'the people'). She also appears to have great power over Parliament. It is she who summons a Parliament, and she who dissolves it before a general election (see chapter 10). Nothing that Parliament has decided can become law until she has agreed to it.

Similarly, it is the Queen, and not any other figure of authority, who embodies the law in the courts. In the USA, when the police take someone to court to accuse them of a crime, the court records show that 'the people' have accused that person. In other countries it might be 'the state' that makes the accusation. But in Britain it is 'the Crown'. This is because of the legal authority of the monarch. And when an accused person is found guilty of a crime, he or she might be sent to one of 'Her Majesty's' prisons.

Other countries have 'citizens'. But in Britain people are legally described as 'subjects' – subjects of Her Majesty the Queen. Moreover, there is a principle of English law that the monarch can do nothing that is legally wrong. In other words, Queen Elizabeth is above the law.

▶ The house of Windsor

Windsor is the family name of the royal family. The press sometimes refers to its members as 'the Windsors'. Queen Elizabeth is only the fourth monarch with this name. This is not because a 'new' royal family took over the throne of Britain four reigns ago. It is because George V, Elizabeth's grandfather, changed the family name. It was Saxe-Coburg-Gotha, but during the First World War it was thought better for the king not to have a German-sounding name.

▸ The royal family

- **Queen Elizabeth the Queen Mother** has been the official title of the mother of the present Queen since the death of her husband, King George VI. She has been popular with the British people ever since her tours of bombed areas of London during the Second World War. She was born in 1900 and is the most consistently popular member of the royal family.
- **Queen Elizabeth II** was born in 1926 and became Queen in 1952 on the death of her father, George VI, who had reigned since 1936 (when his elder brother, Edward VIII, gave up the throne). She is one of the longest-reigning monarchs in British history. She is widely respected for the way in which she performs her duties and is generally popular.
- **Prince Philip Mountbatten,** the Duke of Edinburgh, married the present Queen in 1947. In the 1960s and 1970s, his outspoken opinions on controversial matters were sometimes embarrassing to the royal family.
- **Princess Margaret** is the Queen's younger sister. She is divorced from her husband, Lord Snowdon, who is a professional photographer.
- **Prince Charles,** the Prince of Wales, was born in 1948. As the eldest son of Queen Elizabeth and Prince Philip, he is heir to the throne. He is concerned about the environment and about living conditions in Britain's cities. He sometimes makes speeches which are critical of aspects of modern life.
- **Princess Diana** married Prince Charles in 1981. The couple separated in 1992 and later divorced. Princess Diana died as the result of a car accident in 1997. She was a glamorous and popular figure during her lifetime.
- **Princess Anne**, the Queen's daughter (also known as the Princess Royal), was born in 1950. She separated from her husband after they had one son and one daughter. She married again in 1992. She is widely respected for her charity work, which she does in a spirit of realism.
- **Prince Andrew**, the Duke of York, was born in 1960 and is the Queen's second son. He is divorced from his wife, Sarah Ferguson (who is known to the popular press as 'Fergie'). They have two daughters.
- **Prince Edward**, the Queen's youngest son, was born in 1964. He is involved in theatrical production. He married Sophie Rhys-Jones in 1999. He and his wife are the Duke and Duchess of Wessex.
- **Prince William** (born 1982) and **Prince Henry** (born 1984) are the sons of Charles and Diana. William is next in line to the throne after his father.

Princess Margaret — The Queen Mother — The Queen — Prince Philip — Prince Charles

The reality

In practice, of course, the reality is very different. In fact, the Queen cannot choose anyone she likes to be Prime Minister. She has to choose someone who has the support of the majority of MPs in the House of Commons (the elected chamber of the two Houses of Parliament). This is because the law says that 'her' government can only collect taxes with the agreement of the Commons, so if she did not choose such a person, the government would stop functioning. In practice the person she chooses is the leader of the strongest party in the House of Commons. Similarly, it is really the Prime Minister who decides who the other government ministers are going to be (although officially the Prime Minister simply 'advises' the monarch who to choose).

It is the same story with Parliament. Again, the Prime Minister will talk about 'requesting' a dissolution of Parliament when he or she wants to hold an election, but it would normally be impossible for the monarch to refuse this 'request'. Similarly, while, in theory, the Queen could refuse the royal assent to a bill passed by Parliament – and so stop it becoming law (see chapter 9) – no monarch has actually done so since the year 1708. Indeed, the royal assent is so automatic that the Queen doesn't even bother to give it in person. Somebody else signs the documents for her.

In reality the Queen has almost no power at all. When she opens Parliament each year the speech she makes has been written for her. She makes no secret of this fact. She very obviously reads out the script that has been prepared for her, word for word. If she strongly disagrees with one of the policies of the government, she might ask the government ministers to change the wording in the speech a little beforehand, but that is all. She cannot actually stop the government going ahead with any of its policies.

The role of the monarch

What, then, is the monarch's role? Many opinions are offered by political and legal experts. Three roles are often mentioned. First, the monarch is the personal embodiment of the government of the country. This means that people can be as critical as they like about the *real* government, and can argue that it should be thrown out, without being accused of being unpatriotic. Because of the clear separation between the symbol of government (the Queen) and the actual government (the ministers, who are also MPs), changing the government does not threaten the stability of the country as a whole. Other countries without a monarch have to use something else as the symbol of the country. In the USA, for example, one of these is its flag, and to damage the flag in any way is actually a criminal offence.

Second, it is argued that the monarch could act as a final check on a government that was becoming dictatorial. If the government ever managed to pass a bill through Parliament which was obviously terribly bad and very unpopular, the monarch could refuse the royal assent and the bill would not become law. Similarly, it is possible that if a Prime Minister who had been defeated at a general election (and so no longer commanded a majority in the House of Commons) were to ask immediately for another dissolution of Parliament (so that another election could take place), the monarch could refuse the request and dismiss the Prime Minister.

Third, the monarch has a very practical role to play. By being a figurehead and representing the country, Queen Elizabeth II can perform the ceremonial duties which heads of state often have to spend their time on. This way, the real government has more time to get on with the actual job of running the country.

▶ Honours

Twice a year, an Honours List is published. The people whose names appear on the list are then summoned to Buckingham Palace where the Queen presents them with a token which entitles them to write (and be formally addressed with) KG, or KCB, or CBE, or many other possible combinations of letters, after their names. The letters stand for titles such as 'Knight of the Order of the Garter', 'Knight Commander of the Order of the Bath', 'Commander of the British Empire', and so on. Life peerages are also awarded, which entitle the recipients to a seat in the House of Lords.

Traditionally, it was by giving people titles such as these that the monarch 'honoured' them in return for their services. These days, the decision about who gets which honour is usually taken by the Prime Minister (see chapter 8). And, as you can see, the names of the titles don't seem to make much sense in modern times. But that does not stop people finding it a real 'honour' to be given a title by the monarch herself! A high proportion of honours are given to politicians and civil servants, but they are also given to business people, sports stars, rock musicians and other entertainers.

The Beatles with their MBEs

The Queen, attracting foreign tourists

▸ The economic argument

Every tourist brochure for Britain in every country in the world gives great prominence to the monarchy. It is impossible to estimate exactly how much the British royal family and the events and buildings associated with the monarchy help the tourist industry, or exactly how much money they help to bring into the country. But most people working in tourism think it is an awful lot!

▸ Edward and Mrs Simpson

For the last two centuries the public have wanted their monarch to have high moral standards. In 1936 Edward VIII, the uncle of the present Queen, was forced to abdicate (give up the throne). This happened because he wanted to marry a woman who had divorced two husbands. (On top of that, she was not even a British aristocrat – she was an American!) The government and the major churches in the country insisted that Edward could not marry her and remain king. He chose to marry her. The couple then went to live abroad. In spite of the constitutional crisis that he caused, the Duke of Windsor (as Edward later became) and his wife were popular celebrities in Britain all their lives, and the king's abdication has gone down in popular history as an example of the power of love.

The value of the monarchy

However, all these advantages are hypothetical. It cannot be proved that only a monarch can provide them. Other modern democracies manage perfectly well without one. The British monarchy is probably more important to the economy of the country (▷ *The economic argument*) than it is to the system of government. Apart from this, the monarchy is very popular with the majority of the British people. The monarchy gives British people a symbol of continuity, and a harmless outlet for the expression of national pride. Even in very hard times it has never seemed likely that Britain would turn to a dictator to get it out of its troubles. The grandeur of its monarchy may have been one of the reasons for this.

Occasions such as the state opening of Parliament, the Queen's official birthday, royal weddings, and ceremonial events such as the changing of the guard make up for the lack of colour and ceremony in most people's daily lives. (There is no tradition of local parades as there is in the USA, and very few traditional local festivals survive as they do in other European countries.) In addition the glamorous lives of 'the royals' provide a source of entertainment that often takes on the characteristics of a television soap opera. When, in 1992, it became known that Prince Charles and his wife Princess Diana were separating, even the more 'serious' newspapers discussed a lot more than the possible political implications. *The Sunday Times* published a 'five-page royal separation special'.

The future of the monarchy

For the last 250 years, the British monarchy as an institution has only rarely been a burning political issue. Only occasionally has there been debate about the existence of the monarchy itself. Few people in Britain could be described as either 'monarchists' or 'anti-monarchists', in the sense in which these terms are often used in other countries. Most people are either vaguely in favour or they just don't care one way or the other. There is, however, a great deal of debate about what kind of monarchy Britain should have. During the last two decades of the twentieth century, there has been a general cooling of enthusiasm. The Queen herself remains popular. But the various marital problems in her family have lowered the prestige of royalty in many people's eyes. The problem is that, since Queen Victoria's reign, the public have been encouraged to look up to the royal family as a model of Christian family life.

The change in attitude can be seen by comparing Queen Elizabeth's 25th anniversary as Queen with her 40th anniversary. In 1977, there were neighbourhood street parties throughout the country, most of them spontaneously and voluntarily organized. But in 1992, nothing like this took place. On 20 November 1992, a fire damaged one of the Queen's favourite homes to the value of £60 million. There were expressions of public sympathy for the Queen. But when the government announced that public money was going to pay for the repairs, the sympathy quickly turned to anger. The Queen had recently been reported to be the richest woman in the world, so people didn't see why she shouldn't pay for them herself.

It is, in fact, on the subject of money that 'anti-royalist' opinions are most often expressed. In the early nineties even some Conservative MPs, traditionally strong supporters of the monarchy, started protesting at how much the royal family was costing the country. For the whole of her long reign Elizabeth II had been exempt from taxation. But, as a response to the change in attitude, the Queen decided that she would start paying taxes on her private income. In addition, Civil List payments to some members of the royal family were stopped. (The Civil List is the money which the Queen and some of her relatives get from Parliament each year so that they can carry out their public duties.)

For most people, the most notable event marking Queen Elizabeth's 40th anniversary was a television programme about a year in her life which showed revealing details of her private family life. In the following year parts of Buckingham Palace were, for the first time, opened for public visits (to raise money to help pay for the repairs to Windsor Castle). These events are perhaps an indication of the future royal style – a little less grand, a little less distant.

One's bum year

The Sun is Britain's most popular daily newspaper (see chapter 18). This was its front page headline after the Queen had spoken of 1992 as an *annus horribilis* (Latin for 'a horrible year'). As well as the separation of Charles and Diana, 1992 had included the fire at Windsor Castle and the news that Australia was intending to break its ties with the 'old country' and become a republic.

The headline uses the similarity between 'annus' and 'anus' to make a pun of 'bum' (which, in colloquial British English, can mean both 'anus' and 'horrible'). It also mimics the supposed frequent use by the Queen of the pronoun 'one' to mean 'I/me'. The headline thus mixes the very formal-sounding 'one' with the very colloquial 'bum'. It is impossible to imagine that such a disrespectful (and unsympathetic) headline could have appeared in the 1950s or 1960s.

QUESTIONS

1. Why does the British Prime Minister continue to 'advise' and 'request' the Queen, when everybody knows that he or she is really *telling* her what to do?
2. The attitude of the British people towards their royal family has changed over the last quarter of the twentieth century. In what way has it changed, and what demonstrates that there has been a change? Why do you think this has happened?
3. Would you advise the British to get rid of their monarchy?
4. Do you have a monarch in your country, or someone who fulfils a similar role? If you do, how does their position compare with that of the British monarch? If you don't, do you think your country would benefit from having a figurehead who could perform the functions of a monarch?

SUGGESTIONS

- *The Queen and I* by Sue Townsend (Mandarin) includes humorous characterizations of the main members of the royal family.
- Books about the monarchy abound. Among them are: *The Prince of Wales: A Biography* by Jonathan Dimbleby (Little, Brown and Company), *The Queen* by Kenneth Harris (Orion), *Elizabeth R: The Role of the Monarchy Today* by Antony Jay (BBC Books), *Diana, Her True Story* and *Diana, Her New Life*, both by Andrew Morton (Michael O'Mara Books Limited).

8
The government

Who governs Britain? When the media talk about 'the government' they usually mean one of two things. The term 'the government' can be used to refer to all of the politicians who have been appointed by the monarch (on the advice of the Prime Minister) to help run government departments (there are several politicians in each department) or to take on various other special responsibilities, such as managing the activities of Parliament. There are normally about a hundred members of 'the government' in this sense. Although there are various ranks, each with their own titles (▷ *Ministers and departments*), members of the government are usually known as 'ministers'. All ministers come from the ranks of Parliament, most of them from the House of Commons. Unlike in the USA and in some other countries in Europe, it is rare for a person from outside Parliament to become a minister. (And when this does happen, the person concerned is quickly found a seat in one of the two Houses.)

The other meaning of the term 'the government' is more limited. It refers only to the most powerful of these politicians, namely the Prime Minister and the other members of the cabinet. There are usually about twenty people in the cabinet (though there are no rules about this). Most of them are the heads of the government departments.

Partly as a result of the electoral system (see chapter 10), Britain, unlike much of western Europe, normally has 'single-party government'. In other words, all members of the government belong to the same political party. Traditionally, British politicians have regarded coalition government (with several parties involved) as a bad idea. Since the formation of modern political parties in the nineteenth century, Britain has had a total of only twenty-one years of coalition governments (1915–1922 and 1931–1945). Even when, for brief periods in the 1970s, no single party had a majority of seats in the House of Commons, no coalition was formed. There was a 'minority government' instead.

The habit of single-party government has helped to establish the tradition known as collective responsibility. That is, every member of the government, however junior, shares the responsibility for every policy made by the government. This is true even if, as is often the case, he or she did not play any part in making it. Of course,

▶ Ministers and departments

Most heads of government departments have the title 'Secretary of State' (as in, for example, 'Secretary of State for the Environment'). The minister in charge of Britain's relations with the outside world is known to everybody as the 'Foreign Secretary'. The one in charge of law and order inside the country is the 'Home Secretary'. Their departments are called the Foreign and Commonwealth Office and the Home Office respectively (the words 'exterior' and 'interior' are not used). The words 'secretary' and 'office' reflect the history of government in Britain, in which government departments were at one time part of the domestic arrangements of the monarch.

Another important person is the 'Chancellor of the Exchequer', who is the head of the Treasury (in other words, a sort of Minister of Finance).

A cabinet meeting in progress

individual government members may hold different opinions, but they are expected to keep these private. By convention, no member of the government can criticize government policy in public. Any member who does so must resign.

The cabinet

Obviously, no government wants an important member of its party to start criticizing it. This would lead to divisions in the party. Therefore, the leading politicians in the governing party usually become members of the cabinet, where they are tied to government policy by the convention of collective responsibility.

The cabinet meets once a week and takes decisions about new policies, the implementation of existing policies and the running of the various government departments. Because all government members must be seen to agree, exactly who says what at these meetings is a closely guarded secret. Reports are made of the meetings and circulated to government departments. They summarize the topics discussed and the decisions taken, but they never refer to individuals or what they said.

To help run the complicated machinery of a modern government, there is an organization called the cabinet office. It runs a busy communication network, keeping ministers in touch with each other and drawing up the agendas for cabinet meetings. It also does the same things for the many cabinet committees. These committees are appointed by the cabinet to look into various matters in more detail than the individual members of the cabinet have the time (or knowledge) for. Unlike members of 'the government' itself, the people on these committees are not necessarily politicians.

The Prime Minister

The position of a British Prime Minister (PM) is in direct contrast to that of the monarch. Although the Queen appears to have a great deal of power, in reality she has very little. The PM, on the other hand, appears not to have much power but in reality has a very great

▶ The cabinet

The history of the cabinet is a good example of the tendency to secrecy in British politics. It started in the eighteenth century as an informal grouping of important ministers and officials of the royal household. It had no formal recognition. Officially speaking, the government was run by the Privy Council, a body of a hundred or more people (including those belonging to 'the cabinet'), directly responsible to the monarch (but not to each other). Over the years, the cabinet gradually took over effective power. The Privy Council is now a merely ceremonial organization with no power. Among others, it includes all the present ministers and the most important past ministers.

In the last hundred years, the cabinet has itself become more and more 'official' and publicly recognized. It has also grown in size, and so is now often too rigid and formal a body to take the real decisions. In the last fifty years, there have been unofficial 'inner cabinets' (comprising the Prime Minister and a few other important ministers). It is thought that it is here, and in cabinet committees, that much of the real decision-making takes place.

▶ No. 10 Downing Street

Here is an example of the traditional fiction that Prime Ministers are not especially important people. Their official residence does not have a special name. Nor, from the outside, does it look special. It is not even a detached house! Inside, though, it is much larger than it looks. The cabinet meets here and the cabinet office works here. The PM lives 'above the shop' on the top floor.

The Chancellor of the Exchequer lives next door, at No. 11, and the Government Chief Whip (see chapter 10) at No. 12, so that the whole street is a lot more important than it appears. Still, there is something very domestic about this arrangement. After the government loses an election all three ministers have to throw out their rubbish and wait for the furniture vans to turn up, just like anybody else moving house.

The PM also has an official country residence to the west of London, called 'Chequers'.

deal indeed. As we have seen (chapter 7), the Queen is, in practice, obliged to give the job of Prime Minister to the person who can command a majority in the House of Commons. This normally means the leader of the party with the largest number of MPs.

From one point of view, the PM is no more than the foremost of Her Majesty's political servants. The traditional phrase describes him or her as *primus inter pares* (Latin for 'first among equals'). But in fact the other ministers are not nearly as powerful. There are several reasons for this. First, the monarch's powers of patronage (the power to appoint people to all kinds of jobs and to confer honours on people) are, by convention, actually the PM's powers of patronage. The fiction is that the Queen appoints people to government jobs 'on the advice of the Prime Minister'. But what actually happens is that the PM simply decides. Everybody knows this. The media do not even make the pretence that the PM has successfully persuaded the Queen to make a particular appointment, they simply state that he or she has made an appointment.

The strength of the PM's power of patronage is apparent from the modern phenomenon known as the 'cabinet reshuffle'. For the past thirty years it has been the habit of the PM to change his or her cabinet quite frequently (at least once every two years). A few cabinet members are dropped, and a few new members are brought in, but mostly the existing members are shuffled around, like a pack of cards, each getting a new department to look after.

The second reason for a modern PM's dominance over other ministers is the power of the PM's public image. The mass media has tended to make politics a matter of personalities. The details of policies are hard to understand. An individual, constantly appearing on the television and in the newspapers, is much easier to identify with. Everybody in the country can recognize the Prime Minister, while many cannot put a name to the faces of the other ministers. As a result the PM can, if the need arises, go 'over the heads' of the other ministers and appeal directly to the public.

▶The ideal Prime Minister

Here is another extract (see chapter 6) from *Yes, Prime Minister*, the political satire. It is a section of the private diary of a senior civil servant. In it he describes his conversation with another top civil servant, in which they discussed who should become the new Prime Minister. When he says 'experts' in the last line he means, of course, the civil servants themselves!

> We take a fairly dim view of them both [the two candidates]. It is a difficult choice, rather like asking which lunatic should run the asylum. We both agreed that they would present the same problems. They are both interventionists and they would both have foolish notions about running the country themselves if they became Prime Minister. . . . It is clearly advisable to look for a compromise candidate.
>
> We agreed that such a candidate must have the following qualities: he must be malleable, flexible, likeable, have no firm opinions, no bright ideas, not be intellectually committed, and be without the strength of purpose to change anything. Above all, he must be someone whom we know can be professionally guided, and who is willing to leave the business of government in the hands of experts.

Third, all ministers except the PM are kept busy looking after their government departments. They don't have time to think about and discuss government policy as a whole. But the PM does, and cabinet committees usually report directly to him or her, not to the cabinet as a whole. Moreover, the cabinet office is directly under the PM's control and works in the same building. As a result, the PM knows more about what is going on than the other ministers do. Because there is not enough time for the cabinet to discuss most matters, a choice has to be made about what will be discussed. And it is the PM who makes that choice. Matters that are not discussed can, in effect, be decided by the PM. The convention of collective responsibility then means that the rest of the government have to go along with whatever the PM has decided.

Prime Ministers since 1940

Winston Churchill (1940–45)
Clement Attlee (1945–51)
Winston Churchill (1951–55)
Anthony Eden (1955–57)
Harold Macmillan (1957–63)
Alec Douglas-Home (1963–64)
Harold Wilson (1964–70)
Edward Heath (1970–74)
Harold Wilson (1974–76)
James Callaghan (1976–79)
Margaret Thatcher (1979–91)
John Major (1991–97)
Tony Blair (1997–)

Blue = Conservative
Red = Labour

The civil service

Considering how complex modern states are, there are not really very many people in a British 'government' (as defined above). Unlike some other countries (the USA for example), not even the most senior administrative jobs change hands when a new government comes to power. The day-to-day running of the government and the implementation of its policy continue in the hands of the same people that were there with the previous government – the top rank of the civil service. Governments come and go, but the civil service remains. It is no accident that the most senior civil servant in a government department has the title of 'Permanent Secretary'.

Unlike politicians, civil servants, even of the highest rank, are unknown to the larger public. There are probably less than 10,000 people in the country who, if you asked them, could give you the names of the present secretary to the cabinet (who runs the cabinet office) or the present head of the home civil service; still fewer know the names of more than one of the present permanent secretaries.

For those who belong to it, the British civil service is a career. Its most senior positions are usually filled by people who have been working in it for twenty years or more. These people get a high salary (higher than that of their ministers), have absolute job security (unlike their ministers) and stand a good chance of being awarded an official honour. By comparison, ministers, even those who have been in the same department for several years, are still new to the job. Moreover, civil servants know the secrets of the previous government which the present minister is unaware of.

For all these reasons, it is often possible for top civil servants to exercise quite a lot of control over their ministers, and it is sometimes said that it is they, and not their ministers, who really govern the country. There is undoubtedly some truth in this opinion. Indeed, an interesting case in early 1994 suggests that civil servants now *expect* to have a degree of control. At this time, the association which represents the country's top civil servants made an official complaint

The origins of the civil service

The British 'cult of the talented amateur' (see chapter 5) is not normally expressed openly. But when, in the middle of the nineteenth century, the structure of the modern civil service was established, it was a consciously stated principle, as described by the contemporary historian Lord Macauley:

> We believe that men who have been engaged, up to twenty-one or twenty-two, in studies which have no immediate connection with the business of any profession, and of which the effect is merely to open, to invigorate, and to enrich the mind, will generally be found in the business of every profession superior to men who have, at eighteen or nineteen, devoted themselves to the special studies of their calling.

In other words, it is better to be a non-specialist than a specialist, to have a good brain rather than thorough knowledge. Reforms since then have given greater emphasis to specialist knowledge, but the central belief remains that administration is an art rather than an applied science.

▶ Whitehall

This is the name of the street in London which runs from Trafalgar Square to the Houses of Parliament. The Foreign and Commonwealth Office and the Ministry of Defence are both located here. These are the two oldest government departments. The term 'Whitehall' is sometimes used to refer to the government as a whole (although other departments are in other streets nearby). This is done when the writer or speaker wishes to emphasize the administrative aspects of government. The phrase, 'the opinion in Whitehall . . .' refers not only to the opinions of government ministers but also, and perhaps more so, to the opinions of senior civil servants.

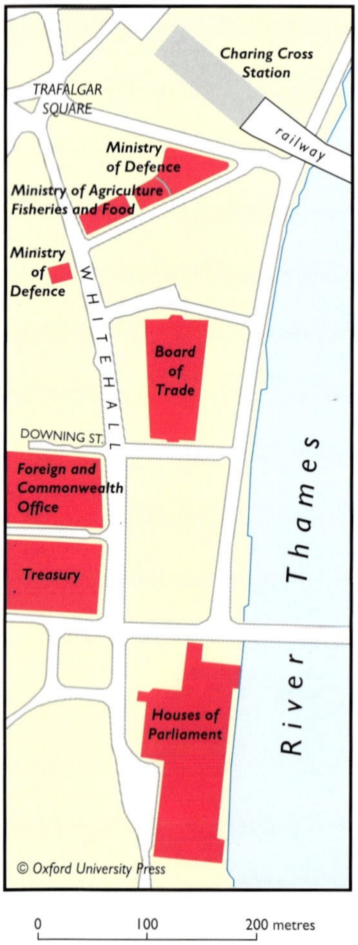

that four government ministers 'verbally abused' their civil service advisers and generally treated them 'with contempt'. It was the first time that such a complaint had been made. It seemed that the unprecedentedly long period of government by the same party (the Conservatives – see chapter 10) had shifted the traditional balance of power.

However, the British civil service has a (largely) deserved reputation for absolute political impartiality. Many ministers have remarked on the struggle for power between them and their top civil servants, but very few have ever complained of any political bias. Top civil servants know that their power depends on their staying out of 'politics' and on their being absolutely loyal to their present minister.

Modern criticism of the civil service does not question its loyalty but its efficiency. Despite reforms, the top rank of the civil service is still largely made up of people from the same narrow section of society – people who have been to public school (see chapter 14) and then on to Oxford or Cambridge, where they studied subjects such as history or classical languages. The criticism is therefore that the civil service does not have enough expertise in matters such as economics or technology, and that it lives too much in its own closed world, cut off from the concerns of most people in society. In the late twentieth century, ministers tried to overcome these perceived deficiencies by appointing experts from outside the civil service to work on various projects and by having their own political advisers working alongside (or, some would say, in competition with) their civil servants.

Central and local government

Some countries, such as the USA and Canada, are federal. They are made up of a number of states, each of which has its own government with its own powers to make laws and collect taxes. In these countries the central governments have powers only because the states have given them powers. In Britain it is the other way around. Local government authorities (generally known as 'councils') only have powers because the central government has given them powers. Indeed, they only exist because the central government allows them to exist. Several times in the last hundred years British governments have reorganized local government, abolishing some local councils and bringing new ones into existence.

The system of local government is very similar to the system of national government. There are elected representatives, called councillors (the equivalent of MPs). They meet in a council chamber in the Town Hall or County Hall (the equivalent of Parliament), where they make policy which is implemented by local government officers (the equivalent of civil servants).

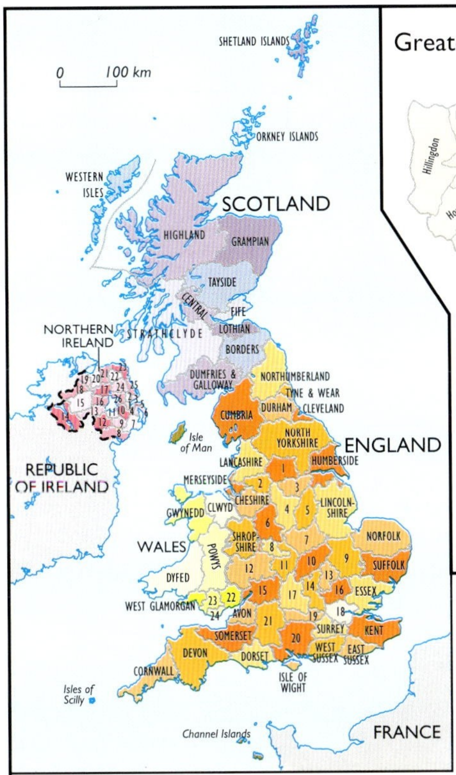

Key to Greater London Boroughs

1	City of London	9	Southwark
2	City of Westminster	10	Lewisham
3	Camden	11	Lambeth
4	Islington	12	Wandsworth
5	Haringey	13	Kensington & Chelsea
6	Hackney	14	Hammersmith
7	Waltham Forest	15	Richmond upon Thames
8	Tower Hamlets	16	Kingston upon Thames

British Isles: Counties and London Boroughs,

as at June 1995

Key to England and Wales

1	WEST YORKSHIRE	13	BEDFORDSHIRE
2	GREATER MANCHESTER	14	BUCKINGHAMSHIRE
3	SOUTH YORKSHIRE	15	GLOUCESTERSHIRE
4	DERBYSHIRE	16	HERTFORDSHIRE
5	NOTTINGHAMSHIRE	17	OXFORDSHIRE
6	STAFFORDSHIRE	18	GREATER LONDON (see inset)
7	LEICESTERSHIRE	19	BERKSHIRE
8	WEST MIDLANDS	20	HAMPSHIRE
9	CAMBRIDGESHIRE	21	WILTSHIRE
10	NORTHAMPTONSHIRE	22	GWENT
11	WARWICKSHIRE	23	MID GLAMORGAN
12	HEREFORD AND WORCESTER	24	SOUTH GLAMORGAN

Key to Northern Ireland

1	BELFAST	14	FERMANAGH
2	NEWTOWNABBEY	15	OMAGH
3	CARRICKFERGUS	16	COOKSTOWN
4	CASTLEREAGH	17	MAGHERAFELT
5	NORTH DOWN	18	STRABANE
6	ARDS	19	DERRY
7	DOWN	20	LIMAVADY
8	NEWRY AND MOURNE	21	COLERAINE
9	BANBRIDGE	22	BALLYMONEY
10	LISBURN	23	MOYLE
11	CRAIGAVON	24	BALLYMENA
12	ARMAGH	25	LARNE
13	DUNGANNON	26	ANTRIM

Most British people have far more direct dealings with local government than they do with national government. Local councils traditionally manage nearly all public services. Taken together, they employ three times as many people as the national government does. In addition, there is no system in Britain whereby a national government official has responsibility for a particular geographical area. (There is no one like a 'prefect' or 'governor'). In practice, therefore, local councils have traditionally been fairly free from constant central interference in their day to day work.

Local councils are allowed to collect one kind of tax. This is a tax based on property. (All other kinds are collected by central government.) It used to be called 'rates' and was paid only by those who owned property. Its amount varied according to the size and location of the property. In the early 1990s it was replaced by the 'community charge' (known as the 'poll tax'). This charge was the

▶ Counties, boroughs, parishes

Counties are the oldest divisions of the country in England and Wales. Most of them existed before the Norman conquest (see chapter 2). They are still used today for local government purposes, although a few have been 'invented' more recently (e.g. Humberside) and others have no function in government but are still used for other purposes. One of these is Middlesex, which covers the western part of Greater London (letters are still addressed 'Middx.') and which is the name of a top-class cricket team. Many counties have 'shire' in their name (e.g. Hertfordshire, Hampshire, Leicestershire). 'Shires' is what the counties were originally called.

Boroughs were originally towns that had grown large and important enough to be given their own government, free of control by the county. These days, the name is used for local government purposes only in London, but many towns still proudly describe themselves as Royal Boroughs.

Parishes were originally villages centred on a local church. They became a unit of local government in the nineteenth century. Today they are the smallest unit of local government in England.

The name 'parish' is still used in the organization of the main Christian churches in England (see chapter 13).

same for everybody who lived in the area covered by a council. It was very unpopular and was quickly replaced by the 'council tax', which is based on the estimated value of a property and the number of people living in it. Local councils are unable to raise enough money in this way for them to provide the services which central government has told them to provide. In addition, recent governments have imposed upper limits on the amount of council tax that councils can charge and now collect the taxes on business properties themselves (and then share the money out between local councils). As a result, well over half of a local council's income is now given to it by central government.

The modern trend has been towards greater and greater control by central government. This is not just a matter of controlling the way local government raises money. There are now more laws governing the way councils can conduct their affairs. On top of this, schools and hospitals can now 'opt out' of local-government control (see chapters 14 and 18). Perhaps this trend is inevitable now that national party politics dominates local politics. Successful independent candidates (candidates who do not belong to a political party) at local elections are becoming rarer and rarer. Most people now vote at local elections according to their national party preferences, if they bother to vote at all, so that these elections become a kind of opinion poll on the performance of the national government.

▶ The Greater London Council

The story of the Greater London Council (GLC) is an example of the struggle for power between central and local government. In the early 1980s Britain had a right-wing Conservative government. At a time when this government was unpopular, the left-wing Labour party in London won the local election and gained control of the GLC. The Labour-controlled GLC then introduced many measures which the national government did not like (for example, it reduced fares on London's buses and increased local taxes to pay for this).

The government decided to abolish the GLC. Using its majority in the House of Commons, it was able to do this. The powers of the GLC were either given to the thirty-two boroughs of London, or to special commitees. It was not until the year 2000 that a single governmental authority for the whole of London came into existence again and the city got its first ever directly-elected mayor.

Local government services

Most of the numerous services that a modern government provides are run at local level in Britain. These include public hygiene and environmental health inspection, the collecting of rubbish from outside people's houses (the people who do this are euphemistically known as 'dustmen'), and the cleaning and tidying of all public places (which is done by 'street sweepers') (▷ *The organization of local government*). They also include the provision of public swimming pools, which charge admission fees, and public parks, which do not. The latter are mostly just green grassy spaces, but they often contain children's playgrounds and playing fields for sports such as football and cricket which can be reserved in advance on payment.

Public libraries are another well-known service (▷ *Public libraries*). Anybody can go into one of these to consult the books, newspapers and magazines there free of charge. If you want to borrow books and take them out of the library, you have to have a library card or ticket (these are available to people living in the area). Sometimes CDs and video cassettes are also available for hire. The popularity of libraries in Britain is indicated by the fact that, in a country without identity cards (see chapter 6), a person's library card is the most common means of identification for someone who does not have a driving licence.

▶ Public libraries

In comparison with the people of other western countries, the British public buy relatively few books. However, this does not necessarily mean that they read less. There are about 5,000 public libraries in Britain (that's about one for every 12,000 people). On average, each one houses around 45,000 books. A recent survey showed that 70% of children between the ages of four and sixteen use their local library at least twice a month, and that 51% of them use it once a week or more.

In addition, and unfortunately, many British people seem to prefer libraries to bookshops even when they want to own a book. Nearly nine million books are stolen from the shelves of libraries every year.

The organization of local government (1995)

CENTRAL GOVERNMENT

↓

Cities and large towns in England and Wales

36 Metropolitan Districts
32 London Boroughs

Responsible for:
- collection of council tax
- planning
- roads and traffic
- housing
- building regulations
- safety in public places
- collection of rubbish
- disposal of rubbish
- education
- social services
- libraries
- leisure and recreation

In these areas some services, such as transport, the police force and the fire brigade, are run by special authorities, some of whose members are councillors.

↓

The rest of England and Wales and all of Scotland

10 Regions (Scotland)
47 Counties (England and Wales)

Responsible for:
- collection of council tax
- planning
- roads and safety
- disposal of rubbish
- education
- social services
- libraries
- police force
- fire brigade

↓

Districts

Responsible for:
- housing
- local planning
- collection of rubbish
- leisure and recreation
- safety in public places

↓

Parishes (England)
Communities (Scotland and Wales)

These have no legal powers but are recognized as neighbourhood or village-level forums of discussion.

QUESTIONS

1 Do you think the theory of collective responsibility is a good one? Does it exist in your country?

2 What would be the equivalent titles in your country for: Chancellor, Home Secretary, Foreign Secretary?

3 A British Prime Minister has no status in law which puts him or her above other politicians. So why are modern British PMs so powerful?

4 How does the relationship between central and local government in Britain compare with that in your country?

5 Local government in Britain is responsible for most of the things that affect people in everyday life. So why do you think so few people bother to vote in local elections in Britain?

SUGGESTIONS

- Margaret Thatcher (Prime Minister from 1979 to 1990) has been the subject of several biographical studies which offer insights into the workings of government. For example, *One of us* by Hugo Young (Pan Books).

9
Parliament

The activities of Parliament in Britain are more or less the same as those of the Parliament in any western democracy. It makes new laws, gives authority for the government to raise and spend money, keeps a close eye on government activities and discusses those activities.

The British Parliament works in a large building called the Palace of Westminster (popularly known as 'the Houses of Parliament'). This contains offices, committee rooms, restaurants, bars, libraries and even some places of residence. It also contains two larger rooms. One of these is where the House of Lords meets, the other is where the House of Commons meets. The British Parliament is divided into two 'houses', and its members belong to one or other of them, although only members of the Commons are normally known as MPs (Members of Parliament). The Commons is by far the more important of the two houses.

▶ **The House of Commons**

1 Speaker's chair
2 government benches
3 opposition benches
4 galleries for visitors
5 press gallery

The atmosphere of Parliament

Look at the picture of the inside of the meeting room of the House of Commons (▷ *The House of Commons*). Its design and layout differ from the interior of the parliament buildings in most other countries. These differences can tell us a lot about what is distinctive about the British Parliament.

First, notice the seating arrangements. There are just two rows of benches facing each other. On the left of the picture are the government benches, where the MPs of the governing party sit. On the right are the opposition benches. There is no opportunity in this layout for a reflection of all the various shades of political opinion (as there is with a semi-circle). According to where they sit, MPs are seen to be either 'for' the government (supporting it) or against it. This physical division is emphasized by the table on the floor of the House between the two rows of benches. The Speaker's chair, which is raised some way off the floor, is also here. From this commanding position, the Speaker chairs (that is, controls) the debates (▷ *The Speaker*). The arrangement of the benches encourages confrontation between government and opposition. It also reinforces psychologically the reality of the British two-party system (see chapter 6). There are no 'cross-benches' for MPs who belong neither to the governing party nor the main opposition party. In practice, these MPs sit on the opposition benches furthest from the Speaker's chair (at the bottom right of the picture).

Plan of the Palace of Westminster (principal floor)

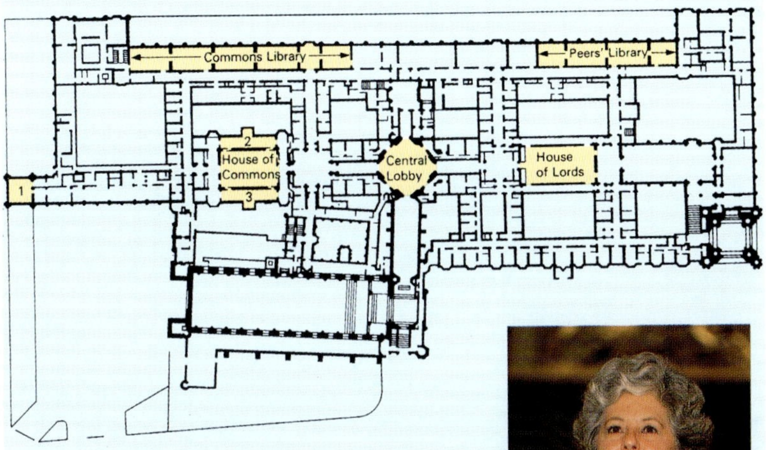

1 Clock-tower (Big Ben)
2 'No' Division Lobby
3 'Aye' Division Lobby

▶ The Speaker

Anybody who happened to be watching the live broadcast of Parliament on 27 April 1992 was able to witness an extraordinary spectacle. A female MP was physically dragged, apparently against her will, out of her seat on the back benches by fellow MPs and was forced to sit in the large chair in the middle of the House of Commons.

What the House of Commons was actually doing was appointing a new Speaker. The Speaker is the person who chairs and controls discussion in the House, decides which MP is going to speak next and makes sure that the rules of procedure are followed. (If they are not, the Speaker has the power to demand a public apology from an MP or even to ban an MP from the House for a number of days). It is a very important position. In fact, the Speaker is, officially, the second most important 'commoner' (non-aristocrat) in the kingdom after the Prime Minister.

Hundreds of years ago, it was the Speaker's job to communicate the decisions of the Commons to the King (that is where the title 'Speaker' comes from). As the king was often very displeased with what the Commons had decided, this was not a pleasant task. As a result, nobody wanted the job. They had to be forced to take it. These days, the position is a much safer one, but the tradition of dragging an unwilling Speaker to the chair has remained.

The occasion in 1992 was the first time that a woman had been appointed Speaker, so that MPs had to get used to addressing not 'Mr Speaker', as they had always done in the past, but 'Madam Speaker' instead. Once a Speaker has been appointed, he or she agrees to give up all party politics and remains in the job for as long as he or she wants it.

Betty Boothroyd, the first woman Speaker of the House of Commons

Second, the Commons has no 'front', no obvious place from which an MP can address everybody there. MPs simply stand up and speak from wherever they happen to be sitting. Third, notice that there are no desks for the MPs. The benches where they sit are exactly and only that – benches, just as in a church. This makes it physically easy for them to drift in and out of the room, which is something that they frequently do during debates. Fourth, notice that the House is very small. In fact, there isn't enough room for all the MPs. There are more than 650 of them, but there is seating for less than 400. A candidate at an election is said to have won 'a seat' in the Commons, but this 'seat' is imaginary. MPs do not have their 'own' place to sit. No names are marked on the benches. MPs just sit down wherever (on 'their' side of the House) they can find room.

All these features result in a fairly informal atmosphere. Individual MPs, without their own 'territory' (which a personal seat and desk would give them), are encouraged to co-operate. Moreover, the small size of the House, together with the lack of a podium or dais from which to address it, means that MPs do not normally speak in the way that they would at a large public rally. MPs normally speak in a conversational tone, and because they have nowhere to place their notes while speaking, they do not normally speak for very long either! It is only on particularly important occasions, when all the MPs are present, that passionate oratory is sometimes used.

One more thing should be noted about the design of the House of Commons. It is deliberate. Historically, it was an accident: in medieval times, the Commons met in a church and churches of that time often had rows of benches facing each other. But after the House was badly damaged by bombing in 1941, it was deliberately rebuilt to the old pattern (with one or two modern comforts such as central heating added). This was because of a belief in the two-way 'for and against' tradition, and also because of a more general desire for continuity.

The ancient habits are preserved today in the many customs and detailed rules of procedure which all new MPs find that they have to learn. The most noticeable of these is the rule that forbids MPs to address one another directly or use personal names. All remarks and questions must go 'through the Chair'. An MP who is speaking refers to or asks a question of 'the honourable Member for Winchester' or 'my right honourable friend'. The MP for Winchester may be sitting directly opposite, but the MP never says 'you'. These ancient rules were originally formulated to take the 'heat' out of debate and decrease the possibility that violence might break out. Today, they lend a touch of formality which balances the informal aspects of the Commons and further increases the feeling of MPs that they belong to a special group of people.

An MP's life

The comparative informality of the Commons may partly result from the British belief in amateurism. Traditionally, MPs were not supposed to be specialist politicians. They were supposed to be ordinary people giving some of their time to representing the people. Ideally, they came from all walks of life, bringing their experience of the everyday world into Parliament with them. This is why MPs were not even paid until the early twentieth century. Traditionally, they were supposed to be doing a public service, not making a career for themselves. Of course, this tradition meant that only rich people could afford to be MPs so that, although they did indeed come from a wide variety of backgrounds, these were always backgrounds of power and wealth. Even now, British MPs do not get paid very much in comparison with many of their European counterparts. Moreover, by European standards, they have incredibly poor facilities. Most MPs have to share an office and a secretary with two or more other MPs.

The ideal of the talented amateur does not, of course, reflect modern reality. Politics in Britain in the last forty years has become professional. Most MPs are full-time politicians, and do another job, if at all, only part-time. But the amateur tradition is still reflected in the hours of business of the Commons. They are 'gentleman's hours'. The House does not sit in the morning. This is when, in the traditional ideal, MPs would be doing their ordinary work or pursuing other interests outside Parliament. From Monday to Thursday, the House does not start its business until 14.30 (on Friday it starts in the morning, but then finishes in the early afternoon for the weekend). It also gives itself long holidays: four weeks at Christmas, two each at Easter and Whitsun (Pentecost), and about eleven weeks in the summer (from the beginning of August until the middle of October).

But this apparently easy life is misleading. In fact, the average modern MP spends more time at work than any other professional in the country. From Monday to Thursday, the Commons never 'rises' (i.e. finishes work for the day) before 22.30 and sometimes it continues sitting for several hours longer. Occasionally, it debates through most of the night. The Commons, in fact, spends a greater total amount of time sitting each year than any other Parliament in Europe.

MPs' mornings are taken up with committee work, research, preparing speeches and dealing with the problems of constituents (the people they represent). Weekends are not free for MPs either. They are expected to visit their constituencies (the areas they represent) and listen to the problems of anybody who wants to see them. It is an extremely busy life that leaves little time for pursuing another career. It does not leave MPs much time for their families either. Politicians have a higher rate of divorce than the (already high) national average.

▶ Hansard

This is the name given to the daily verbatim reports of everything that has been said in the Commons. They are published within forty-eight hours of the day they cover.

▶ The parliamentary day in the Commons from Mondays to Thursdays

14.30
Prayers

14.35
Question time

15.30
Any miscellaneous business, such as a statement from a minister, after which the main business of the day begins. On more than half of the days, this means a debate on a proposal for a new law, known as a 'bill'. Most of these bills are introduced by the government but some days in each year are reserved for 'private members' bills'; that is, proposals for laws made by individual MPs. Not many of these become law, because there is not enough interest among other MPs and not enough time for proper discussion of them.

22.00
Motion on the adjournment: the main business of the day stops and MPs are allowed to bring up another matter for general discussion.

22.30
The House rises (usually).

Parliamentary business

The basic procedure for business in the Commons is a debate on a particular proposal, followed by a resolution which either accepts or rejects this proposal. Sometimes the resolution just expresses a viewpoint, but most often it is a matter of framing a new law or of approving (or not approving) government plans to raise taxes or spend money in certain ways. Occasionally, there is no need to take a vote, but there usually is, and at such times there is a 'division'. That is, MPs have to vote for or against a particular proposal. They do this by walking through one of two corridors at the side of the House – one is for the 'Ayes' (those who agree with the proposal) and the other is for the 'Noes' (those who disagree).

But the resolutions of the Commons are only part of its activities. There are also the committees. Some committees are appointed to examine particular proposals for laws, but there are also permanent committees whose job is to investigate the activities of government in a particular field. These committees comprise about forty members and are formed to reflect the relative strengths of the parties in the Commons as a whole. They have the power to call certain people, such as civil servants, to come and answer their questions. They are becoming a more and more important part of the business of the Commons.

The party system in Parliament

Most divisions take place along party lines. MPs know that they owe their position to their party, so they nearly always vote the way that their party tells them to. The people who make sure that MPs do this are called the Whips. Each of the two major parties has several MPs who perform this role. It is their job to inform all MPs in their party how they should vote. By tradition, if the government loses a vote in Parliament on a very important matter, it has to resign. Therefore, when there is a division on such a matter, MPs are expected to go to the House and vote even if they have not been there during the debate.

The Whips act as intermediaries between the backbenchers and the frontbench (▷ *Frontbenchers and backbenchers*) of a party. They keep the party leadership informed about backbench opinion. They are powerful people. Because they 'have the ear' of the party leaders, they can have an effect on which backbenchers get promoted to the front bench and which do not. For reasons such as this, 'rebellions' among a group of a party's MPs (in which they vote against their party) are very rare.

Sometimes the major parties allow a 'free vote', when MPs vote according to their own beliefs and not according to party policy. Some quite important decisions, such as the abolition of the death penalty and the decision to allow television cameras into the Commons, have been made in this way.

▶ Frontbenchers and backbenchers

Although MPs do not have their own personal seats in the Commons, there are two seating areas reserved for particular MPs. These areas are the front benches on either side of the House. These benches are where the leading members of the governing party (i.e. ministers) and the leading members of the main opposition party sit. These people are thus known as 'frontbenchers'. MPs who do not hold a government post or a post in the shadow cabinet (see chapter 8) are known as 'backbenchers'.

Tony Blair, Prime Minister from 1997, answering questions in the House of Commons

▶ How a bill becomes a law

Before a proposal for a new law starts its progress through Parliament, there will have been much discussion. If it is a government proposal, Green and White Papers will probably have been published, explaining the ideas behind the proposal. After this, lawyers draft the proposal into a bill.

Most bills begin life in the House of Commons, where they go through a number of stages.

First reading
This is a formal announcement only, with no debate

↓

Second reading
The house debates the general principles of the bill and, in most cases, takes a vote.

↓

Committee stage
A committee of MPs examines the details of the bill and votes on amendments (changes) to parts of it.

↓

Report stage
The House considers the amendments.

↓

Third reading
The amended bill is debated as a whole.

↓

The bill is sent to the **House of Lords**, where it goes through the same stages. (If the Lords make new amendments, these will be considered by the Commons.)

↓

After both Houses have reached agreement, the bill receives the **royal assent** and becomes an Act of Parliament which can be applied as part of the law.

▶ Question time

This is the most well-attended, and usually the noisiest, part of the parliamentary day. For about an hour there is no subject for debate. Instead, MPs are allowed to ask questions of government ministers. In this way they can, in theory at least, force the government to make certain facts public and to make its intentions clear. Opposition MPs in particular have an opportunity to make government ministers look incompetent or perhaps dishonest.

The questions and answers, however, are not spontaneous. Questions to ministers have to be 'tabled' (written down and placed on the table below the Speaker's chair) two days in advance, so that ministers have time to prepare their answers. In this way the government can usually avoid major embarrassment. The trick, though, is to ask an unexpected 'supplementary' question. After the minister has answered the tabled question, the MP who originally tabled it is allowed to ask a further question relating to the minister's answer. In this way, it is sometimes possible for MPs to catch a minister unprepared.

Question time has been widely copied around the world. It is also probably the aspect of Parliament most well-known among the general public. The vast majority of television news excerpts of Parliament are taken from this period of its day. Especially common is for the news to show an excerpt from the half-hour on Wednesdays when it is the Prime Minister's turn to answer questions.

Lords legal and spiritual

As well as life peers, there are two other kinds of peer in the House of Lords who do not have seats there by hereditary right, but because of their position. First, there are the twenty-six bishops of the Church of England. Second, there are the Lords of Appeal (known as the 'Law Lords'), the twenty or so most senior judges in the land. By tradition, the House of Lords is the final court of appeal in the country. In fact, however, when the Lords acts in this role, it is only the Law Lords who vote on the matter.

Reforming the House of Lords

In 1910 the Liberal government proposed heavy taxes on the rich. The House of Lords rejected the proposal. This rejection went against a long-standing tradition that the House of Commons had control of financial matters.

The government then asked the king for an election and won it. Again, it passed its tax proposals through the Commons, and also a bill limiting the power of the Lords. Again, the Lords rejected both bills, and again the government won another election. It was a constitutional crisis.

What was to happen? Revolution? No. What happened was that the king let it be known that if the Lords rejected the same bills again, he would appoint hundreds of new peers who *would* vote for the bills – enough for the government to have a majority in the Lords. So, in 1911, rather than have the prestige of their House destroyed in this way, the Lords agreed to both bills, including the one that limited their own powers. From that time, a bill which had been agreed in the Commons for three years in a row could become law without the agreement of the Lords. This period of time was further reduced in 1949.

The House of Lords

A unique feature of the British parliamentary system is its hereditary element. Unlike MPs, members of the House of Lords (known as 'peers') are not elected. They are members as of right. In the case of some of them, this 'right' is the result of their being the holder of an inherited aristocratic title. The House of Lords is therefore a relic of earlier, undemocratic, times. The fact that it still exists is perhaps typically British. It has been allowed to survive but it has had to change, losing most of its power and altering its composition in the process.

The House of Lords (like the monarchy) has little, if any, real power any more. All proposals must have the agreement of the Lords before they can become law. But the power of the Lords to refuse a proposal for a law which has been agreed by the Commons is now limited. After a period which can be as short as six months the proposal becomes law anyway, whether or not the Lords agree.

The composition of the Lords has changed since 1958, when it became possible to award 'life peerages' through the honours system (see chapter 7). Entitlement to sit in the Lords does not pass to the children of life peers. The life peerage system has established itself as a means of finding a place in public life for distinguished retired politicians who may no longer wish to be as busy as MPs in the Commons, but who still wish to voice their opinions in a public forum. At the time of writing, four of the last five Prime Ministers, as well as about 300 past ministers and other respected politicians, have accepted the offer of a life peerage. Political parties are, in fact, especially keen to send their older members who once belonged to the leadership of the party to the House of Lords. It is a way of rewarding them with prestige while at the same time getting them out of the way of the present party leaders in the Commons, where their status and reputation might otherwise create trouble for party unity. Informally, this practice has become known as being 'kicked upstairs'. As a result of the life peerage system there are more than 300 people in the House of Lords who are not aristocrats and who have expertise in political life. In fact, as a result of recent reforms, these life peers now form a majority at its sittings.

The modern House of Lords is a forum for public discussion. Because its members do not depend on party politics for their position, it is sometimes able to bring important matters that the Commons has been ignoring into the open. More importantly, it is the place where proposals for new laws are discussed in great detail – much more detail than the busy Commons has time for – and in this way irregularities or inconsistencies in these proposals can be removed before they become law. More important still, it is argued, the Lords is a check on a government that, through its control of the Commons, could possibly become too dictatorial. Few people in politics are perfectly happy with the present arrangement. Most

▶ **The state opening of Parliament**

These photographs show two scenes from the annual state opening of Parliament. This is an example of a traditional ceremony which reminds MPs of their special status and of their 'togetherness'. In the first photograph, 'Black Rod', a servant of the Queen, is knocking on the door of the House of Commons and demanding that the MPs let the Queen come in and tell them what 'her' government is going to do in the coming year. The Commons always refuse her entry. This is because, in the seventeenth century, Charles I once burst in to the chamber and tried to arrest some MPs. Ever since then, the monarch has not been allowed to enter the Commons. Instead, the MPs agree to come through to the House of Lords and listen to the monarch in there. This is what they are doing in the second photograph. By tradition they always come through in pairs, each pair comprising MPs from two different parties.

people agree that having two Houses of Parliament is a good idea, and that this second house could have a more useful function if it were constituted in a different way (without the hereditary element). However, at this time, nobody can agree on what would be the best way to reform the composition of the second house, and so, despite recent reforms which have reduced the hereditary element, it remains as a fascinating (but valuable) anachronism in a modern state.

QUESTIONS

1 Where would an MP of the Scottish Nationalist party probably sit in the House of Commons?
2 In what ways do the seating arrangements, general facilities and pay for British MPs differ from those of parliamentary representatives in your country? Why are they different?
3 Many MPs in modern times are experts in various fields of government. Because of the complexity of modern government, this is something which seems to be necessary. But it could be said to have disadvantages, too. What do you think these disadvantages are?
4 When the Commons decide to vote, they do not vote immediately. Instead, a 'division bell' rings throughout the Palace of Westminster, after which MPs have ten minutes in which to vote. Why?
5 Many of the members of the House of Lords are hereditary aritsocrats. Why do the British put up with such an undemocratic element in their parliamentary system?

10 Elections

Look at the table below. You can see that the electoral system used in Britain doesn't seem to add up. In the 1997 election, the Labour party received less than half of the votes but won nearly two-thirds of the seats in the House of Commons. It won two-and-a-half times as many seats as the Conservative party, even though it received less than one-and-a-half times as many votes. The Liberal Democrat party did very badly out of the system. One in every six people voted for it, but it won only one in fourteen of the seats in the Commons. And yet it was much luckier than last time! The arithmetical absurdity of the system becomes clear when we examine the fortunes of the Liberal Democrats at the last two elections. In 1997 it received slightly fewer votes than it did in 1992, but won more than twice as many seats! What's going on? As is often the case with British institutions, the apparently illogical figures are the result of history.

The system

Unlike in any other country in the world, the system of political representation that is used in Britain evolved before the coming of democracy. It also evolved before national issues became more important to people than local ones. In theory, the House of Commons is simply a gathering of people who each represent a particular place in the kingdom. Originally, it was not the concern of anybody in government as to how each representative was chosen. That was a matter for each town or county to decide for itself. Not until the nineteenth century were laws passed about how elections were to be conducted (▷ *The evolution of the electoral system*).

▶ British general election results 1997

	Labour	Conservative	Liberal Democrat	All other parties
Votes	13,551,381 (43%)	9,590,565 (30%)	5,243,322 (17%)	3,130,392 (10%)
MPs	418 (64%)	165 (25%)	46 (7%)	29 (4%)
Votes per MP	32,342	58,125	113,985	107,945

This system was in place before the development of modern political parties (see chapter 6). These days, of course, nearly everybody votes for a candidate because he or she belongs to a particular party. But the tradition remains that an MP is first and foremost a representative of a particular locality. The result of this tradition is that the electoral system is remarkably simple. It works like this. The country is divided into a number of areas of roughly equal population (about 90,000), known as constituencies. Anybody who wants to be an MP must declare himself or herself as a candidate in one of these constituencies. On polling day (the day of the election), voters go to polling stations and are each given a single piece of paper (the ballot paper) with the names of the candidates for that constituency (only) on it. Each voter then puts a cross next to the name of one candidate. After the polls have closed, the ballot papers are counted. The candidate with the largest number of crosses next to his or her name is the winner and becomes the MP for the constituency.

And that's the end of it. There is no preferential voting (if a voter chooses more than one candidate, that ballot paper is 'spoiled' and is not counted); there is no counting of the proportion of votes for each party (all votes cast for losing candidates are simply ignored); there is no extra allocation of seats in Parliament according to party strengths. At the 1997 election, there were 659 constituencies and 659 MPs were elected. It was called a general election, and of course control of the government depended on it, but in formal terms it was just 659 separate elections going on at the same time.

Here are the results from two constituencies in 1997.

	Chesterfield	Votes	Totnes	Votes
Conservative	Martin Potter	4,752	Sir Anthony Steen	19,637
Liberal Democrat	Tony Rogers	20,330	Rob Chave	18,760
Labour	Tony Benn	26,105	Victor Ellery	8,796

If we add the votes received for each party in these two constituencies together, we find that the Liberal Democrats got more votes than Conservative or Labour. And yet, these two parties each won a seat while the Liberal Democrats did not. This is because they were not first in either constituency. It is coming first that matters. In fact, the system is known as the 'first-past-the-post' system (an allusion to horse-racing).

Formal arrangements

In practice, it is the government which decides when to hold an election. The law says that an election has to take place at least every five years. However, the interval between elections is usually a bit shorter than this. A party in power does not normally wait until the last possible moment. In 1983 and 1987, for example, the Conservative government called elections after only four years. When a party

The evolution of the electoral system

1832
The *Great Reform Bill* is passed.

Very small boroughs, where electors can easily be persuaded who to vote for, are abolished.

Seats are given to large new towns such as Birmingham and Manchester, which have until now been unrepresented in Parliament.

The franchise (the right to vote) is made uniform throughout the country, although differences between rural and urban areas remain. It depends on the value of property owned. About 5% of the adult population now has the right to vote in elections.

1867
The franchise is extended to include most of the male workers in towns.

1872
The secret ballot is introduced. (Until now, voting has been by a show of hands.)

1884
The franchise is extended to include male rural labourers.

1918
Women over the age of thirty are given the right to vote.

1928
Women are given the franchise on the same basis as men. All adults over twenty-one now have the right to vote.

1969
The minimum voting age is lowered to eighteen, and candidates are now allowed to enter a 'political description' of themselves next to their names on the ballot paper. Until now, the only information about a candidate that has been allowed on the ballot paper was his or her address.

▶ Crazy candidates

You don't have to belong to an important party to be a candidate. You don't even have to live in the constituency. All you need is £500. Look at this list of candidates from the 1992 election for the constituency of Huntingdon.

Miss Deborah Birkhead *Green*
Lord Buckethead *Gremloids*
Charles Cockell *Forward to Mars Party*
Andrew Duff *Liberal Democrat*
Michael Flanagan *Conservative Thatcherite*
John Major *Conservative*
Hugh Seckleman *Labour*
David Shepheard *Natural Law Party*
Lord David Sutch *Official Monster Raving Loony Party*
Paul Wiggin *Liberal*

Seven of these ten candidates did not get their money back. But there are always some people who are willing to be candidates even when they know they have no chance of winning. Sometimes they are people fighting for a single cause that they feel very strongly about. Sometimes they are people who just like to be candidates for a joke. In this case they tend to be candidates in constituencies where they will get a lot of publicity. Huntingdon is where the Prime Minister at that time, John Major, was a candidate, so it was a natural choice.

The most famous of these 'silly' candidates was 'Lord' David Sutch. He was a candidate in the same constituency as the Prime Minister in every election from 1966 to 1997. The intention of the £500 deposit is to discourage joke candidates such as 'Lord' Sutch, but they certainly add colour and amusement to the occasion.

has a very small majority in the House of Commons, or no majority at all, the interval can be much shorter.

After the date of an election has been fixed, people who want to be candidates in a constituency have to deposit £500 with the Returning Officer (the person responsible for the conduct of the election in each constituency). They get this money back if they get 5% of the votes or more. The local associations of the major parties will have already chosen their candidates (see chapter 6) and will pay the deposits for them. However, it is not necessary to belong to a party to be a candidate. It is a curious feature of the system that, legally speaking, parties do not exist. That is to say, there is no written law which tries to define them or regulate them. The law allows candidates, if they wish, to include a short 'political description' of themselves on the ballot paper. In practice, of course, most of these descriptions simply state 'Conservative', 'Labour' or 'Liberal Democrat'. But they can actually say anything that a candidate wants them to say (▷ *Crazy candidates*).

To be eligible to vote, a person must be at least eighteen years old and be on the electoral register. This is compiled every year for each constituency separately. People who have moved house and have not had time to get their names on the electoral register of their new constituency can arrange to vote by post. Nobody, however, is obliged to vote.

The campaign

British elections are comparatively quiet affairs. There is no tradition of large rallies or parades as there is in the USA. However, because of the intense coverage by the media, it would be very difficult to be in Britain at the time of a campaign and not realize that an election was about to take place.

The campaign reflects the contrast between the formal arrangements and the political reality. Formally, a different campaign takes place in each constituency. Local newspapers give coverage to the candidates; the candidates themselves hold meetings; party supporters stick up posters in their windows; local party workers spend their time canvassing (▷ *Canvassing*). The amount of money that candidates are allowed to spend on their campaigns is strictly limited. They have to submit detailed accounts of their expenses for inspection. Any attempt to influence voters improperly is outlawed.

But the reality is that all these activities and regulations do not usually make much difference. Nearly everybody votes for a candidate on the basis of the party which he or she represents, not because of his or her individual qualities or political opinions. Few people attend candidates' meetings; most people do not read local newspapers. In any case, the size of constituencies means that candidates cannot meet most voters, however energetically they go from door to door.

It is at a national level that the real campaign takes place. The parties spend millions of pounds advertising on hoardings and in newspapers (▷ *Party money*). By agreement, they do not buy time on television as they do in the USA. Instead, they are each given a number of strictly timed 'party political broadcasts'. Each party also holds a daily televised news conference. All of this puts the emphasis on the national party personalities rather than on local candidates. Only in the 'marginals' – constituencies where only a small shift in voting behaviour from last time would change the result – might the qualities of an individual candidate, possibly, affect the outcome.

Polling day

General elections always take place on a Thursday. They are not public holidays. People have to work in the normal way, so polling stations are open from seven in the morning till ten at night to give everybody the opportunity to vote. The only people who get a holiday are schoolchildren whose schools are being used as polling stations.

Each voter has to vote at a particular polling station. After being ticked off on the electoral register, the voter is given a ballot paper. Elections on the British mainland are always very fairly conducted. Northern Ireland, however, is a rather different story. There, the political tensions of so many years have had a negative effect on democratic procedures. Matters have improved since the 1960s, but the traditional, albeit joking, slogan in Ulster on polling day is 'vote early and vote often' – that is, try to vote as many times as you can by impersonating other people.

After the polls close, the marked ballot papers are taken to a central place in the constituency and counted. The Returning Officer then makes a public announcement of the votes cast for each candidate and declares the winner to be the MP for the constituency. This declaration is one of the few occasions during the election process when shouting and cheering may be heard.

An election result being declared

▶ Canvassing

This is the activity that occupies most of the time of local party workers during an election campaign. Canvassers go from door to door, calling on as many houses as possible and asking people how they intend to vote. They rarely make any attempt to change people's minds, but if a voter is identified as 'undecided', the party candidate might later attempt to pay a visit.

The main purpose of canvassing seems to be so that, on election day, transport can be offered, if needed, to those who claim to be supporters. (This is the only form of material help that parties are allowed to offer voters.) It also allows party workers to estimate how well they are doing on election day. They stand outside polling stations and record whether their supporters have voted. If it looks as if these people are not going to bother to vote, party workers might call on them to remind them to do so. Canvassing is an awful lot of work for very little benefit. It is a kind of election ritual.

▶ Party money

There is no law which regulates political parties, so there is no legal limit to the amount of money that national parties can spend on election campaigns. Nor is any money given to the parties by the state for their campaigns. (These are two more ways in which the British system differs from that in most other western countries.)

Furthermore, there is no law which obliges parties to say where they get their money from. This last point is a matter of heated debate among the parties. The Conservatives get a lot of their money from large single donations by individuals, sometimes from people outside Britain. The other parties would like to pass a law which forced parties to reveal the sources of large donations and which forbade donations from foreigners.

▶ The great television election show!

British people are generally not very enthusiastic about politics. But that does not stop them enjoying a good, political fight. Notice the images of sport and of generals planning a military campaign in this extract from the *Radio Times* from just before the 1992 general election.

> What a night it's going to be! As in all the best horseraces there is no clear favourite. Not since 1974 have the two main parties been so closely matched. We may even keep you up all night without being able to tell you who's won . . .
>
> On BBCI's 'Election 92', I'll have a whole array of electronic wizardry – including our Battleground – to help explain and illustrate what is shaping the new Parliament.
>
> Over 30 million people will have voted by 10 p.m. on the Thursday, but the decisive verdict will be pronounced by the five million people who vote in the marginal seats – and these are the ones we feature in our Battleground.
>
> Labour's aim is to colour the seats on the Battleground red. The Conservatives' task is to keep them blue . . .
>
> So sit back in your armchair and enjoy the excitement.

Radio Times, April 1992

Election night

The period after voting has become a television extravaganza. Both BBC and ITV start their programmes as soon as voting finishes. With millions watching, they continue right through the night. Certain features of these 'election specials', such as the 'swingometer' have entered popular folklore (▷ *The Swingometer*).

The first excitement of the night is the race to declare. It is a matter of local pride for some constituencies to be the first to announce their result. Doing so will guarantee that the cameras will be there to witness the event. If the count has gone smoothly, this usually occurs at just after 11.00 p.m. By midnight, after only a handful of results have been declared, experts (with the help of computers) will be making predictions about the composition of the newly elected House of Commons. Psephology (the study of voting habits) has become very sophisticated in Britain so that, although the experts never get it exactly right, they can get pretty close.

By two in the morning at least half of the constituencies will have declared their results and, unless the election is a very close one (as, for example, in 1974 and 1992), the experts on the television will now be able to predict with confidence which party will have a majority in the House of Commons, and therefore which party leader is going to be the Prime Minister.

Some constituencies, however, are not able to declare their results until well into Friday afternoon. This is either because they are very rural (mostly in Scotland or Northern Ireland), and so it takes a long time to bring all the ballot papers together, or because the race has been so close that one or more 'recounts' have been necessary. The phenomenon of recounts is a clear demonstration of the ironies of the British system. In most constituencies it would not make any difference to the result if several thousand ballot papers were lost. But in a few, the result depends on a handful of votes. In these cases, candidates are entitled to demand as many recounts as they want until the result is beyond doubt. The record number of recounts is seven (and the record margin of victory is just one vote!).

Recent results and the future

Since the middle of the twentieth century, the contest to form the government has effectively been a straight fight between the Labour and Conservative parties. As a general rule, the north of England and most of the inner areas of English cities return Labour MPs to Westminster, while the south of England and most areas outside the inner cities have a Conservative MP. Which of these two parties forms the government depends on which one does better in the suburbs and large towns of England.

Scotland used to be good territory for the Conservatives. This changed, however, during the 1980s and the vast majority of MPs from there now represent Labour. Wales has always returned mostly

Swingometers from 1970 and 1992

▶ The swingometer

This is a device used by television presenters on election night. It indicates the percentage change of support from one party to another party since the previous election – the 'swing'. Individual constituencies can be placed at certain points along the swingometer to show how much swing is necessary to change the party affiliation of their MPs. The swingometer was first made popular by Professor Robert McKenzie on the BBC's coverage of the 1964 election. Over the years, it has become more colourful and complicated. Most people enjoy it but say they are confused by it!

Labour MPs. Since the 1970s, the respective nationalist parties in both countries (see chapter 6) have regularly won a few seats in Parliament.

Traditionally, the Liberal party was also relatively strong in Scotland and Wales (and was sometimes called the party of the 'Celtic fringe'). Its modern successor, the Liberal Democrat party (see chapter 6), is not so geographically restricted and has managed to win some seats all over Britain, with a concentration in the south-west of England.

Northern Ireland always has about the same proportion of Protestant Unionist MPs and Catholic Nationalist MPs (since the 1970s, about two-thirds the former, the third the latter). The only element of uncertainty is how many seats the more extremist (as opposed to the more moderate) parties will win on either side of this invariant political divide (see chapter 12).

▶ By-elections

Whenever a sitting MP can no longer fulfil his or her duties, there has to be a special new election in the constituency which he or she represents. (There is no system of ready substitutes.) These are called by-elections and can take place at any time. They do not affect who runs the government, but they are watched closely by the media and the parties as indicators of the current level of popularity (or unpopularity) of the government.

A by-election provides the parties with an opportunity to find a seat in Parliament for one of their important people. If a sitting MP dies, the opportunity presents itself; if not, an MP of the same party must be persuaded to resign.

The way an MP resigns offers a fascinating example of the importance attached to tradition. It is considered wrong for an MP simply to resign; MPs represent their constituents and have no right to deprive them of this representation. So the MP who wishes to resign applies for the post of 'Steward of the Chiltern Hundreds'. This is a job with no duties and no salary. Technically, however, it is 'an office of profit under the Crown' (i.e. a job given by the monarch with rewards attached to it). According to ancient practice, a person cannot be both an MP and hold a post of this nature at the same time because Parliament must be independent of the monarch. (This is why high ranking civil servants and army officers are not allowed to be MPs.) As a result, the holder of this ancient post is automatically disqualified from the House of Commons and the by-election can go ahead!

In the thirteen elections from 1945 to 1987, the Conservatives were generally more successful than Labour. (▷ *Party performance in general elections since 1945*). Although Labour achieved a majority on five occasions, on only two of these was the majority comfortable. On the other three occasions it was so small that it was in constant danger of disappearing as a result of by-election defeats (▷ *By-elections*). In the same period, the Conservatives won a majority seven times, nearly always comfortably.

Then, in the 1992 election, the Conservatives won for the fourth time in a row – the first time this had been achieved for more than 160 years. Moreover, they achieved it in the middle of an economic recession. This made many people wonder whether Labour could ever win again. It looked as if the swingometer's pendulum had stuck on the right. Labour's share of the total vote had gradually decreased in the previous four decades while support for the third party had grown since the early 1970s. Many sociologists believed this trend to be inevitable because Britain had developed a middle-class majority (as opposed to its former working-class majority). Many political observers were worried about this situation. It is considered to be basic to the British system of democracy that power should change hands occasionally, and yet Britain appeared to be in danger of becoming a 'one-party state'. There was much talk about a possible reorganization of

Size of overall majority in the House of Commons
(with name of leader of winning party)

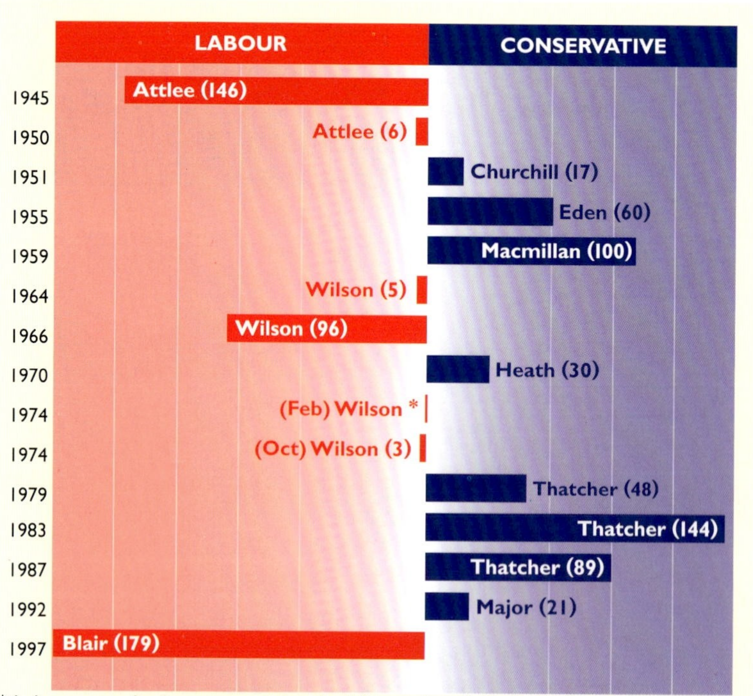

* Labour was the largest party but had fewer than half the seats.

British politics, for example a change to a European-style system of proportional representation (so that Labour could at least share in a coalition government), or a formal union between Labour and the Liberal Democrats (so that together they could defeat the Conservatives).

However, in 1997 the picture changed dramatically. Labour won the largest majority in the House of Commons achieved by any party for 73 years and the Conservative share of the total vote was their lowest in 165 years. What happened? The answer seems to be that voting habits in Britain, reflecting the weakening of the class system, are no longer tribal. There was a time when the Labour party was regarded as the political arm of the trade unions, representing the working class of the country. Most working-class people voted Labour all their lives and nearly *all* middle-class people voted Conservative all their lives. The winning party at an election was the one who managed to get the support of the small number of 'floating voters'. But Labour has now got rid of its trade-union image. It is capable of winning as many middle-class votes as the Conservatives, so that the middle-class majority in the population, as identified by sociologists (see above), does not automatically mean a Conservative majority in the House of Commons.

QUESTIONS

1 The British electoral system is said to discriminate against smaller parties. But look at the table at the beginning of this chapter again. How can it be that the very small parties had much better luck at winning parliamentary seats than the (comparatively large) Liberal Democrats?

2 In what ways is political campaigning in your country different from that in Britain as described in this chapter?

3 Is there a similar level of public interest in learning about election results in your country as there is in Britain? Does it seem to reflect the general level of enthusiasm about, and interest in, politics which exist at other times – in Britain and in your own country?

4 Britain has 'single-member constituencies'. This means that one MP alone represents one particular group of voters (everybody in his or her constituency). Is this a good system? Or is it better to have several MPs representing the same area? What are the advantages and disadvantages of the two systems?

5 Do you think that Britain should adopt the electoral system used in your country? Or perhaps you think that your country should adopt the system used in Britain? Or are the two different systems the right ones for the two different countries? Why?

SUGGESTIONS

- If you can get British television or radio, watch or listen in on the night of the next British general election.

11 The law

▶ The organization of the police force

There is no national police force in Britain. All police employees work for one of the forty or so separate forces which each have responsibility for a particular geographical area. Originally, these were set up locally. Only later did central government gain some control over them. It inspects them and has influence over senior appointments within them. In return, it provides about half of the money to run them. The other half comes from local government.

The exception to this system is the Metropolitan Police Force, which polices Greater London. The 'Met' is under the direct control of central government. It also performs certain national police functions such as the registration of all crimes and criminals in England and Wales and the compilation of the missing persons register. New Scotland Yard is the famous building which is the headquarters of its Criminal Investigation Department (CID).

The police and the public

There was a time when a supposedly typical British policeman could be found in every tourist brochure for Britain. His strange-looking helmet and the fact that he did not carry a gun made him a unique symbol for tourists. The image of the friendly British 'bobby', with his fatherly manner, was also well-known within the country and was reinforced by popular television serials such as *Dixon of Dock Green* (▷ *Images of the police: past and present*). This positive image was not a complete myth. The system of policing was based on each police officer having his own 'beat', a particular neighbourhood which it was his duty to patrol. He usually did this on foot or sometimes by bicycle. The local bobby was a familiar figure on the streets, a reassuring presence that people felt they could trust absolutely.

In the 1960s the situation began to change in two ways. First, in response to an increasingly motorized society, and therefore increasingly motorized crime, the police themselves started patrolling in cars. As a result, individual police officers became remote figures and stopped being the familiar faces that they once were. A sign of this change was the new television police drama, *Z Cars*. This programme showed police officers as people with real problems and failings who did not always behave in the conventionally polite and reassuring manner. Some police were relieved to be presented as ordinary human beings. But the comparatively negative image of the police which this programme portrayed caused uproar and several senior police officials complained to the BBC about it! At the same time, the police found themselves having to deal increasingly with public demonstrations and with the activities of a generation who had no experience of war and therefore no obvious enemy-figure on which to focus their youthful feelings of rebellion. These young people started to see the police as the symbol of everything they disliked about society. Police officers were no longer known as 'bobbies' but became the 'fuzz' or the 'cops' or the 'pigs'.

Since the middle years of the twentieth century, the police in Britain have lost much of their positive image. A child who is lost is still advised to find a police officer, but the sight of one no longer creates a general feeling of reassurance. In the 1980s there were a large number of cases in which it was found that police officers had lied and cheated in order to get people convicted of crimes (▷ *The Stefan Kizsko case*). As a result, trust in the honesty and incorruptibility of the police has declined.

Nevertheless, there is still a great deal of public sympathy for the police. It is felt that they are doing an increasingly difficult job under difficult circumstances. The assumption that their role is to serve the public rather than to be agents of the government persists. Police officers often still address members of the public as 'sir' or 'madam'. Senior officers think it is important for the police to establish a relationship with local people, and the phrase 'community policing' is now fashionable. Some police have even started to patrol on foot again. Generally speaking, the relationship between police and public in Britain compares quite favourably with that in some other European countries. British police still do not carry guns in the course of normal duty (although all police stations have a store of weapons).

Crime and criminal procedure

There is a widespread feeling among the British public that crime is increasing. Figures on this matter are notoriously difficult to evaluate, however. One reason for this is that not all actual crimes are necessarily reported. Official figures suggest that the crime of rape increased by more than 50% between 1988 and 1992. But these figures may represent an increase in the number of victims willing to report rape rather than a real increase in cases of rape.

▶ Images of the police: past and present

The traditional image: Dixon of Dock Green speaking fatherly words of wisdom to the television audience in the 1960s.

The modern image: a scene from the popular 1990s television series *The Bill*.

▶ The Stefan Kizsko case

On 18 February 1992, a man who had spent the previous sixteen years of his life in prison serving a sentence for murder was released. It had been proved that he did not in fact commit the crime.

In the early 1990s a large number of people were let out of British gaols after spending several years serving sentences for crimes they did not commit. The most famous of these were 'the Guildford Four' and 'the Birmingham Six', both groups of people convicted of terrorist bombings. In every case, previous court judgements were changed when it became clear that the police had not acted properly (for example, they had falsified the evidence of their notebooks or had not revealed important evidence).

Public confidence in the police diminished. In the case of the alleged bombers, there remained some public sympathy. The police officers involved may have been wrong but they *were* trying to catch terrorists. The Kizsko case was different. He did not belong to an illegal organization. His only 'crime' was that he was in the wrong place at the wrong time. He also conformed to a stereotype, which made him an easy victim of prejudice. He was of below average intelligence and he had a foreign name, so a jury was likely to see him as a potential murderer.

▶ Caution!

'You do not have to say anything unless you wish to do so, but what you say may be given in evidence'. These words are well-known to almost everybody in Britain. They have been heard in thousands of police dramas on television. For a long time they formed what is technically known as the caution, which must be read out to an arrested person in order to make the arrest legal. But, in 1994, the British government decided that the 'right to silence' contained in the caution made things too easy for criminals. This right meant that the refusal of an arrested person to answer police questions could not be used as part of the evidence against him or her. Now, however, it can.

To accord with the new law, the words of the caution have had to be changed. The new formula is: 'You do not have to say anything. But if you do not mention now something which you later use in your defence, the court may decide that your failure to mention it now strengthens the case against you. A record will be made of anything you say and it may be given in evidence if you are brought to trial'.

Civil liberties groups in Britain are angry about this change. They say that many arrested people find it too difficult to understand and that it is not fair to encourage people to defend themselves immediately against charges about which they do not yet know the details. They are also afraid it encourages false confessions.

▶ Is crime increasing in Britain?

British people think that crime is rising in Britain, but it is impossible to give a completely reliable answer to this question. Figures vary from year to year. In 1993 for instance, the total number of recorded crimes in the London area actually went down by around 10%. And the murder rate is no higher, or even lower, than it was during the second half of the nineteenth century. However, there is no doubt that in the last quarter of the twentieth century there was a definite increase in certain *types* of crime. Crimes with firearms (guns, rifles etc) are an example, as the graph shows.

Offences involving firearms recorded by the police in England and Wales

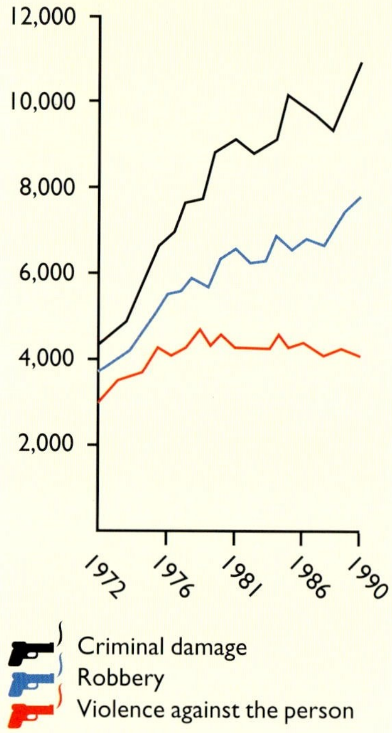

Source: Criminal Statistics, Home Office

Nevertheless, it is generally accepted that in the last quarter of the twentieth century, the number of crimes went up (▷ *Is crime increasing in Britain?*). And the *fear* of crime seems to have increased a lot. This has gone together with a lack of confidence in the ability of the police to catch criminals. In the early 1990s private security firms were one of the fastest-growing businesses in the country. Another response to the perceived situation has been the growth of Neighbourhood Watch schemes. They attempt to educate people in crime prevention and to encourage the people of a particular neighbourhood to look out for anything suspicious. In 1994 the government was even considering helping members of these schemes to organize patrols.

There has also been some impatience with the rules of criminal procedure under which the police and courts have to operate. The police are not, of course, above the law. When they arrest somebody on suspicion of having committed a crime, they have to follow certain procedures. For example, unless they obtain special permission, they are not allowed to detain a person for more than twenty-four hours without formally charging that person with having committed a crime. Even after they have charged somebody, they need permission to remand that person in custody (i.e. to keep him or her in prison) until the case is heard in court. In 1994 public concern about criminals 'getting away with it' led the government to make one very controversial change in the law (▷ *Caution!*).

Source: International Home Office Crime Survey

The system of justice

The system of justice in England and Wales, in both civil and criminal cases, is (as it is in North America) an adversarial system. In criminal cases there is no such thing as an examining magistrate who tries to discover the real truth about what happened. In formal terms it is not the business of any court to find out 'the truth'. Its job is simply to decide 'yes' or 'no' to a particular proposition (in criminal cases, that a certain person is guilty of a certain crime) after it has heard arguments and evidence from both sides (in criminal cases these sides are known as the defence and the prosecution).

There are basically two kinds of court. More than 90% of all cases are dealt with in magistrates' courts. Every town has one of these. In them, a panel of magistrates (usually three) passes judgement. In cases where they have decided somebody is guilty of a crime, they can also impose a punishment. This can be imprisonment for up to a year, or it can be a fine, although if it is a person's 'first offence' and the crime is not serious, they often impose no punishment at all (▷ *The sentence of this court is . . .*).

Magistrates' courts are another example of the importance of amateurism in British public life. Magistrates, who are also known as Justices of the Peace (JPs), are not trained lawyers. They are just ordinary people of good reputation who have been appointed to the job by a local committee. They do not get a salary or a fee for their work (though they get paid expenses). Inevitably, they tend to come

▶ How many victims?

One way of estimating the level of crime is to interview people and ask them whether they have been the victims of crime. On the left are some of the results of a survey in 1990 which interviewed 2,000 people in several countries. The figures show the percentages of interviewees who said they had been victims.

▶ The sentence of this court is . . .

If it is someone's first offence, and the crime is a small one, even a guilty person is often **unconditionally discharged**. He or she is set free without punishment.

The next step up the ladder is a **conditional discharge**. This means that the guilty person is set free but if he or she commits another crime within a stated time, the first crime will be taken into account. He or she may also be put **on probation**, which means that regular meetings with a social worker must take place.

A very common form of punishment for minor offences is a **fine**, which means that the guilty person has to pay a sum of money.

Another possibility is that the convicted person is sentenced to a certain number of hours of **community service**.

Wherever possible, magistrates and judges try not to **imprison** people. This costs the state money, the country's prisons are already overcrowded and prisons have a reputation for being 'schools for crime'. Even people who are sent to prison do not usually serve the whole time to which they were sentenced. They get 'remission' of their sentence for 'good behaviour'.

There is no **death penalty** in Britain, except for treason. It was abolished for all other offences in 1969. Although public opinion polls often show a majority in favour of its return, a majority of MPs has always been against it. For murderers, there is an obligatory **life sentence**. However, 'life' does not normally mean life.

Some terms connected with the legal system

acquitted found not guilty by the court

bail a sum of money guaranteed by somebody on behalf of a person who has been charged with a crime so that he or she can go free until the time of the trial. If he or she does not appear in court, the person 'standing bail' has to pay the money.

convicted found guilty by the court

defendant the party who denies a claim in court; the person accused of a crime

on remand in prison awaiting trial

party one of the sides in a court case. Because of the adversarial system, there must always be two parties in any case: one to make a claim and one to deny this claim.

plaintiff the party who makes a claim in court. In nearly all criminal cases, the plaintiff is the police.

verdict the decision of the court

from the wealthier sections of society and, in times past, their prejudices were very obvious. They were especially harsh, for instance, on people found guilty of poaching (hunting animals on private land), even though these people sometimes had to poach in order to put food on their families' tables. In modern times, however, some care is taken to make sure that JPs are recruited from as broad a section of society as possible.

Even serious criminal cases are first heard in a magistrate's court. However, in these cases, the JPs only need to decide that there is a *prima facie* case against the accused (in other words, that it is possible that he or she may be guilty). They then refer the case to a higher court. In most cases this will be a crown court, where a professional lawyer acts as the judge and the decision regarding guilt or innocence is taken by a jury. Juries consist of twelve people selected at random from the list of voters. They do not get paid for their services and are obliged to perform this duty. In order for a verdict to be reached, there must be agreement among at least ten of them. If this does not happen, the judge has to declare a mistrial and the case must start all over again with a different jury. A convicted person may appeal to the Court of Criminal Appeal (generally known just as the Appeal Court) in London either to have the conviction quashed (i.e. the jury's previous verdict is overruled and they are pronounced 'not guilty') or to have the sentence (i.e. punishment) reduced. The highest court of all in Britain is the House of Lords (see chapter 9).

The duty of the judge during a trial is to act as the referee while the prosecution and defence put their cases and question witnesses, and to decide what evidence is admissible and what is not (what can or can't be taken into account by the jury). It is also, of course, the judge's job to impose a punishment (known as 'pronouncing sentence') on those found guilty of crimes.

A typical courtroom scene showing the judge, the jury, and a witness being questioned by a barrister (cameras are not allowed in court)

The legal profession

There are two distinct kinds of lawyer in Britain. One of these is a solicitor. Everybody who needs a lawyer has to go to one of these. They handle most legal matters for their clients, including the drawing up of documents (such as wills, divorce papers and contracts), communicating with other parties, and presenting their clients' cases in magistrates' courts. However, only since 1994 have solicitors been allowed to present cases in higher courts. If the trial is to be heard in one of these, the solicitor normally hires the services of the other kind of lawyer – a barrister. The only function of barristers is to present cases in court.

The training of the two kinds of lawyer is very different. All solicitors have to pass the Law Society exam. They study for this exam while 'articled' to established firms of solicitors where they do much of the everyday junior work until they are qualified.

Barristers have to attend one of the four Inns of Court in London. These ancient institutions are modelled somewhat on Oxbridge colleges (see chapter 14). For example, although there are some lectures, the only attendance requirement is to eat dinner there on a certain number of evenings each term. After four years, the trainee barristers then sit exams. If they pass, they are 'called to the bar' and are recognized as barristers. However, they are still not allowed to present a case in a crown court. They can only do this after several more years of association with a senior barrister, after which the most able of them apply to 'take silk'. Those whose applications are accepted can put the letters QC (Queen's Counsel) after their names.

Neither kind of lawyer needs a university qualification. The vast majority of barristers and most solicitors do in fact go to university, but they do not necessarily study law there. This arrangement is typically British (see chapter 14).

The different styles of training reflect the different worlds that the two kinds of lawyer live in, and also the different skills that they develop. Solicitors have to deal with the realities of the everyday world and its problems. Most of their work is done away from the courts. They often become experts in the details of particular areas of the law. Barristers, on the other hand, live a more rarefied existence. For one thing, they tend to come from the upper strata of society. Furthermore, their protection from everyday realities is increased by certain legal rules. For example, they are not supposed to talk to any of their clients, or to their client's witnesses, except in the presence of the solicitor who has hired them. They are experts on general principles of the law rather than on details, and they acquire the special skill of eloquence in public speaking. When they present a case in court, they, like judges, put on the archaic gown and wig which, it is supposed, emphasize the impersonal majesty of the law.

It is exclusively from the ranks of barristers that judges are appointed. Once they have been appointed, it is almost impossible

A barrister in the gown and wig that must be worn in court

▶ Ministry of justice?

Actually there is no such thing in Britain. The things that such a ministry takes care of in other countries are shared between a number of authorities, in particular the Home Office, which administers prisons and supervises the police, and the office of the Lord Chancellor, which oversees the appointment of judges, magistrates and other legal officers.

▶ The law in Scotland

Scotland has its own legal system, separate from the rest of the United Kingdom. Although it also uses an adversarial system of legal procedure, the basis of its law is closer to Roman and Dutch law. The names of several officials in Scotland are also different from those in England and Wales. A very noticeable feature is that there are three, not just two, possible verdicts. As well as 'guilty' and 'not guilty', a jury may reach a verdict of 'not proven', which means that the accused person cannot be punished but is not completely cleared of guilt either.

for them to be dismissed. The only way that this can be done is by a resolution of both Houses of Parliament, and this is something that has never happened. Moreover, their retiring age is later than in most other occupations. They also get very high salaries. These things are considered necessary in order to ensure their independence from interference, by the state or any other party. However, the result of their background and their absolute security in their jobs is that, although they are often people of great learning and intelligence, some judges appear to have difficulty understanding the problems and circumstances of ordinary people, and to be out of step with general public opinion. The judgements and opinions that they give in court sometimes make the headlines because they are so spectacularly out of date. (The inability of some of them to comprehend the meaning of racial equality is one example. A senior Old Bailey judge in the 1980s once referred to black people as 'nig-nogs' and to some Asians involved in a case as 'murderous Sikhs'.)

QUESTIONS

1 The public perception of British police officers has changed over the last thirty years. In what ways has it changed, and why do you think this is?

2 It is one of the principles of the British legal system that you are innocent until proven guilty. However, miscarriages of justice do occur. How did the ones described in this chapter come about?

3 What are the main differences between the legal system in your country and that in Britain? Is there anything like the 'right to silence'? Are there any unpaid 'amateur' legal officers similar to Justices of the Peace? What kind of training do lawyers undergo? Compared with the system in your country, what do you see as the strengths and weaknesses of the British system?

4 British people believe that there is more crime in Britain than there used to be. What reasons could there be for this? Is it true? Do you think of Britain as a 'safe' or 'dangerous' place? What about your own country – has crime increased there, or do people think that it has?

5 Many people in Britain argue that imprisonment is an ineffective and expensive form of punishment. Do you agree with this view? What alternative forms of punishment in use in Britain or in your country do you think are better, if any?

SUGGESTIONS

- There are many contemporary British writers who concentrate on the theme of crime and detection, among them Colin Dexter, whose books (such as *The Dead of Jericho*, *Last Bus to Woodstock* and *The Wench is Dead*) feature Inspector Morse. (Many of them have been adapted for television.) P D James and Ruth Rendell are two other highly respected writers of crime fiction.

12
International relations

The relationship between any country and the rest of the world can reveal a great deal about that country.

The end of empire

The map below shows the British empire in 1919, at the time of its greatest extent. By this time, however, it was already becoming less of an empire and more of a confederation. At the same international conference at which Britain acquired new possessions (formerly German) under the Treaty of Versailles, Australia, Canada, New Zealand and South Africa were all represented separately from Britain.

The real dismantling of the empire took place in the twenty-five years following the Second World War and with the loss of empire went a loss of power and status. These days, Britain's armed forces can no longer act unilaterally, without reference to the international community. Two events illustrate this. First, Suez. In 1956, Egypt, without prior agreement, took over the Suez canal from the international company owned by Britain and France. British and French

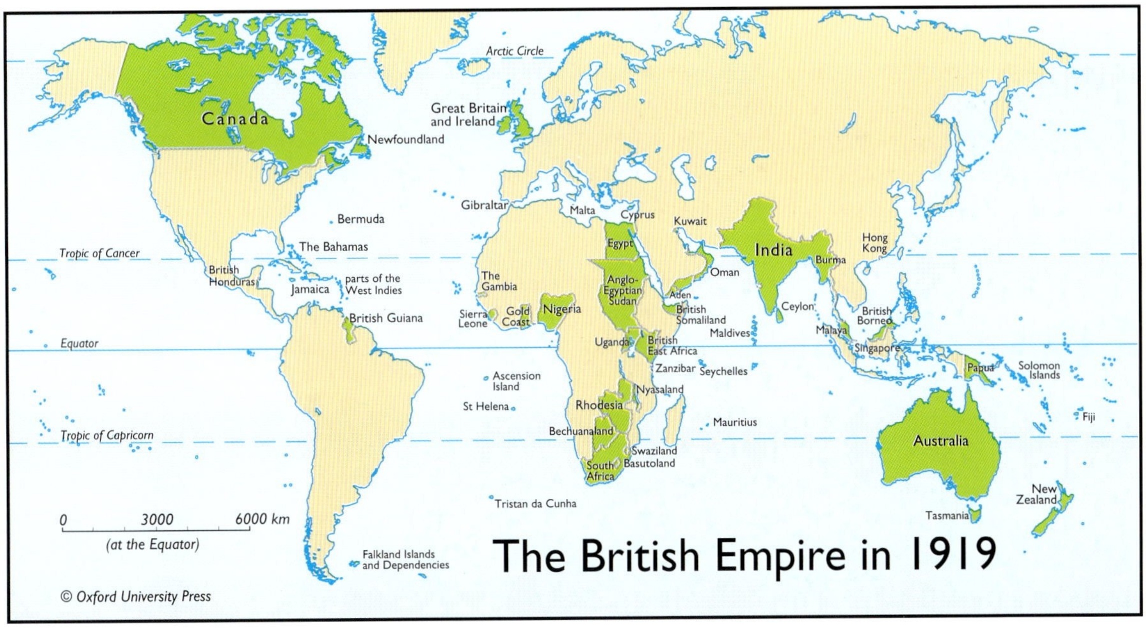

The British Empire in 1919

The opening ceremony of the Commonwealth Games in 1994. This athletics contest is held every four years.

military action to stop this was a diplomatic disaster. The USA did not support them and their troops were forced to withdraw. Second, Cyprus. When this country left the British empire, Britain became one of the guarantors of its independence from any other country. However, when Turkey invaded the island in 1974, British military activity was restricted to airlifting the personnel of its military base there to safety.

After the Second World War and throughout the 1950s, it was understood that a conference of the world's great powers involved the USA, the Soviet Union and Britain. However, in 1962, the Cuban missile crisis, one of the greatest threats to global peace since the war, was resolved without reference to Britain. By the 1970s it was generally accepted that a 'superpower' conference involved only the USA and the Soviet Union.

Despite Britain's loss of power and status on the world stage, some small remnants of the empire remain. Whatever their racial origins, the inhabitants of Gibraltar, St Helena, the Ascension Islands, the Falklands/Malvinas and Belize have all wished to continue with the imperial arrangement (they are afraid of being swallowed up by their nearest neighbours). For British governments, on the one hand this is a source of pride, but on the other hand it causes embarrassment and irritation: pride, because it suggests how beneficial the British imperial administration must have been; embarrassment, because the possession of colonial territories does not fit with the image of a modern democratic state; and irritation because it costs the British taxpayer money.

The old imperial spirit is not quite dead. In 1982 the British government spent hundreds of millions of pounds to recapture the Falklands/Malvinas Islands from the invading Argentinians. We cannot know if it would have done so if the inhabitants had not been in favour of remaining British and if Argentina had not had a military dictatorship at the time. But what we do know is that the government's action received enormous popular support at home. Before the 'Falklands War', opinion polls showed that the government was extremely unpopular; afterwards, it suddenly became extremely popular and easily won the general election early in the following year.

▶The Commonwealth

The dismantling of the British empire took place comparatively peacefully, so that good relations between Britain and the newly independent countries were established. As a result, and with the encouragement of Queen Elizabeth II, an international organization called the Commonwealth, composed of the countries that used to be part of the empire, has continued to hold annual meetings. Some countries in the Commonwealth have even kept the British monarch as head of state.

There are no formal economic or political advantages involved in belonging to the Commonwealth, but it has helped to keep cultural contacts alive, and does at least mean that every year the leaders of a sixth of the world's population sit down and talk together. Until quite recently it did have economic importance, with special trading agreements between members. But since Britain became a full member of the EEC, all but a few of these agreements have gradually been discontinued.

The armed forces

The loyalty of the leaders of the British armed forces to the government has not been in doubt since the Civil War (with the possible exception of a few years at the beginning of the twentieth century – see chapter 2). In addition, and with the exception of Northern Ireland, the army has only rarely been used to keep order within Great Britain in the last 100 years.

'National Service' (a period of compulsory military service for all men) was abolished in 1957. It had never been very popular. It was contrary to the traditional view that Britain should not have a large standing army in peacetime. Moreover, the end of empire, together with the increasing mechanization of the military, meant that it was more important to have small, professional forces staffed by specialists. The most obviously specialist area of the modern military is nuclear weapons. Since the 1950s, the Campaign for Nuclear Disarmament (CND) has argued, on both moral and economic grounds, that Britain should cease to be a nuclear power. At certain periods the CND has had a lot of popular support (▷ *Greenham Common*). However, this support has not been consistent. Britain still has a nuclear force, although it is tiny compared to that of the USA.

The end of the 'Cold War' between the west and the Soviet Union at the end of 1980s caused the British government to look for the 'peace dividend' and to reduce further the size of the armed forces. This caused protest from politicians and military professionals who were afraid that Britain would not be able to meet its 'commitments' in the world. These commitments, of course, are now mostly on behalf of the United Nations or the European Union. There is still a feeling in Britain that the country should be able to make significant contributions to international peacekeeping efforts. The reduction also caused bad feeling within sections of the armed forces themselves. Its three branches (the Army, the Royal Navy and the Royal Air Force) have distinct traditions and histories that it was felt were being threatened. The army in particular was unhappy when several famous old regiments, each with their own distinct traditions, were forced to merge with others. At one time, a number of upper-middle class families maintained a tradition down the generations of belonging to a particular regiment. Fewer and fewer such families exist today. However, a career in the armed forces is still highly respectable. In fact, Britain's armed forces are one of the few institutions that its people admit to being proud of.

▸ The senior service

This is a phrase sometimes used to describe the Royal Navy. It was the first of the three armed forces to be established. Traditionally, it traces its history right back to King Alfred (see chapter 2).

▸ Greenham Common

Greenham Common is the Royal Air Force base in Berkshire which became the focus for anti-nuclear campaigners (mainly women) in the 1980s. American Cruise nuclear missiles were based there from 1983 to 1991.

Protestors at Greenham Common

Transatlantic relations

Since the Second World War, British governments have often referred to the 'special relationship' which exists between Britain and the USA. There have been occasional low points, such as Suez (see above) and when the USA invaded the Caribbean island of Grenada (a member of the British Commonwealth). But generally speaking it has persisted. It survived the Falklands War, when the USA offered Britain important material help, but little public support, and regained its strength in 1991 during the Gulf War against Iraq, when Britain gave more active material support to the Americans than any other European country.

Public feeling about the relationship is ambiguous. On the one hand, it is reassuring to be so diplomatically close to the most powerful nation in the world, and the shared language gives people some sense of brotherhood with Americans. On the other hand, there is mild bitterness about the sheer power of the USA. There is no distrust, but remarks are often made about Britain being nothing more than the fifty-first state of the USA. Similarly, while some older people remember with gratitude the Americans who came to their aid in two world wars, others resent the fact that it took them so long to get involved!

In any case, the special relationship has inevitably declined in significance since Britain joined the European Community. In the world trade negotiations of the early 1990s, there was nothing special about Britain's position with regard to the USA – it was just part of the European trading bloc. The opening of the Channel tunnel in 1994 has emphasized that Britain's links are now mainly with Europe. Tourist statistics also point this way. In 1993, for the first time, it was not American visitors who arrived in the greatest numbers, it was the French, and there were almost as many German visitors as Americans. The majority of visitors to Britain are now from Europe.

Is Britain really part of Europe?

The government says it is, but look at this report from *The Sunday Times* of 18 April 1993.

Britain bans EC medals

British members of the European Community monitoring mission in former Yugoslavia have been banned from a formal presentation of medals struck by the EC to honour their bravery.

The British monitors have been told that they may only receive the medals privately and keep them as momentoes. They must never wear them on their uniforms because of government rules against the acceptance of decorations from 'foreign powers'.

... Many are angered by the decision to count the EC as a foreign power.

The sovereignty of the union: Europe

When the European Coal and Steel Community was formed in 1951, Britain thought it was an excellent idea, but nothing to do with Britain! Long years of an empire based on sea power meant that the traditional attitude to Europe had been to encourage stability there, to discourage any expansionist powers there, but otherwise to leave it well alone.

As the empire disappeared, and the role of 'the world's policeman' was taken over by the USA, the British government decided to ask for membership of the newly-formed European Communities. It took more than ten years for this to be achieved (in 1973). From the very start, the British attitude to membership has been ambiguous. On the one hand, it is seen as an economic necessity and a political advantage (increasing Britain's status as a regional power). The referendum on continued membership in 1975 (the first in British history) produced a two-to-one majority in favour. On the other hand, acceptance does not mean enthusiasm. The underlying attitude – that Britain is somehow special – has not really changed and there are fears that Britain is gradually giving up its autonomy. Changes in European

▶ The British sausage

Below is an extract from the script of the BBC satirical comedy *Yes, Prime Minister*. It is part of a speech made by James Hacker MP, in which he expresses anti-European sentiments. It is fiction, of course, but it does capture part of the British attitude to Europe. In the story, Hacker's speech makes him so popular that he becomes the new Prime Minister!

Notice how, in the speech, sovereignty is not connected with matters of conventional political power, but rather with matters of everyday life and habits. (For the references to pints, yards, tanners etc, see chapter 5.)

I'm a good European. I believe in Europe. I believe in the European ideal! Never again shall we repeat the bloodshed of two World Wars. Europe is here to stay.

But this does not mean that we have to bow the knee to every directive from every bureaucratic Bonaparte in Brussels. We are a sovereign nation still and proud of it. [*applause*]

We have made enough concessions to the European Commissar for agriculture. We have swallowed the wine lake, we have swallowed the butter mountain, we have watched our French 'friends' beating up British lorry drivers carrying good British lamb to the French public. We have bowed and scraped, tugged our forelocks and turned the other cheek. But I say enough is enough! [*prolonged applause*]

The Europeans have gone too far. They are now threatening the British sausage. They want to standardize it – by which they mean they'll force the British people to eat salami and bratwurst and other garlic-ridden greasy foods that are **totally alien** to the British way of life. [*cries of 'hear hear', 'right on' and 'you tell 'em, Jim'*].

Do you want to eat salami for breakfast with your egg and bacon? I don't. And I won't! [*massive applause*]

They've turned our pints into litres and our yards into metres, we gave up the tanner and the threepenny bit, the two bob and the half-crown. But they cannot and will not destroy the British sausage! [*applause and cheers*]. Not while I'm here. [*tumultuous applause*].

In the words of Martin Luther: Here I stand, I can do no other. [*Hacker sits down. Shot of large crowd rising to its feet in appreciation*]

domestic policy, social policy or sovereignty arrangements tend to be seen in Britain as a threat (▷ *The British sausage*). Throughout the 1980s and 1990s it has been Britain more than any other member of the European Union (as it is now called) which has slowed down progress towards further European unity. Meanwhile, there is a certain amount of popular distrust of the Brussels bureaucracy.

This ambiguous attitude can partly be explained by the fact that views about Britain's position in Europe cut across political party lines. There are people both for and against closer ties with Europe in both the main parties. As a result, 'Europe' has not been promoted as a subject for debate to the electorate. Neither party wishes to raise the subject at election time because to do so would expose divisions within that party (a sure vote-loser).

▶ Up yours, Delors

This was the front page headline of the *Sun*, Britain's most popular newspaper, on 1 November 1990. It gives voice, in a vulgar manner, to British dislike of the Brussels bureaucracy. Jacques Delors was president of the European Commission at the time. The expression 'up yours' is the spoken equivalent of a rude, two fingered gesture. Notice how the full effect of the phrase is only possible if the French name 'Delors' is pronounced in an English way, rhyming the second syllable of 'Delors' with 'yours'. Even serious, so-called 'quality' British newspapers can sometimes get rather hysterical about the power of Brussels. When, in 1991, the British government refused to agree the social chapter in the Maastricht Treaty, *The Sunday Times* published an article warning that the EU might still try to impose the chapter on Britain. The headline described this possibility as 'Ambush'.

▶ The European history book

Sir Francis Drake is a well-known English historical character. In 1588 he helped to defeat the Spanish Armada which was trying to invade England. Or did he? Historians know that there was a terrible storm which broke up the Spanish fleet.

In 1992 an EC history 'textbook' for secondary schools, written by a committee of historians from every member state, was published. The first version of the book decided that it was the weather which caused the failure of the Spanish invasion, the second that it was Drake. The book was published at the same time in Dutch, French, German, Greek, Italian and Portuguese. But, strangely enough, no publisher for either a British or a Spanish edition could be found.

▶ Scotland

This was the front page of the *Sun's* Scottish edition on 23 January 1992, when it decided to support the campaign for Scottish independence (see chapter 18). The design shows the cross of St Andrew, the national flag of Scotland.

▶ Ulster

Ulster is the name often used to describe the part of Ireland which is in the UK. It is the name of one of the four ancient kingdoms of Ireland. (The others are Leinster, Munster and Connaught). In fact, the British province does not embrace all of Ulster's nine counties; three of its counties belong to the republic. The name 'Northern Ireland' is not used by some nationalists; they think it gives validity to an entity which they do not recognize. One of the alternative names they use is 'the six counties'

The sovereignty of the union: Scotland and Wales

There is another reason for a distrust of greater European cohesion among politicians at Westminster. It is feared that this may not just be a matter of giving extra power to Brussels. It may also be a matter of giving extra powers to the regions of Britain, especially its different nations.

Until recently most Scottish people, although they insisted on many differences between themselves and the English, were happy to be part of the UK. But there has always been some resentment in Scotland about the way that it is treated by the central government in London. In the 1980s and early 1990s this resentment increased because of the continuation in power of the Conservative party, for which only around a quarter of the Scottish electorate had voted. Opinion polls consistently showed that between half and three-quarters of the Scottish population wanted either 'home rule' (internal self-government) within the UK or complete independence.

The realization that, in the EU, home rule, or even independence, need not mean isolation has caused the Scottish attitude to Europe to change. Originally, Scotland was just as cautious as England. But now the Scottish, as a group, have become the most enthusiastic Europeans in the UK. Scotland now has its own parliament which controls its internal affairs and even has the power to vary slightly the levels of income tax imposed by the UK government. It is not clear whether complete independence will eventually follow, but this is the policy of the Scottish National Party (SNP), which is well represented in the new parliament.

In Wales, the situation is different. The southern part of this nation is thoroughly Anglicized and the country as a whole has been fully incorporated into the English governmental structure for more than 400 years. Nationalism in Wales is felt mostly in the central and northern part of the country, where it tends to express itself not politically, but culturally (see chapter 4). Many people in Wales would like to have greater control over Welsh affairs, but not much more than some people in some regions of England would like the same. Wales also now has its own assembly with responsibility for many internal affairs.

The sovereignty of the union: Northern Ireland

In this section, the word 'Ulster' is used to stand for the British province of Northern Ireland (▷ *Ulster*). Politics here is dominated by the historic animosity between the two communities there (see chapter 4). The Catholic viewpoint is known as 'nationalist' or 'republican' (in support of the idea of a single Irish nation and its republican government); the Protestant viewpoint is known as 'unionist' or 'loyalist' (loyal to the union with Britain).

A little modern history is necessary to explain the present situation. By the beginning of the twentieth century, when Ireland was still part of the United Kingdom, the vast majority of people in Ireland wanted either home rule or complete independence from Britain. Liberal governments in Britain had accepted this and had attempted at various times to make it a reality. However, the one million Protestants in Ulster were violently opposed to this idea. They did not want to belong to a country dominated by Catholics. They formed less than a quarter of the total population of the country, but in Ulster they were in a 65% majority.

After the First World War the British government partitioned the country between the (mainly Catholic) south and the (mainly Protestant) north, giving each part some control of its internal affairs. But this was no longer enough for the south. There, support for complete independence had grown as a result of the British government's savage repression of the 'Easter Rising' in 1916. War followed. The eventual result was that the south became independent of Britain. Ulster, however, remained within the United Kingdom, with its own Parliament and Prime Minister. The Protestants had always had the economic power in the six counties (▷ *Ulster*). Internal self-government allowed them to take all the political power as well. Matters were arranged so that positions of official power were always filled by Protestants.

In the late 1960s a Catholic civil rights movement began. There was violent Protestant reaction and frequent fighting broke out. In 1969 British troops were sent in to keep order. At first they were welcomed, particularly among the Catholics. But troops, inevitably, often act without regard to democratic rights. In the tense atmosphere, the welcome disappeared. Extremist organizations from both communities began committing acts of terrorism, such as shootings and bombings. One of these groups, the Provisional IRA (▷ *Extremist groups*), then started a bombing campaign on the British mainland. In response, the British government reluctantly imposed certain measures not normally acceptable in a modern democracy, such as imprisonment without trial and the outlawing of organizations such as the IRA. The application of these measures caused resentment to grow. There was a hardening of attitudes in both communities and support for extremist political parties increased.

There have been many efforts to find a solution to 'the troubles' (as they are known in Ireland). In 1972 the British government decided to rule directly from London. Over the next two decades most of the previous political abuses disappeared, and Catholics now have almost the same political rights as Protestants. In addition, the British and Irish governments have developed good relations and new initiatives are presented jointly. The troubles may soon be over. However, despite reforms, inequalities remain. At the time of writing, unemployment among Ulster's Catholics is the highest of

▶ Extremist groups

The most well-known republican group is the IRA (Irish Republican Army). Seventy years ago this name meant exactly what it says. The IRA was composed of many thousands of people who fought for, and helped to win, Irish independence. Members of the modern IRA are also known as 'the Provisionals'. They are a group that split off from the 'official' IRA in the 1960s. They have used a name that once had great appeal to Irish patriotic sentiments. In fact, the IRA has little support in the modern Irish Republic and no connection at all with its government.

The most well-known loyalist groups are the UFF (Ulster Freedom Fighters), the UVF (Ulster Volunteer Force) and the UDA (Ulster Defence Association).

A republican message (the republicans call Londonderry 'Derry')

A loyalist mural

any area in the UK, while that among its Protestants is one of the lowest. Members of the police force, the Royal Ulster Constabulary (RUC), are still almost entirely Protestant. Most of all, the basic divisions remain. The Catholics identify with the south. Most of them would like the Irish government in Dublin to have at least a share in the government of Ulster. In 1999 the Republic removed the part of its constitution which included a claim to the six counties. This has calmed Protestant fears about being swallowed up. In return for its gesture, the Republic now has a role to play in a number of all-Ireland bodies which have been set up. Some Protestants still have misgivings about this initiative. It should be noted here that the names 'loyalist' and 'unionist' are somewhat misleading. The Ulster Protestants are distinct from any other section of British society. While it is important to them that they belong to the United Kingdom, it is just as important to them that they do *not* belong to the Republic of Ireland. From their point of view, and also from the point of view of some Catholics, a place for Ulster in a federated Europe is a possible solution.

In Ulster there is now a general disgust at the activities of extremists, and a strong desire for peace. At the time of writing, nearly all terrorist activities have ceased and a Northern Ireland government which includes representatives of all political views has been set up.

QUESTIONS

1 What indications can you find in this chapter that British people like to think of their country as an important and independent power in the world?
2 Would you say that the British people feel closer to the USA or the European Union? What evidence do you have for your view?
3 The people of Scotland have changed from being 'anti-Europe' to being 'pro-Europe' in the last twenty years of the twentieth century. Why?
4 In 1994, Prime Minister John Major announced that he would like to hold a referendum in Ulster on that area's future constitutional position. Some people said that the referendum should include the whole of Ireland. Which people do you think they were? Why did they say this?
5 Do you think that the present boundaries of the UK should remain as they are or should they change? Do you think they *will* stay as they are?

SUGGESTIONS

- *A Passage to India* by E M Forster is set in India at the height of the British Empire and reflects colonial attitudes. (There is also a film of the book.) *The Raj Quartet*, by Paul Scott (originally four novels, but published in a combined version under this title) is similarly set in India, but in the last years of British rule in the 1940s.

13
Religion

The vast majority of people in Britain do not regularly attend religious services. Many do so only a few times in their lives. Most people's everyday language is no longer, as it was in previous centuries, enriched by their knowledge of the Bible and the English Book of Common Prayer. It is significant that the most familiar and well-loved English translation of the Bible, known as the King James Bible, was written in the early seventeenth century and that no later translation has achieved similar status.

It therefore seems that most people in Britain cannot strictly be described as religious. However, this does not mean that they have no religious or spiritual beliefs or inclinations. Surveys have suggested that nearly three-quarters of the population believe in God and between a third and a half believe in concepts such as life after death, heaven and hell (and that half or more of the population believe in astrology, parapsychology, ghosts and clairvoyance). In addition, a majority approve of the fact that religious instruction at state schools is compulsory. Furthermore, almost nobody objects to the fact that the Queen is queen 'by the grace of God', or the fact that she, like all previous British monarchs, was crowned by a religious

▶ **Religious participation in Britain**

Here are two graphs showing the extent of active participation in organized religion in 1990 and the change in these numbers from five years before. Of course, what exactly is meant by 'active participation' can vary. Nevertheless, the figures give a reasonably accurate picture. The category 'Independent Christian' denotes the various charismatic and Pentecostalist groups mentioned in the text.

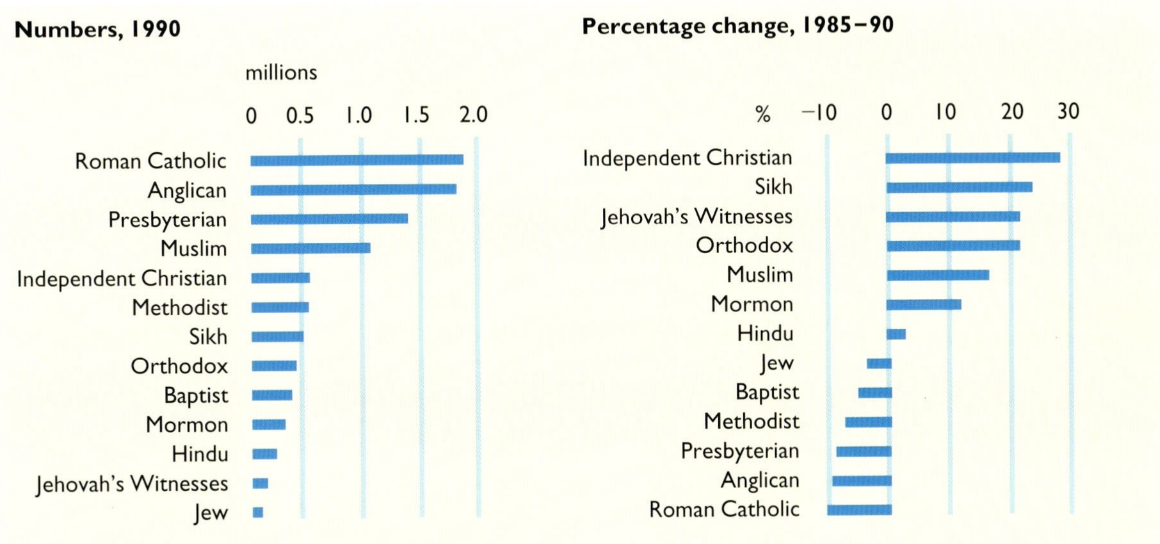

Source: UK Christian Handbook, 1992–93

figure (the Archbishop of Canterbury) in a church (Westminster Abbey) and that the British national anthem (God Save Our Queen) invokes God's help in protecting her.

The general picture, as with so many aspects of British life, is of a general tolerance and passive approval of the status quo. The majority attitude towards organized religion is rather similar to that towards the monarchy. Just as there is no serious republican movement in the country, so there is no widespread anti-clericalism. And just as there is no royalist movement either, so most people are not active participants in organized religion, but they seem to be glad it is there!

Religion and politics

Freedom of religious belief and worship (and also the freedom to be a non-believer) is taken for granted in modern Britain. With the notable exception of Northern Ireland (see chapter 4), a person's religion has almost no political significance. There are no important 'Christian' or anti-clerical political parties. Except perhaps for Muslims, there is no recognizable political pressure group in the country which is based on a particular religious ideology. To describe oneself as 'Catholic' or 'Church of England' or 'Methodist' or any other recognized label is to indicate one's personal beliefs but not the way one votes.

The religious conflicts of the past and their close relationship with politics (see chapter 2) have left only a few traces in modern times, and the most important of these are institutional rather than political: the fact that the monarch cannot, by law, be a Catholic; the fact that the twenty-six senior bishops in one particular church (the Church of England) are members of the House of Lords (where they are known as the 'Lords Spiritual'); the fact that the government has the right of veto on the choice of these bishops; the fact that the ultimate authority for this same church is the British Parliament. These facts point to a curious anomaly. Despite the atmosphere of tolerance and the separation of religion and politics, it is in Britain that we find the last two cases in Europe of 'established' churches, that is churches which are, by law, the official religion of a country. These cases are the Church of Scotland (see 'other Christian denominations' below) and the Church of England. The monarch is the official head of both, and the religious leader of the latter, the Archbishop of Canterbury, is appointed by the government.

However, the privileged position of the Church of England (also known as the Anglican Church) is not, in modern times, a political issue. Nobody feels that they are discriminated against if they do not belong to it. In any case, the Anglican Church, rather like the BBC (see chapter 16), has shown itself to be effectively independent of government and there is general approval of this independence.
In fact, there is a modern politics-and-religion debate, but now it is the other way around. That is, while it is accepted that politics should

▶ The road to tolerance

Until 1828 nonconformists were not allowed to hold any kind of government post or public office or even to go to university. Excluded from public life, many developed interests in trade and commerce as an outlet for their energies and were the leading commercial figures in the industrial revolution. For example, all the big British chocolate manufacturing companies were started by Quaker families (note also the well-known 'Quaker' brand of cereals).

Catholics were even worse off, having to worship in secret, or, later, at least with discretion. The last restriction on their freedom was lifted in 1924, when bells to announce the celebration of Catholic Mass were allowed to ring as long as they liked (previously, Mass had to be announced with a single chime of the bell only). Catholics were given the right to hold public office in 1829. There is still a law today which forbids Catholic priests to sit in Parliament (though it is doubtful that any would want to!).

A service in a Pentecostalist church

stay out of religion, it is a point of debate as to whether religion should stay out of politics.

The Anglican Church used to be half-jokingly described as 'the Conservative party at prayer'. This reputation was partly the result of history (see chapter 6) and partly the result of the fact that most of its clergy and regular followers were from the higher ranks of society. However, during the 1980s and early 1990s it was common for the Church to publicly condemn the widening gap between rich and poor in British society. Its leaders, including the Archbishop of Canterbury himself, repeatedly spoke out against this trend, implying that the Conservative government was largely to blame for it – despite comments from government ministers that politics should be left to the politicians. The Archbishop also angered some Conservative Anglicans when, at the end of the Falklands/Malvinas War in 1982, he did not give thanks to God for a British victory. Instead, he prayed for the victims of the war on both sides.

In 1994 the Catholic Church in Britain published a report which criticized the Conservative government. Since the general outlook of Britain's other conventional Christian denominations has always been anti-Conservative, it appears that all the country's major Christian churches are now politically broadly left of centre.

Anglicanism

Although the Anglican Church apparently has much the largest following in England, and large minorities of adherents in the other nations of Britain, appearances can be deceptive. It has been estimated that less than 5% of those who, if asked, might describe themselves as Anglicans regularly attend services. Many others are christened, married and buried in Anglican ceremonies but otherwise hardly ever go to church. Regular attendance for many Anglicans is tradition-

▶ The Christian churches in Britain

The organization of the Anglican and Catholic churches is broadly similar. At the highest level is an archbishop, who presides over a province. There are only two of these in the Church of England, Canterbury and York. The senior Catholic archbishopric is Westminster and its archbishop is the only cardinal from Britain. At the next level is the diocese, presided over by a bishop. In the Anglican Church there are other high-ranking positions at the level of the diocese, whose holders can have the title dean, canon or archdeacon. Other Christian churches do not have such a hierarchical organization, though the Methodists have a system of circuits.

At the local level, the terms verger, warden and sexton are variously used for lay members of churches (i.e. not trained clergy) who assist in various ways during services or with the upkeep of the church. Note also that a priest who caters for the spiritual needs of those in some sort of institution (for example, a university or a hospital) is called a chaplain.

An Anglican service in progress

▶ Women priests

On Wednesday 11 November 1992, at five in the evening, Dr George Carey, the Archbishop of Canterbury, rose to announce a momentous decision. By just two votes more than the required two-thirds majority, the General Synod of the Anglican Church (its governing body) had voted to allow the ordination of women priests. The debate in the Synod had lasted more than six hours, and had been going on for years before that, both inside and outside the church, all over the country.

About eighteen months afterwards, the first women priests were ordained. Those who support this development believe that it will help to give the Church of England a greater relevance to the modern world and finally bring it up to date. (Unlike the Catholic Church, it has always allowed its clergy to be married.) Some who were opposed to the change have not accepted the Synod's decision, and there are a few local cases of attempts to set up a rebel church. Some members of the Anglican Church have decided to 'go over to Rome' – that is, to join the Catholic Church, which does not have women priests.

Women priests waiting to be ordained

ally as much a social as a religious activity, and predominantly one for the upper and middle classes.

The doctrine of the Church of England was set out in the sixteenth century, in a document called the Thirty-Nine Articles. However, the main motivation for the birth of Anglicanism was more patriotic and political than doctrinal (see chapter 2). As a result, it has always been what is called a 'broad church', willing to accommodate a wide variety of beliefs and practices. For example, the nature of its religious services varies quite widely from church to church, depending partly on the inclinations of the local priest and partly on local tradition.

Three main strands of belief can be identified. One strand is evangelical, or 'low church'. This places great emphasis on the contents of the Bible and is the most consciously opposed to Catholicism. It therefore adheres closely to those elements of the Thirty-Nine Articles that reject Papal doctrines and is suspicious of the hierarchical structure of the Church. It prefers plain services with a minimum of ceremony. In contrast, the beliefs of the 'Anglo-Catholic', or 'high church', strand are virtually identical to those of Catholicism – except that it does not accept the Pope as the ultimate authority. High church services are more colourful and include organ music and elaborate priestly clothing. Both these strands are traditional in their outlook. But there is also a liberal wing, which is willing to question some of the traditional Christian beliefs, is more inclined to view the Bible as merely a historical document, is more tolerant towards homosexuality and was the first to support moves to ordain women priests (▷ *Women priests*).

But to many, perhaps most, of its members, it is the 'Englishness' of the Anglican Church which is just as important as its religious doctrine. This is what gives it meaning and holds its various strands together. Without it, many Anglo-Catholics would be Catholic, many low churchers and liberals would form their own sects or join existing nonconformist groups (see below), and a very large number would simply cease to have anything to do with organized religion at all. Perhaps this is why an opinion poll in the 1980s showed that most people, displaying apparently uncharacteristic intolerance, approve of the law that does not permit a Catholic monarch.

At present, this national distinctiveness is emphasized by the Anglican Church's position as the official religion. It has been argued that the tie between Church and State should be broken; that is, that the Church should be disestablished so that, after losing its extreme members to other churches, it could spend less time on internal disagreement and more on the moral and spiritual guidance of its remaining members. Those who are against this move fear that it would cause the obvious Englishness of the Church to disappear and thus for the number of its adherents to drop sharply.

Catholicism

After the establishment of Protestantism in Britain (see chapter 2), Catholicism was for a time an illegal religion and then a barely tolerated religion. Not until 1850 was a British Catholic hierarchy re-established. Only in the twentieth century did it become fully open about its activities. Although Catholics can now be found in all ranks of society and in all occupations, the comparatively recent integration of Catholicism means that they are still under-represented at the top levels. For example, although Catholics comprise more than 10% of the population, they comprise only around 5% of MPs.

A large proportion of Catholics in modern Britain are those whose family roots are in Italy, Ireland or elsewhere in Europe. The Irish connection is evident in the large proportion of priests in England who come from Ireland (they are sometimes said to be Ireland's biggest export!).

Partly because of its comparatively marginal status, the Catholic Church, in the interests of self-preservation, has maintained a greater cohesiveness and uniformity than the Anglican Church. In modern times it is possible to detect opposing beliefs within it (there are conservative and radical/liberal wings), but there is, for example, more centralized control over practices of worship. Not having had a recognized, official role to play in society, the Catholic Church in Britain takes doctrine and practice (for example, weekly attendance at mass) a bit more seriously than it is taken in countries where Catholicism is the majority religion – and a lot more seriously than the Anglican Church in general does.

This comparative dedication can be seen in two aspects of Catholic life. First, religious instruction is taken more seriously in Catholic schools than it is in Anglican ones, and Catholic schools in Britain usually have a head who is either a monk, a friar or a nun. Second, there is the matter of attendance at church. Many people who hardly ever step inside a church still feel entitled to describe themselves as 'Anglican'. In contrast, British people who were brought up as Catholics but who no longer attend mass regularly or receive the sacraments do not normally describe themselves as 'Catholic'. They qualify this label with 'brought up as' or 'lapsed'. Despite being very much a minority religion in most places in the country, as many British Catholics regularly go to church as do Anglicans.

▶ Episcopalianism

The Anglican Church is the official state religion in England only. There are, however, churches in other countries (such as Scotland, Ireland, the USA and Australia) which have the same origin and are almost identical to it in their general beliefs and practices. Members of these churches sometimes describe themselves as 'Anglican'. However, the term officially used in Scotland and the USA is 'Episcopalian' (which means that they have bishops), and this is the term which is often used to denote all of these churches, including the Church of England, as a group.

Every ten years the bishops of all the Episcopalian churches in the world gather together in London for the Lambeth Conference, which is chaired by the Archbishop of Canterbury.

Despite the name 'Canterbury', the official residence of the head of the Church of England is Lambeth Palace in London.

Other conventional Christian churches

In many ways, Anglicanism represents a compromise between Protestantism and Catholicism. Its stated doctrine, which rejects the authority of the Pope and other important aspects of Catholic doctrine, is Protestant. But its style, as shown by its hierarchical structure and its forms of worship, is rather Catholic.

When Protestantism first took root in Britain, there were many people who rejected not only Catholic doctrine but also 'Romish' style. These people did not join the newly-established Anglican Church. They regarded both the authority given to its clergy and its continuation of orthodox ritual as obstacles to true worship. Instead, they placed great importance on finding the truth for oneself in the words of the Bible and on living an austere life of hard work and self-sacrifice. They disapproved of the pursuit of pleasure and therefore frowned on public entertainments such as the theatre, on drinking, on gambling and on any celebration of the sexual aspect of life.

This is the origin of the Puritan/Calvinist tradition in Britain (see chapter 2). The first church within this tradition was the Presbyterian Church. In Scotland, this form of Protestantism was so strong that it became the nation's established church. The Church of Scotland has a separate organization from the Anglican Church. It has no bishops. Its head, or 'Moderator', is elected by its general assembly. It is the biggest religion in Scotland, where it is often known simply as 'the kirk' (the Scots word for 'church'). There are also many Presbyterians in England and a large number in Northern Ireland.

In England, those Protestants who did not accept the authority of the Anglican Church were first known as 'dissenters' and later, as

▶ Keeping the sabbath

In the last two centuries, the influence of the Calvinist tradition has been felt in laws relating to Sundays. These laws have recently been relaxed, but shop opening hours, gambling and professional sport on Sundays are still all restricted in small ways. In some places in rural Wales, where nonconformism is traditionally strong, Sundays are still 'dry'; that is, the pubs stay closed.

▶ What is it called?

	Anglican	Catholic	Presbyterian and other nonconformist
Local unit	parish	parish	congregation
Place of worship	church	church	chapel kirk[1] meeting house[2]
Clergy	vicar/rector/parson[3] priests curate[4]	priest	minister pastor
New member of clergy	deacon	novice	
Residence of clergy	vicarage rectory		manse[1]

[1] Church of Scotland only
[2] Mainly Quaker
[3] One of these is used when referring to an individual; 'priests' is used collectively.
[4] A junior member of the clergy

tolerance grew, as 'nonconformists'. These days, when refusal to conform to the established church is irrelevant, they are simply called 'members of the free churches'. A great many different free-church groups have come into being over the centuries. In the details of their organization, styles of worship and doctrinal emphasis, the various nonconformist groups differ considerably. However, they all share, in varying degrees, certain characteristics: they regard simplicity and individual prayer as more important than elaborate ritual and public ceremony; there is comparatively little difference between their clergy (if they have any at all) and their lay members; they praise self-denial, although to a lesser extent than the original Puritans. For example, many are teetotal (their members do not drink alcohol).

After Presbyterians, the largest traditional nonconformist group in Britain is the Methodist Society. Methodists follow the teachings of John Wesley, an eighteenth century preacher who started his career as an Anglican clergyman. He had little doctrinal disagreement with the established church. However, he and his followers considered that it did not care enough about the needs of ordinary people and that its hierarchy was not serious enough about the Christian message. The Salvation Army (see chapter 18) grew out of the Wesleyan movement.

Two other nonconformist groups with a long history are the Baptists and the Quakers. The former are comparatively strict both in their interpretation of the Bible and in their dislike of worldly pleasures. The latter, also known as the Society of Friends, are a very small group whose notable characteristics are their complete lack of clergy and their pacifism. They refuse to fight in any war, though they will do ambulance and hospital work.

Ecumenicalism

This term is used to describe the trend in the last half of the twentieth century towards greater co-operation, and even unity, among the various Christian churches in Britain. Cynics say that this spirit is the result of the fact that active participation in any form of Christianity has become the activity of a rather small minority. However, the churches themselves are quite sincere about it. With political and social divisions far enough behind them, they find that they do indeed have a lot in common.

The only actual union that ecumenicalism has yet produced is the unification of Presbyterians and Congregationalists, who, in 1972, became the United Reformed Church. Anglicans and Methodists came very close (but not quite close enough) to a union in 1968.

The possibility of the Anglican Church rejoining world Catholicism seems to have receded since the introduction of women priests.

Other religions, churches and religious movements

Since it is a multicultural country where the pressure to conform is comparatively weak, Britain is home to followers of almost every religion and sect imaginable. Some of these are offshoots, or local combinations, of those already mentioned. For example, the only Church of distinctly Welsh origin calls itself both 'Calvinistic Methodist' and 'Presbyterian Church of Wales'.

The numbers of followers of all the traditional Christian churches have been slowly but steadily declining in the second half of the twentieth century. Other Christian sects and churches have been growing. Because of their energetic enthusiasm and their desire to attract new followers, they are sometimes characterized by the term 'evangelical'. Most of them are similar to traditional nonconformist groups in that they avoid rigid ritual and place great emphasis on scripture. In the case of some groups, their interpretations of the Bible are often literal: the Mormons, Jehovah's Witnesses and Seventh Day Adventists (all of which originated in the USA) are examples. These groups, and others, also provide a strict code of behaviour for their followers.

▶ Church of Wales?

There is no Welsh equivalent of the Church of England or the Church of Scotland. That is to say, Wales has no officially established Church. The Anglican Church was disestablished in Wales, where it has always had only a tiny following, in 1914. Wales is predominantly nonconformist.

▶ As quiet as a church mouse

Conventional church services in Britain are typically very quiet, except when hymns are being sung. British people attending church services abroad have often been amazed, even shocked, by the noisiness and liveliness of the congregation. They chatter among themselves, they walk in and out . . . In Britain, respect and reverence have traditionally been expressed by silence and stillness. Many people, however, find the atmosphere at traditional services rather repressive and unwelcoming. This could help to explain the trend towards evangelical and charismatic Christian churches.

The fastest-growing type of evangelical Christianity, however, places less emphasis on dogma, sin, or giving people a code of behaviour. Instead, the emphasis is on the spiritual and miraculous; on revelation. Gatherings often involve joyful singing. There is a belief in spiritual healing of the sick. The oldest existing church of this type in Britain is called Pentecostal, and this term is sometimes used to denote all such groups. Pentecostalism has had a small working-class following for many years. Its recent growth is among the middle class. Many groups began with meetings in people's living rooms, where formality is at a minimum. Another term sometimes used of these groups is 'charismatic', reflecting both their enthusiasm and their emphasis on the miraculous. The growth of these groups might indicate that many British people feel a gap in their lives which neither the material benefits of modern life nor the conventional churches can fill.

Some people are turning even further afield, beyond the bounds of the Christian tradition. The term 'New Age' is used to cover a very wide range of beliefs which can involve elements of Christianity, eastern religions and ancient pagan beliefs all mixed in together. Interests and beliefs of this kind are not new in Britain. Theosophy, Druidism, Buddhism, Christian Scientism (which believes in the control of the body through the mind) and many other beliefs have all had their followers in this country for a hundred years or more. Until the 1960s such people came exclusively from a small set of the upper middle class. Since then, however, New Age beliefs have filtered downwards to other sections of the social scale. Despite their great variety and lack of exclusiveness, two features seem to be common to all New Age beliefs: first, an emphasis on personal development (often seen as spiritual development); second, respect for the natural environment.

The remaining religious groups with significant numbers of followers in Britain are all associated with racial minorities. The most well-established of these are the Jews. Anti-Semitism exists in Britain, but for a long time it has been weaker than it is in most other parts of Europe. The security and confidence of Judaism in Britain can be seen both in the healthy proportion of Jews in Parliament and in the fact that within it there is, quite openly, the same struggle between orthodox/conservative and liberal/radical viewpoints as there is in the Anglican and Catholic churches.

The numbers of followers of the Christian Orthodox, Sikh, Hindu and Muslim religions are all growing, mainly because of high birth rates among families belonging to them. The last of these is by far the largest. Its continued growth is also for another reason. Relative poverty, racial discrimination and occasional conflicts with the authorities have caused people brought up as Muslims to be politicized – more so than any other religious group in the country. As a result, young Muslims are less likely to drift away from their religion

A Buddhist monastery in Scotland

Samye Ling

In February 1993 thirty-five monks emerged from a four-year retreat. It was a very strict retreat. The monks never left their sleeping quarters. They spent most of their time meditating in wooden boxes, the same boxes in which they slept. They never once listened to the radio, watched television or read a newspaper.

If you know something about religion, you will not be surprised to learn that these monks were Tibetan Buddhists and that the name of the monastery in which the retreat took place is Samye Ling. But what you may be surprised to learn is that Samye Ling is in Eskdalemuir, near Lockerbie, in Scotland. It was set up in 1968 when a group of Tibetan monks arrived in the area. They soon collected a large number of European followers and set them to work building Europe's largest Buddhist temple. Since then, Samye Ling has continued to attract new followers. So many Buddhists now live in the area that in 1993 the local primary school had only one Christian pupil.

than the young of other faiths. One example of conflict is the Salman Rushdie affair (see chapter 6). Another is the question of Muslim schools. There have been both Catholic and Jewish state schools for some time now. The country's Muslims are demanding the same opportunity.

Finally, it is necessary to mention what are called 'cults'. The beliefs of these groups vary so widely that it is impossible to generalize about them. What they seem to have in common is the style of their belief, involving absolute commitment to and unquestioning obedience of the leader around whom they are centred (it is often only in this sense that they can be called religions). Cults have a bad reputation for using mind-control techniques. Their extremist tendencies are often offensive to most people and, with a few exceptions, each individual cult is tiny. However, it has been estimated that there are between 500 and 700 of them in the country and that, taken together, they have nearly half a million followers.

QUESTIONS

1. What reasons have been put forward for disestablishing the Anglican Church? What are the arguments in favour of keeping it in its favoured position?
2. In what ways, and to what extent, can different churches and religions in Britain be associated with particular geographical areas and particular social classes?
3. How does the relation between religion and politics differ between your country and Britain?
4. It could be argued that in both the nature of their services and their general attitude, the charismatic churches are surprisingly un-British in their approach to religion. In contrast, it could be said that the general attitude of the New Age movement fits quite comfortably into the traditional British approach. Do you agree?

14 Education

▶ **Public means private!**

Terminology to do with the school system in Britain can be confusing. Schools funded by the government, either directly or via local education authorities, are called 'state schools' and education provided in this way is known as 'state education'. This distinguishes it from 'private education', which comprises 'independent schools'. Some independent schools (a varying number, because the term is not exact) are known as 'public schools'.

The possibility of confusion is especially great because in the USA schools organized by the government are called 'public schools' and the education provided by the government is called the 'public school system'.

In Britain today, about 8% of children are educated outside the state system.

The basic features of the British educational system are the same as they are anywhere else in Europe: full-time education is compulsory up to the middle teenage years; the academic year begins at the end of summer; compulsory education is free of charge, but parents may spend money on educating their children privately if they want to (▷ *Public means private!*). There are three recognized stages, with children moving from the first stage (primary) to the second stage (secondary) at around the age of eleven or twelve. The third (tertiary) stage is 'further' education at university or college. However, there is quite a lot which distinguishes education in Britain from the way it works in other countries.

Historical background

The British government attached little importance to education until the end of the nineteenth century. It was one of the last governments in Europe to organize education for everybody. Britain was leading the world in industry and commerce, so, it was felt, education must somehow be taking care of itself. Today, however, education is one of the most frequent subjects for public debate in the country. To understand the background to this debate, a little history is needed.

Schools and other educational institutions (such as universities) existed in Britain long before the government began to take an interest in education. When it finally did, it did not sweep these institutions away, nor did it always take them over. In typically British fashion, it sometimes incorporated them into the system and sometimes left them outside it. Most importantly, the government left alone the small group of schools which had been used in the nineteenth century (and in some cases before then) to educate the sons of the upper and upper-middle classes. At these 'public' schools (▷ *The public school system*), the emphasis was on 'character-building' and the development of 'team spirit' rather than on academic achievement. This involved the development of distinctive customs and attitudes, the wearing of distinctive clothes and the use of specialized items of vocabulary. They were all 'boarding schools' (that is, the pupils lived in them), so they had a deep and lasting influence on their pupils. Their aim was to prepare young men to take up positions in the higher ranks of the army, in business, the legal profession, the civil service and politics.

▶ The public school system

Stereotypical public schools:

- are for boys only from the age of thirteen onwards, most of whom attended a private 'prep' (= preparatory) school beforehand;
- take fee-paying pupils (and some scholarship pupils who have won a place in a competitive entrance exam and whose parents do not pay);
- are boarding schools (the boys live there during term-time);
- are divided into 'houses', each 'house' being looked after by a 'housemaster';
- make some of the senior boys 'prefects', which means that they have authority over the other boys and have their own servants (called 'fags'), who are appointed from amongst the youngest boys;
- place great emphasis on team sports;
- enforce their rules with the use of physical punishment;
- have a reputation for a relatively great amount of homosexual activity;
- are not at all luxurious or comfortable.

However, this traditional image no longer fits the facts. These days, there is not a single public school in the country in which all of the above features apply. There have been a fairly large number of girls' public schools for the last hundred years, and more recently a few schools have started to admit both boys and girls. Many schools admit day pupils as well as boarders, and some are day-schools only; prefects no longer have so much power or have been abolished altogether; fagging has disappeared; there is less emphasis on team sport and more on academic achievement; life for the pupils is more physically comfortable than it used to be.

Among the most famous public schools are Eton, Harrow, Rugby and Winchester.

Public schoolboys from Eton

When the pupils from these schools finished their education, they formed the ruling élite, retaining the distinctive habits and vocabulary which they had learnt at school. They formed a closed group, to a great extent separate from the rest of society. Entry into this group was difficult for anybody who had had a different education. When, in the twentieth century, education and its possibilities for social advancement came within everybody's reach, new schools tended to copy the features of the public schools. (After all, they provided the only model of a successful school that the country had.)

Many of the more distinctive characteristics of British education outlined below can be ascribed, at least partly, to this historical background. Of more recent relevance is Britain's general loss of confidence in itself (see chapters 4 and 6). This change of mood has probably had a greater influence on education than on any other aspect of public life (▷ *Looking towards Germany*). The modern educational system has been through a period of constant change and it is difficult to predict what further changes will occur in the next decade. At the same time, however, there are certain underlying characteristics that seem to remain fixed.

▶ Looking towards Germany

The accepted wisdom in modern Britain is that the education systems of many other countries are better than the British one, especially the German system. Queen Victoria was known to have remarked on this in the nineteenth century. But that, of course, was in the days when Britain ruled the world, so who cared?

These days, however, the British take their inadequacies seriously. In 1991 *The Economist* reported that pilgrimages to Germany from British educationalists, education ministers and business people had become so common that the British embassy in Bonn employed a full-time official to look after these visitors and put them in touch with the right educational experts.

▶ School days

Look at these comparisons.

Age of compulsory full-time school education (1989)

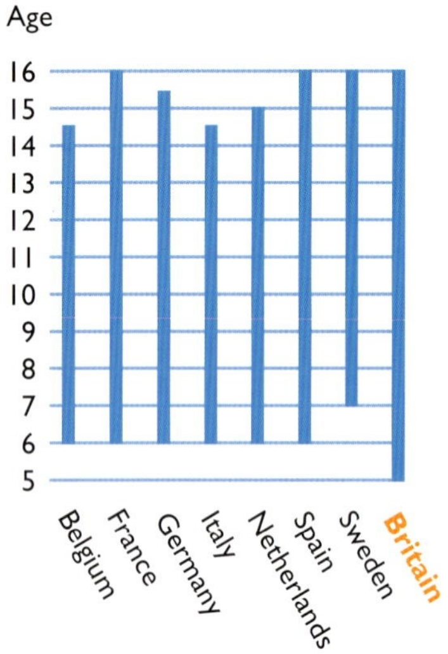

Average number of weeks in school year (discounting short 'half-term' breaks)

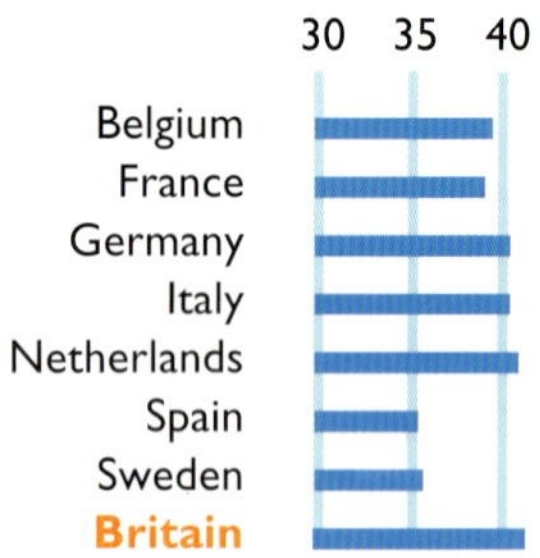

Source: Selected National Education Systems (Department of Education and Science)

Education in Britain is compulsory for the most years and the school year is the longest. The number of hours in the school week is no less than the average for Europe. But look at ▷*Before and after school*.

Organization

Despite recent changes, it is a characteristic of the British system that there is comparatively little central control or uniformity. For example, education is managed not by one, but by three, separate government departments: the Department for Education and Employment is responsible for England and Wales alone – Scotland and Northern Ireland have their own departments. In fact, within England and Wales education has traditionally been seen as separate from 'training', and the two areas of responsibility have only recently been combined in a single department.

None of these central authorities exercises much control over the details of what actually happens in the country's educational institutions. All they do is to ensure the availability of education, dictate and implement its overall organization and set overall learning objectives (which they enforce through a system of inspectors) up to the end of compulsory education.

Central government does not prescribe a detailed programme of learning or determine what books and materials should be used. It says, in broad terms, what schoolchildren should learn, but it only offers occasional advice about how they should learn it. Nor does it dictate the exact hours of the school day, the exact dates of holidays or the exact age at which a child must start in full-time education. It does not manage an institution's finances either, it just decides how much money to give it. It does not itself set or supervise the marking of the exams which older teenagers do. In general, as many details as possible are left up to the individual institution or the Local Education Authority (LEA, a branch of local government).

One of the reasons for this level of 'grass-roots' independence is that the system has been influenced by the public-school tradition that a school is its own community. Most schools develop, to some degree at least, a sense of distinctiveness. Many, for example, have their own uniforms for pupils. Many, especially those outside the state system, have associations of former pupils. It is considered desirable (even necessary) for every school to have its own school hall, big enough to accommodate every pupil, for daily assemblies and other occasional ceremonies. Universities, although financed by the government, have even more autonomy. Each one has complete control over what to teach, how to teach it, who it accepts as students and how to test these students.

Style

Learning for its own sake, rather than for any particular practical purpose, has traditionally been given a comparatively high value in Britain. In comparison with most other countries, a relatively strong emphasis has been put on the quality of *person* that education produces (as opposed to the qualities of *abilities* that it produces). The balance has changed in the last quarter of the twentieth century (for example, there is now a high degree of concern about levels of literacy), but much of the public debate about educational policy still focuses not so much on how to help people develop useful knowledge and skills as on how education might help to bring about a better society – on social justice rather than on efficiency.

This approach has had a far-reaching effect on many aspects of the educational system. First of all, it has influenced the general style of teaching, which has tended to give priority to developing understanding rather than acquiring factual knowledge and learning to apply this knowledge to specific tasks. This is why British young people do not appear to have to work as hard as their counterparts in other European countries. Primary schoolchildren do not have as much formal homework to do and university students have fewer hours of programmed attendance than students on the continent do. (On the other hand, they receive greater personal guidance with their work). A second effect has been an emphasis on academic ability rather than practical ability (despite English anti-intellectualism – see chapter 5). This has resulted in high-quality education for the intelligent and academically inclined (at the upper secondary and university levels) with comparatively little attention given to the educational needs of the rest.

The traditional approach, together with the dislike of centralized authority, also helps to explain why the British school system got a national curriculum (a national specification of learning objectives) so much later than other European countries. If your aim is so vague and universal, it is difficult to specify what its elements are. It is for the same reason that British schools and universities have tended to give such a high priority to sport. The idea is that it helps to develop the 'complete' person. The importance of school as a 'community' can increase this emphasis. Sporting success enhances the reputation of an institution. Until the last quarter of the twentieth century, certain sports at some universities (especially Oxford and Cambridge) and medical schools were played to an international standard. People with poor academic records were sometimes accepted as students because of their sporting prowess (although, unlike in the USA, this practice was always unofficial).

Recent developments

Some of the many changes that took place in British education in the second half of the twentieth century simply reflected the wider social process of increased egalitarianism. The élitist institutions which first set the pattern no longer set the trend, and are themselves less élitist.

In other cases the changes have been the result of government policy. Before 1965 most children in the country had to take an exam at about the age of eleven, at the end of their primary schooling. If

▶ **Before and after school**

Look at these comparisons for attendance in education *outside* the compulsory years.

Four-year-olds attending nursery school (1989)

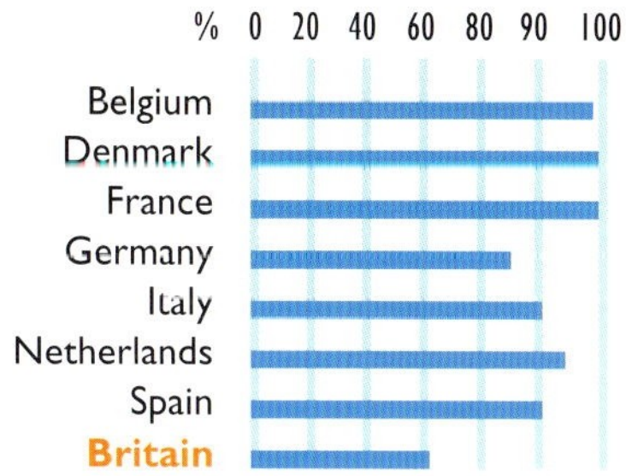

Students in full-time education and training in the year after the end of compulsory schooling (1985–86)

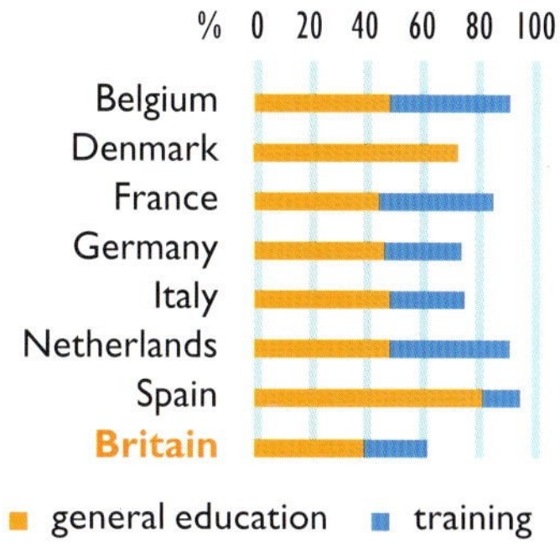

Sources: Selected National Education Systems (Department of Education and Science), Key Data and Europe in Figures

It seems that the British are comparatively unenthusiastic about education when it is not something that they have to do.

The 1994 Parent's Charter, explaining changes in the education system

they passed this exam, they went to a grammar school where they were taught academic subjects to prepare them for university, the professions, managerial jobs or other highly-skilled jobs; if they failed, they went to a secondary modern school, where the lessons had a more practical and technical bias. Many people argued that it was wrong for a person's future life to be decided at so young an age. The children who went to 'secondary moderns' tended to be seen as 'failures'. Moreover, it was noticed that the children who passed this exam (known as the 'eleven plus') were almost all from middle-class families. The system seemed to reinforce class distinctions. It was also unfair because the proportion of children who went to a grammar school varied greatly from area to area (from 15% to 40%). During the 1960s these criticisms came to be accepted by a majority of the public. Over the next decade the division into grammar schools and secondary modern schools was changed. These days, most eleven-year-olds all go on to the same local school. These schools are known as comprehensive schools. (The decision to make this change was in the hands of LEAs, so it did not happen at the same time all over the country. In fact, there are still one or two places where the old system is still in force.)

However, the comprehensive system has also had its critics. Many people felt that there should be more choice available to parents and disliked the uniformity of education given to teenagers. In addition, there is a widespread feeling that educational standards fell during the 1980s and that the average eleven-year old in Britain is significantly less literate and less numerate than his or her European counterpart.

Starting in the late 1980s, two major changes were introduced by the government. The first of these was the setting up of a national curriculum. For the first time in British education there is now a set of learning objectives for each year of compulsory school and all state schools are obliged to work towards these objectives. The national curriculum is being introduced gradually and will not be operating fully in all parts of Britain until the end of the 1990s. The other major change is that schools can now decide to 'opt out' of the control of the LEA and put themselves directly under the control of the appropriate government department. These 'grant-maintained' schools get their money directly from central government. This does not mean, however, that there is more central control. Provided they fulfil basic requirements, grant-maintained schools do not have to ask anybody else about how to spend their money.

One final point about the persistence of decentralization: there are really three, not one, national curricula. There is one for England and Wales, another for Scotland and another for Northern Ireland. The organization of subjects and the details of the learning objectives vary slightly from one to the other. There is even a difference between England and Wales. Only in the latter is the Welsh language part of the curriculum.

▶ Learning for its own sake

One effect of the traditional British emphasis on academic learning as opposed to practical training can be seen in the way that people gain qualifications for certain professions. In many cases this has not traditionally been done within universities. Instead, people go to specialized institutions which are separate from any university. You *can* study architecture at university, but most architects have learnt their profession at a separate School of Architecture. You *can* study law at university but this alone does not qualify you to be a lawyer (see chapter 11). You cannot get a teacher's qualification by doing an ordinary university course – most teachers get theirs at teacher training colleges. Until recently, schools were not usually involved in helping people to get qualifications for skilled manual jobs such as bricklaying or carpentry or machine-operating.

The introduction of the national curriculum is also intended to have an influence on the subject-matter of teaching. At the lower primary level, this means a greater emphasis on what are known as 'the three Rs' (Reading, wRiting and aRithmetic). At higher levels, it means a greater emphasis on science and technology. A consequence of the traditional British approach to education had been the habit of giving a relatively large amount of attention to the arts and humanities (which develop the well-rounded human being), and relatively little to science and technology (which develop the ability to do specific jobs). The prevailing belief at the time of writing is that Britain needs more scientists and technicians (▷ *A nation of ignoramuses?*).

School life

There is no countrywide system of nursery (i.e. pre-primary) schools. In some areas primary schools have nursery schools attached to them, but in others there is no provision of this kind. Many children do not begin full-time attendance at school until they are about five and start primary school. Almost all schools are either primary or secondary only, the latter being generally larger.

Nearly all schools work a five-day week, with no half-day, and are closed on Saturdays. The day starts at or just before nine o'clock and finishes between three and four, or a bit later for older children. The lunch break usually lasts about an hour-and-a-quarter. Nearly two-thirds of pupils have lunch provided by the school. Parents pay for this, except for the 15% who are rated poor enough for it to be free. Other children either go home for lunch or take sandwiches.

Methods of teaching vary, but there is most commonly a balance between formal lessons with the teacher at the front of the classroom, and activities in which children work in small groups round a table with the teacher supervising. In primary schools, the children are mostly taught by a class teacher who teaches all subjects. At the ages of seven and eleven, children have to take national tests in English, mathematics and science. In secondary schools, pupils have different teachers for different subjects and are given regular homework.

▶ A nation of ignoramuses?

Does the earth go around the sun or does the sun go around the earth? This was one of the questions a representative sample of 13,000 adults was asked in a study conducted by the European Commission in 1993. Guess which state in the European Union came last in knowledge of basic astronomical and evolutionary facts! A third of those questioned in Britain got that sun–earth question wrong, and half of them did not know how long it takes for the earth to go around the sun. Most spectacularly, nearly half thought that early human beings were alive at the same time as dinosaurs.

These results reinforced the feeling in Britain that people's basic scientific knowledge is unacceptably low. But the results of the EC survey were not all depressing for British scientists and educationalists. In biology, the British appeared comparatively knowledgeable (although still not top of the European league). The survey also showed that, contrary to what was supposed, scientists are very highly respected.

▶ The school year

Schools usually divide their year into three 'terms', starting at the beginning of September.

Autumn term	Christmas holiday (about 2 weeks)	Spring term	Easter holiday (about 2 weeks)	Summer term	Summer holiday (about 6 weeks)

In addition, all schools have a 'half-term' (= half-term holiday), lasting a few days or a week in the middle of each term.

The older children get, the more likely they are to be separated into groups according to their perceived abilities, sometimes for particular subjects only, sometimes across all subjects. But some schools teach all subjects to 'mixed ability' classes. The rights and wrongs of this practice have generated heated debate for several decades and there is great variety from school to school and area to area.

Public exams

The organization of the exams which schoolchildren take from the age of about fifteen onwards exemplifies both the lack of uniformity in British education and also the traditional 'hands-off' approach of British governments. First, these exams are not set by the government, but rather by independent examining boards. There are several of these. Everywhere except Scotland (which has its own single board), each school or LEA decides which board's exams its pupils take. Some schools even enter their pupils for the exams of more than one board.

Second, the boards publish a separate syllabus for each subject. There is no unified school-leaving exam or school-leaving certificate. Some boards offer a vast range of subjects. In practice, nearly all pupils do exams in English language, maths and a science subject, and most also do an exam in technology and one in a foreign language, usually French. Many students take exams in three or more additional subjects.

Third, the exams have nothing to do with school years as such. They are divorced from the school system. There is nothing to stop a sixty-five year-old doing a few of them for fun. In practice, of course, the vast majority of people who do these exams are school pupils, but formally it is individual people who enter for these exams, not pupils in a particular year of school.

An example of the independence of the examining boards is the decision of one of them (the Northern Examinations Board) in 1992 to include certain popular television programmes on their English literature syllabus. This was against the spirit of the government's education policy at that time. The idea of 100,000 schoolchildren settling down to watch the Australian soap opera *Neighbours* as part of their homework made government ministers very angry, but there was nothing they could do to stop it.

Education beyond sixteen

At the age of sixteen people are free to leave school if they want to. With Britain's newfound enthusiasm for continuing education (and because there are not enough unskilled jobs to go round), far fewer sixteen-year-olds go straight out and look for a job than used to. About a third of them still take this option, however. Most do not find employment immediately and many take part in training schemes which involve on-the-job training combined with part-time college courses.

Exams and qualifications

GCSE = General Certificate of Secondary Education. The exams taken by most fifteen- to sixteen-year-olds in England, Wales and Northern Ireland. Marks are given for each subject separately. The syllabuses and methods of examination of the various examining boards differ. However, there is a uniform system of marks, all being graded from A to G. Grades A, B and C are regarded as 'good' grades.

SCE = Scottish Certificate of Education. The Scottish equivalent of GCSE. These exams are set by the Scottish Examinations Board. Grades are awarded in numbers (1 = the best).

A Levels = Advanced Levels. Higher-level academic exams set by the same examining boards that set GCSE exams. They are taken mostly by people around the age of eighteen who wish to go on to higher education.

SCE 'Highers' = The Scottish equivalent of A-levels.

GNVQ = General National Vocational Qualification. Courses and exams in job-related subjects. They are divided into five levels, the lowest level being equivalent to GCSEs/SCEs and the third level to A-levels/'Highers'. Most commonly, GNVQ courses are studied at Colleges of Further Education, but more and more schools are also offering them.

Degree: A qualification from a university. (Other qualifications obtained after secondary education are usually called 'certificate' or 'diploma'). Students studying for a first degree are called undergraduates. When they have been awarded a degree, they are known as graduates. Most people get honours degrees, awarded in different classes. These are:
Class I (known as 'a first')
Class II,I ('a 2,1' or 'an upper second')
Class II,II ('a 2,2' or 'a lower second')
Class III ('a third')
A student who is below one of these gets a pass degree (i.e. not an honours degree).

Bachelor's Degree: The general name for a first degree, most commonly a BA (= Bachelor of Arts) or BSc (= Bachelor of Science).

Master's Degree: The general name for a second (postgraduate) degree, most commonly an MA or MSc. At Scottish universities, however, these titles are used for first degrees.

Doctorate: The highest academic qualification. This usually (but not everywhere) carries the title PhD (= Doctor of Philosophy). The time taken to complete a doctorate varies, but it is generally expected to involve three years of more-or-less full-time study.

The growth of higher education

In 1960 there were less than twenty-five universities in the whole of Britain. By 1980 there were more than forty, and by now there are well over a hundred institutions which have university status.

Nineteen to twenty-two year-olds in full-time education

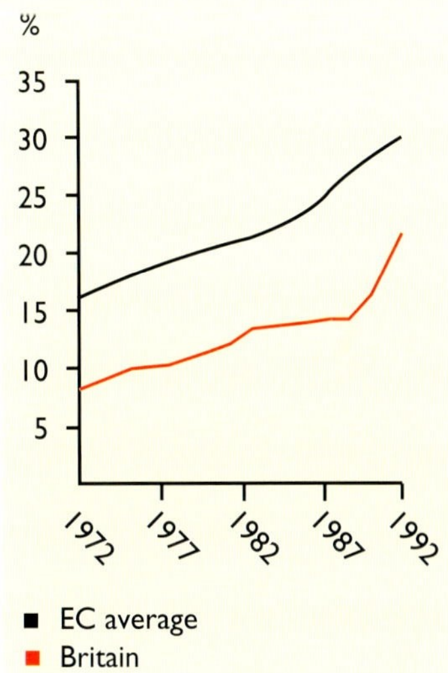

Sources: Europe in Figures, Government Statistical Service and Key Data

There has been a great increase in educational opportunities for people at this age or older in the last quarter of the twentieth century. About half of those who stay in full-time education will have to leave their school, either because it does not have a sixth form (▷ *The sixth form*) or because it does not teach the desired subjects, and go to a Sixth-form College, or College of Further Education. An increasing number do vocational training courses for particular jobs and careers. Recent governments have been keen to increase the availability of this type of course and its prestige (which used to be comparatively low).

The sixth form

The word 'form' was the usual word to describe a class of pupils in public schools. It was taken over by some state schools. With the introduction of the national curriculum it has become common to refer to 'years'. However, 'form' has been universally retained in the phrase 'sixth form', which refers to those pupils who are studying beyond the age of sixteen.

▶ The Open University

This is one development in education in which Britain can claim to have led the world. It was started in 1969. It allows people who do not have the opportunity to be ordinary 'students' to study for a degree. Its courses are taught through television, radio and specially written coursebooks. Its students work with tutors, to whom they send their written work and with whom they then discuss it, either at meetings or through correspondence. In the summer, they have to attend short residential courses of about a week.

In England and Wales, for those who stay in education and study conventional academic subjects, there is more specialization than there is in most other countries. Typically, a pupil spends a whole two years studying just three subjects, usually related ones, in preparation for taking A-level exams (▷ *Exams and qualifications*), though this is something else which might change in the near future.

The independence of Britain's educational institutions is most noticeable in universities. They make their own choices of who to accept on their courses. There is no right of entry to university for anybody. Universities normally select students on the basis of A-level results and an interview. Those with better exam grades are more likely to be accepted. But in principle there is nothing to stop a university accepting a student who has no A-levels at all and conversely, a student with top grades in several A-levels is not guaranteed a place.

The availability of higher education has increased greatly in the second half of the twentieth century (▷ *The growth of higher education*). Nevertheless, finding a university place is not easy. Universities only take the better students. Because of this, and also because of the relatively high degree of personal supervision of students which the low ratio of students to staff allows, nearly all university students complete their studies – and in a very short time too! In England, Wales and Northern Ireland, it is only for modern languages and certain vocational studies that students take more than three years. In Scotland, four years is the norm for most subjects.

Another reason for the low drop-out rate is that 'full-time' really means full-time. A large proportion of students live 'on campus', (or, in Oxford and Cambridge, 'in college') or in rooms nearby, which tends to mean that the student is surrounded by a university atmosphere.

However, the expansion of higher education is putting a strain on these characteristics. More students means more expense for the state. The government's response has been to abolish the student grant which, at one time, covered most of a student's expenses during the thirty-week teaching year. On top of that, most students have to pay fees. As a result, many more students cannot afford to live away from home. In 1975 it was estimated that 80% of all university students were non-local. This percentage is becoming lower and lower. In addition, more than a third of students now have part-time jobs, which means that they cannot spend so much time on their studies. A further result of increased numbers of students without a corresponding increase in budgets is that the student/staff ratio has been getting higher. All of these developments threaten to reduce the traditionally high quality of British university education. They also threaten to reduce its availability to students from low-income families.

University College, Oxford

Types of university

There are no important official or legal distinctions between the various types of university in the country. But it is possible to discern a few broad categories.

• Oxbridge

This name denotes the universities of Oxford and Cambridge, both founded in the medieval period. They are federations of semi-independent colleges, each college having its own staff, known as 'Fellows'. Most colleges have their own dining hall, library and chapel and contain enough accommodation for at least half of their students. The Fellows teach the college students, either one-to-one or in very small groups (known as 'tutorials' in Oxford and 'supervisions' in Cambridge). Oxbridge has the lowest student/staff ratio in Britain. Lectures and laboratory work are organized at university level. As well as the college libraries, there are the two university libraries, both of which are legally entitled to a free copy of every book published in Britain. Before 1970 all Oxbridge colleges were single-sex (mostly for men). Now, the majority admit both sexes.

• The old Scottish universities

By 1600 Scotland boasted four universities. They were Glasgow, Edinburgh, Aberdeen and St Andrews. The last of these resembles Oxbridge in many ways, while the other three are more like civic universities (see below) in that most of the students live at home or find their own rooms in town. At all of them the pattern of study is closer to the continental tradition than to the English one – there is less specialization than at Oxbridge.

• The early nineteenth-century English universities

Durham University was founded in 1832. Its collegiate living arrangements are similar to Oxbridge, but academic matters are organized at university level. The University of London started in 1836 with just two colleges. Many more have joined since, scattered widely around the city, so that each college (most are non-residential) is almost a separate university. The central organization is responsible for little more than exams and the awarding of degrees.

• The older civic ('redbrick') universities

During the nineteenth century various institutes of higher education, usually with a technical bias, sprang up in the new industrial towns and cities such as Birmingham, Manchester and Leeds. Their buildings were of local material, often brick, in contrast to the stone of older universities (hence the name, 'redbrick'). They catered only for local people. At first, they prepared students for London University degrees, but later they were given the right to award their own degrees, and so became universities themselves. In the mid twentieth century they started to accept students from all over the country.

• The campus universities

These are purpose-built institutions located in the countryside but close to towns. Examples are East Anglia, Lancaster, Sussex and Warwick. They have accommodation for most of their students on site and from their beginning, mostly in the early 1960s, attracted students from all over the country. (Many were known as centres of student protest in the late 1960s and early 1970s.) They tend to emphasize relatively 'new' academic disciplines such as social sciences and to make greater use than other universities of teaching in small groups, often known as 'seminars'.

• The newer civic universities

These were originally technical colleges set up by local authorities in the first half of the twentieth century. Their upgrading to university status took place in two waves. The first wave occurred in the mid 1960s, when ten of them (e.g. Aston in Birmingham, Salford near Manchester and Strathclyde in Glasgow) were promoted in this way. Then, in the early 1970s, another thirty became 'polytechnics', which meant that as well as continuing with their former courses, they were allowed to teach degree courses (the degrees being awarded by a national body). In the early 1990s most of these (and also some other colleges) became universities. Their most notable feature is flexibility with regard to studying arrangements, including 'sandwich' courses (i.e. studies interrupted by periods of time outside education). They are now all financed by central government.

Warwick University, a campus university

QUESTIONS

1 From your reading of this chapter, what can you say about the trends in the British educational system? Is it moving towards greater or lesser uniformity? Towards more or less provision before and after the years of compulsory schooling? Concentrating more on purely academic subjects or on more practical ones?
2 Here are the ten subjects which, according to the national curriculum for England, must be taught in the first three years of secondary education: English, Mathematics (Maths), Science, Technology, History, Geography, a modern foreign language (French is the most common), Art, Music and Physical Education (PE). Is there anything here that surprises you? Do you think any other subjects should be included? Are these the main subjects taught in your country?
3 Would you say that people in your country are more or less enthusiastic about university education than they are in Britain?
4 In what ways has the pursuit of equality for all affected the development of the educational system in Britain? Would you say that there was equality of opportunity in the present system?
5 What would you say are the successes and failures of the British educational system? What things, if any, does it appear to do well, and what areas does it seem to neglect or do badly in?

SUGGESTIONS

- Any British Council library has lots of information about educational institutions in Britain. For example, a look at a few university prospectuses would help you to get the flavour of British universities (but remember, of course, that these prospectuses function as advertisements!). Alternatively, you could write to British universities (including the Open University) for free information or prospectuses.
- David Lodge's contemporary social comedies *Small World* and *Nice Work* have a university background. *Brideshead Revisited* by Evelyn Waugh paints a romantic view of life as lived by Oxford undergraduates in the nineteen twenties and *Porterhouse Blue* by Tom Sharpe is a comedy of contemporary Oxbridge student life. *Educating Rita* is a play by Willy Russell (which has also been made into a film) about a working-class woman from Liverpool whose life is transformed by studying with the Open University.

15 The economy and everyday life

The one thing the English will never forgive the Germans for is working too hard.

GEORGE MIKES

This statement was written by a Hungarian humourist who emigrated to Britain in 1938. He wrote it in the 1960s, when the German economy was rapidly overtaking Britain's. Living standards in Britain have risen steadily since then, but not as fast, perhaps, as they have in other EU countries. Britain used to be one of the wealthiest countries in Europe. These days it is often, by most standards of measurement, poorer than the EU average. (In fact, in 1992 it was even poor enough to qualify for special EU funding for poorer member states, though national pride prevented it from applying.)

Earning money

The statement above is, of course, not literally true. However, it does reflect a certain lack of enthusiasm for work in general. At the upper end of the social scale this attitude to work exists because leisure has always been the main outward sign of aristocracy. And because of Britain's class system, it has had its effects throughout society. If you have to work, then the less it looks like work the better. Traditionally therefore, a major sign of being middle class (as opposed to working class) has been that you do non-manual work. The fact that skilled manual (or 'blue-collar') workers have been paid more highly than the lower grades of 'white-collar' (i.e. non-manual) worker for several decades has only slightly changed this social perception. This 'anti-work' outlook among the working class has led to a relative lack of ambition or enthusiasm and a belief that high earnings are more important than job satisfaction.

These attitudes are slowly changing. For example, at least half of the workforce now does non-manual work, and yet a majority describe themselves as working class (see chapter 4). It would therefore seem that the connection between being middle class and doing non-manual work is growing weaker. Nevertheless, the connection between class distinctions and types of work lives on in a number of ways. One illustration of this is the different way in which earnings

▶ Top people

In Britain, particular occupations are no longer as closely associated with particular classes as they used to be. The feminist movement, the expansion of higher education and an egalitarian atmosphere have reduced the influence of old-established, male-dominated institutions such as public schools and Oxbridge (see chapter 14). A popular claim is that in modern Britain people achieve their positions by exercising their abilities rather than as a result of their backgrounds. In the early 1990s it was true that even the Prime Minister (John Major) had been educated at a state school and had left full-time education at the age of sixteen.

However, there is a limit to these changes. In 1992 *The Economist* magazine drew up a list of the holders of 100 of the most important positions in the country (in politics, the civil service, the armed forces, academia, the arts, business and finance). The backgrounds of these 'top' people were then compared with those of people in similar positions in 1972. Here are the results:

% who...	1972	1992
went to public school	67	66
of which Eton College	14	8
attended higher education	78	89
of which Oxbridge	52	54
are women	2	4

In both years two-thirds of the top people had been to public school (to which less than 5% of the population goes) and an astonishing proportion to just one of these. It was more important in 1992 to be highly educated than it was in 1972. But still half of all the top jobs were held by people from just two of the country's universities. And women are almost completely excluded (in both years' lists, one of those women was the Queen!).

▶ How they are paid

	Manual (and lowest grades of non-manual)	Non-manual
Rate quoted	per hour/week	per year
Known as	wages	salary
Paid every	week	month
Method	usually in cash	by cheque or into bank

are conventionally expressed and paid (▷ *How they are paid*). Another is the fact that certain organizations of professional workers, such as the National Union of Teachers (NUT), have never belonged to the Trades Union Congress (see below). The connection can also be seen if we look at those people who hold the most important jobs in the country (▷ *Top people*).

Perhaps the traditional lack of enthusiasm for work is the reason why the working day, in comparison with most European countries, starts rather late (usually at eight o'clock for manual workers and around nine for non-manual workers). However, measured by the number of hours worked in a week, the British reputation for not working hard enough appears to be false (▷ *The industrious British*). The normal lunch break is an hour or less, and most people (unless they work part-time) continue working until five or later. Many people often work several hours overtime a week. In addition, a comparatively large proportion of British people stay in the workforce for a comparatively large part of their lives. The normal retiring age for most people is sixty-five (sixty for some, including a greater proportion of women).

There are three main ways in which people look for work in Britain: through newspapers (national ones for the highest-qualified, otherwise local ones), through the local job centre (which is run as a government service) and through privately-run employment agencies (which take a commission from employers). The overall trend in employment over the last quarter of the twentieth century has been basically the same as elsewhere in western Europe. The level of unemployment has gradually risen and most new job opportunities are in the service sector (in communications, health care and social care, for example).

This situation has led to an interesting irony with regard to the two sexes. The decline of heavy industry means fewer jobs in stereotypical 'men's work', while the rise in service occupations means an increase in vacancies for stereotypical 'women's work'. In 1970 around 65% of all those in work in Britain were men. In 1993 men made up only 51% of the workforce. When the law against sex discrimination in employment was passed in 1975, it was intended

Average length of working week (1989)

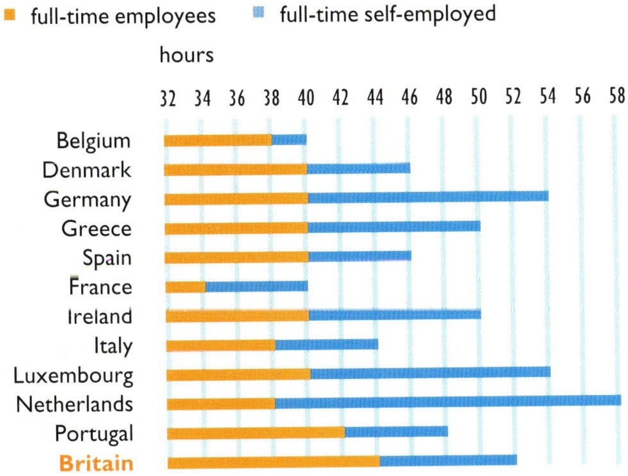

Percent of population in the labour force (1989)

Those either in work or looking for work

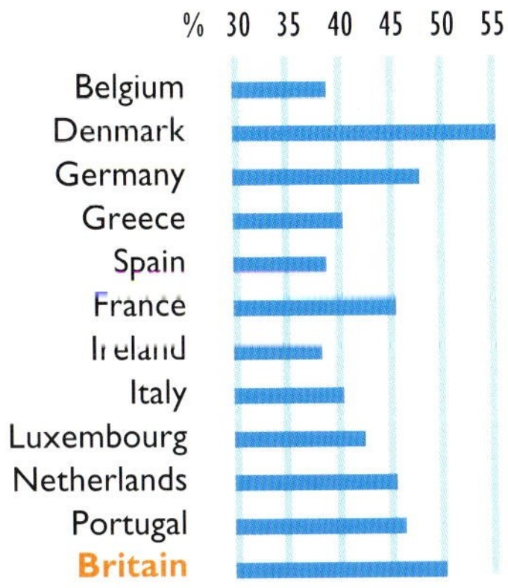

Source: Europe in Figures

mainly to protect women. However, in 1994 nearly half of the complaints received by the Equal Opportunities Commission (which helps to enforce the law) came from men. In that year there were two-and-a-half times as many unemployed men as there were unemployed women. Many men now seek employment as nurses, child carers, shop assistants, secretaries and other kinds of office worker. But they often find that, for no justifiable reason, they are not hired. It seems that these jobs are still considered to be more suitable for women. One of the reasons for this may be the low rates of pay in these areas of work. Although it is illegal for women to be paid less than men for the same job, in 1993 the average full-time male employee earned about 50% more than the average full-time female worker.

Work organizations

The organization which represents employers in private industry is called the Confederation of British Industry (CBI). Most employers belong to it and so the advice which it gives to trade unions and the government is quite influential. The Trades Union Congress (TUC) is a voluntary association of the country's trade unions. There are more than a hundred of these, representing employees in all types of business.

Most British unions are connected with particular occupations. Many belong to the Labour party (see chapter 6) to which their members pay a 'political levy'. That is, a small part of their union membership subscription is passed on to the party, although they have the right to 'contract out' of this arrangement if they want to. However, the unions themselves are not usually formed along party lines; that is, there is usually only one union for each group of

▶ The industrious British

The British may not like work very much. But they seem to spend a lot of time doing it. Look at the European comparisons above. The figures show that in Britain, full-time employees work the longest hours in Europe, self-employed people work longer than in most other European countries and more people between the ages of twenty-five and sixty, especially women, stay in 'the job market' than they do in most other European countries. Moreover, holiday periods in Britain are comparatively short and the country has a comparatively small number of public holidays (see chapter 23).

▶ Labour relations: a glossary

When there is a dispute between employees and management, the matter sometimes goes to **arbitration**; that is, both sides agree to let an independent investigator settle the dispute for them.

Refusing to work in the normal way is generally referred to as **industrial action** (even when the work has nothing to do with industry). This can take various forms. One of these is a **work-to-rule**, in which employees follow the regulations concerning their jobs exactly and refuse to be flexible or co-operative in the normal way. Another is a **go slow**.

Finally, the employees might **go on strike**. Strikes can be **official**, if all the procedures required to make them legal have taken place, or **unofficial** (when they are sometimes referred to as **wildcat strikes**). When there is a strike, some strikers act as **pickets**. They stand at the entrance to the worksite and try to dissuade any fellow-workers who might not want to strike (whom they call **blacklegs**) from going into work.

Striking miners in 1984

employees rather than a separate one for each political party within that group.

Unions have local branches, some of which are called 'chapels', reflecting a historical link with nonconformism (see chapter 13). At the work site, a union is represented by a shop steward, who negotiates with the on-site management. His (very rarely is it 'her') struggles with the foreman, the management-appointed overseer, became part of twentieth century folklore.

Union membership has been declining since 1979 (▷ *The decline of the unions*). Immediately before then, the leader of the TUC (its General Secretary) was one of the most powerful people in the country and was regularly consulted by the Prime Minister and other important government figures. At that time the members of unions belonging to the TUC made up more than half of all employed people in the country. But a large section of the public became disillusioned with the power of the unions and the government then passed laws to restrict this power. Perhaps the decline in union membership is inevitable in view of the history of British unions as organizations for full-time male industrial workers. To the increasing numbers of female and part-time workers in the workforce, the traditional structure of British unionism has seemed less relevant. In an effort to halt the decline, the TUC declared in 1994 that it was loosening its contacts with the Labour party and was going to forge closer contacts with other parties.

One other work organization needs special mention. This is the National Union of Farmers (NUF). It does not belong to the TUC, being made up mostly of agricultural employers and independent farmers. Considering the small number of people involved in agriculture in Britain (the smallest proportion in the whole of the EU), it has a remarkably large influence. This is perhaps because of the special fascination that 'the land' holds for most British people (see chapter 5), making it relatively easy for the NUF to make its demands heard, and also because many of its members are wealthy.

The structure of trade and industry

The 'modernization' of business and industry happened later in Britain than it did in most other European countries. It was not until the 1960s that large corporations started to dominate and that a 'management class', trained at business school, began to emerge. Even after that time, many companies still preferred to recruit their managers from people who had 'worked their way up' through the company ranks and/or who were personally known to the directors. Only in the 1980s did graduate business qualifications become the norm for newly-hired managers.

British industry performed poorly during the decades following the Second World War (some people blamed this on the above characteristics). In contrast, British agriculture was very successful. In this industry, large scale organization (i.e. big farms) had been more common in Britain than in other European countries for quite a long time.

As in all European countries, the economic system in Britain is a mixture of private and public enterprise. Exactly how much of the country's economy is controlled by the state has fluctuated a great deal in the last fifty years and has been the subject of continual political debate. From 1945 until 1980 the general trend was for the state to have more and more control. Various industries became nationalized (in other words, owned by the government), especially those concerned with the production and distribution of energy. So too did the various forms of transport and communication services (as well, of course, as the provision of education, social welfare and health care). By 1980, 'pure' capitalism probably formed a smaller part of the economy than in any other country in western Europe.

From 1980 the trend started going in the other direction. A major part of the philosophy of the Conservative government of the 1980s was to let 'market forces' rule (which meant restricting the freedom of business as little as possible) and to turn state-owned companies into companies owned by individuals (who became shareholders). This approach was a major part of the thinking of Thatcherism (Margaret Thatcher was Prime Minister at that time). Between 1980 and 1994 a large number of companies were privatized (or 'de-nationalized'). That is, they were sold off by the government. By 1988 there were more shareholders in the country than there were members of unions. In addition, local government authorities were encouraged to 'contract out' their responsibility for services to commercial organizations.

The privatization of services which western people now regard as essential has necessitated the creation of various public 'watchdog' organizations with regulatory powers over the industries which they monitor. For example, Offtel monitors the activities of the privatized telephone industry, and OffWat monitors the privatized water companies.

▶ The decline of the unions

In the 1980s the British government passed several laws to restrict the power of the unions. One of these abolished the 'closed shop' (an arrangement which employers made with unions to hire only people who belonged to a union). Another made strikes illegal unless a postal vote of all union members had been conducted. In 1984 there was a long miners' strike. The National Union of Miners refused to follow the new regulations. Its leader, Arthur Scargill, became a symbol (depending on your point of view) of either all the worst lunacies of unionism or the brave fight of the working classes against the rise of Thatcherism. Previous miners' strikes in the twentieth century had been mostly successful. But this one was not (the miners did not achieve their aims); a sign of the decline in union power. Here is another sign (the TUC is the Trades Union Congress, the national association of trade unions):

Total membership of the TUC

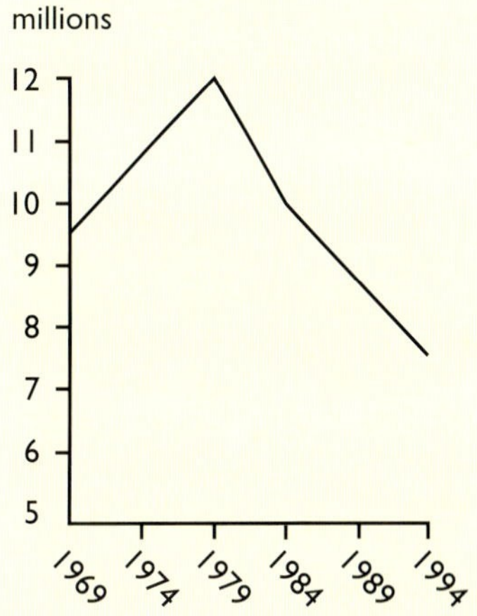

The widening gap between rich and poor

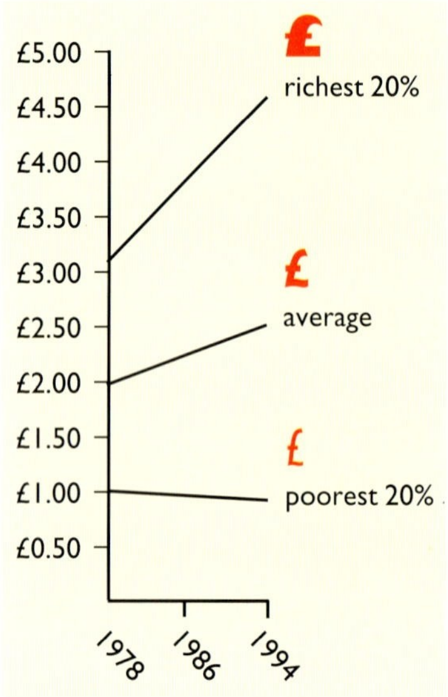

Source: Social Trends 1994

The graph shows that for every pound that the poorest 20% of the population in Britain had in 1978, most people had two pounds and the richest 20% of the population had three pounds. In 1994 the gap in wealth had grown. The richest people were about 50% richer, and most people were about 25% richer. The poorest people had, however, become slightly poorer.

Collecting taxes

The government organization which is responsible for collecting taxes in Britain is called the Inland Revenue. For employees, paying their income tax is not something they have to worry about. It is deducted from their pay cheque or pay packet before they receive it. This system is known as PAYE (= pay as you earn). The tax added to the price of something you buy is called VAT (= value added tax).

The distribution of wealth

In the early 1970s Britain had one of the most equitable distributions of wealth in western Europe. By the early 1990s it had one of the least equitable. The rich had got richer but the poor had not. Some surveys suggested that, by this time, the gap between the richest 10% of the population and the poorest 10% was as great as it had been in the late nineteenth century and that large numbers of households were living below the 'poverty line', which meant that they did not have enough money for basic things such as food and heating.

Class and wealth do not run parallel in Britain (see chapter 4), so it is not a country where people are especially keen to flaunt their wealth. Similarly, people are generally not ashamed to be poor. Of course, they don't like being poor, but they do not feel obliged to hide the fact. This can sometimes lead to an acceptance of poverty which is surprising for an 'advanced' country. When, in 1992, news of its increasing extent came to wider public attention, the government neither pretended that greater poverty did not exist, nor promised to do anything radical about it. Instead, it issued, through the Ministry of Agriculture, a suggested diet which it claimed even the poorest could afford. There were, of course, public comments about the patronizing nature of this action, but criticism in the press concentrated on how unrealistic the diet was, on how the figures didn't add up (and on the mystery of how a person should prepare and eat the recommended half an egg a week!).

One reason for the increasing disparity of wealth in Britain in the 1970s and 1980s is that rates of income tax changed. For a short period in the 1960s the basic rate was 40%. By the early eighties it was 30% and it then went down to 25%. During the same period, the top rate of income tax fell from a high of 98% to 40%. Of course, these figures do not mean that this is how much is deducted from a person's earnings. People in different situations are allowed to earn varying amounts before tax is deducted. People earning twice the average wage have about 25% of their gross income deducted. Somebody earning less than half the average wage pays very little tax at all. Nevertheless, there is, at the time of writing, a great disparity in different people's 'take-home pay'. During the 1980s, rates of pay for the best-paid jobs increased faster than those for badly-paid jobs. People in the best-paid jobs now take home about ten times as much as those in the lowest paid jobs. Many company directors, for example, take home seven times as much as the average wage.

Finance and investment

Wealth (and poverty) are relative concepts. Despite its relative economic decline, Britain is still one of the wealthiest places in the world. The empire has gone, the great manufacturing industries have nearly gone, but London is still one of the centres of the financial world. The Financial Times-Stock Exchange (FT-SE) Index of the 100 largest British companies (known popularly as the 'Footsie') is one of the main indicators of world stock market prices.

The reason for this is not hard to find. The same features that contributed to the country's decline as a great industrial and political power – the preference for continuity and tradition rather than change, the emphasis on personal contact as opposed to demonstrated ability when deciding who gets the important jobs – are exactly the qualities that attract investors. When people want to invest a lot of money, what matters to them is an atmosphere of stability and a feeling of personal trust. These are the qualities to be found in the 'square mile' of the old City of London (see chapter 3), which has one of the largest concentrations of insurance companies, merchant banks, joint-stock banks and stockbrokers in the world. As regards stability, many of the institutions in what is known as 'the City' can point to a long and uninterrupted history. Some of them have directors from the same family which started them perhaps over 200 years ago. Although there have been adaptations to modern conditions, and the stereotyped bowler-hatted 'city gent' is a thing of the past, the sense of continuity, epitomized by the many old buildings in the square mile, is still strong. As regards trust, the city has a reputation for habits of secrecy that might be thought of as undesirable in other aspects of public life, but which in financial dealings become an advantage. In this context, 'secrecy' means 'discretion'.

Although more than half of the British population has money invested in the city indirectly (because the insurance companies and pension funds to which they have entrusted their money invest it on the stock market), most people are unaware of what goes on in the world of 'high finance'. To most people, money is just a matter of the cash in their pockets and their account with one of the 'high street' banks (▷ *The high street banks*). Not every adult has a bank account. In 1970 only about 30% used these banks. But with the increasing habit of paying wages by cheque and the advent of cash dispensing machines, a majority now do so. Many, however, still prefer to use their National Savings account at the post office or one of the country's many building societies (see chapter 19).

An indication of the importance of bank accounts in people's lives is the strong dislike of the banks that has developed. During the 1990s the newspapers carried horror stories about their practices. In the years 1988 to 1993 banking profits rose by 50% while charges to customers rose by 70%. It is often difficult for people to do anything about bank charges – if they try to discuss them with their bank, they get charged for the phone calls and letters! So far, the one clear improvement has been in bank opening times. These used to be from nine-thirty to three-thirty, Mondays to Fridays only. Now, many banks stay open later and also open on Saturday mornings.

▶ The old lady of Threadneedle Street

This is the nickname of the Bank of England, the institution which controls the supply of money in Britain and which is located, of course, in the 'square mile'. Notice how the name suggests both familiarity and age – and also conservative habits. The bank has been described as 'fascinated by its own past'. It is also notable that the people who work there are reported to be proud of the nickname.

A doorman at the Bank of England

▶ The high street banks

The so-called 'big four' banks, which each have a branch in almost every town in Britain are: the National Westminster Bank (NatWest); Barclays Bank; Lloyds Bank; Midland Bank. The Bank of Scotland also has a very large number of branches. So does the Trustee Savings Bank (TSB).

NatWest

BARCLAYS

MIDLAND
The Listening Bank
Member HSBC Group

Lloyds Bank

The company logos of the 'big four' high street banks

▶ Currency and cash

The currency of Britain is the pound sterling, whose symbol is '£', always written before the amount. Informally, a pound is sometimes called a 'quid', so £20 might be expressed as 'twenty quid'. There are 100 pence (written 'p', pronounced 'pea') in a pound.

The one-pound coin has four different designs: an English one, a Scottish one, a Northern Irish one and a Welsh one (on which the inscription on the side is in Welsh; on all the others it is in Latin).

In Scotland, banknotes with a Scottish design are issued. These notes are perfectly legal in England, Wales and Northern Ireland, but banks and shops are not obliged to accept them if they don't want to and nobody has the right to demand change in Scottish notes.

Before 1971 Britain used the 'LSD' system. There were twelve pennies in a shilling and twenty shillings in a pound. Amounts were written like this: £3 12s. 6d. (= three pounds, twelve shillings and sixpence). If you read any novels set in Britain before 1971, you may come across the following:

a farthing = a quarter of a penny (not used after 1960)
a ha'penny (halfpenny) = half of a penny
a threepenny bit = threepence
a tanner = an informal name for a sixpenny coin
a bob = an informal name for a shilling
a half crown = two-and-a-half shillings (or two and sixpence)

People were not enthusiastic about the change to what they called 'new money'. For a long time afterwards, the question 'what's that in old money?' was used to imply that what somebody had just said was too complicated to be clear. In fact, money provides frequent opportunities for British conservatism (see chapter 5) to show itself. When the one-pound coin was introduced in 1983, it was very unpopular. People said they were sad to see the end of the pound note, which it replaced, and that a mere coin didn't seem to be worth as much. Another example is the reaction to the European euro. Since 1991 this has had the same status in Britain as Scottish banknotes have in England. But the first signs were that most shops and banks were refusing to accept them.

▶ How much do you want?

On tins and packets of food in British shops, the weight of an item is written in the kilos and grams familiar to people from continental Europe. However, most British people have little idea of what these terms mean (see chapter 5). Therefore, many of their packets and tins also record their weight in pounds (written as 'lbs') and ounces (written as 'oz'). Moreover, nobody ever asks for a kilo of apples or 200 grams of cheese. If those were the amounts you wanted, you would have to ask for 'two pounds or so' of apples and 'half a pound or less' of cheese and you would be about right.

Shoe and clothing sizes are also measured on different scales in Britain. The people who work in shops which sell these things usually known about continental and American sizes too, but most British people don't.

Spending money: shopping

The British are not very adventurous shoppers. They like reliability and buy brand-name goods wherever possible, preferably with the price clearly marked (they are not very keen on haggling over prices). It is therefore not surprising that a very high proportion of the country's shops are branches of chain stores.

Visitors from northern European countries are sometimes surprised by the shabbiness of shop-window displays, even in prosperous areas. This is not necessarily a sign of economic depression. It is just that the British do not demand art in their shop windows. In general, they have been rather slow to take on the idea that shopping might actually be fun. On the positive side, visitors are also sometimes struck by the variety of types of shop. Most shops are chain stores, but among those that are not, there is much individuality. Independent shopowners feel no need to follow conventional ideas about what a particular shop does and doesn't sell.

In the last quarter of the twentieth century supermarkets began moving out of town, where there was lots of free parking space. As they did so, they became bigger, turning into 'hypermarkets' stocking a wider variety of items. For example, most of them now sell alcoholic drinks, which are conventionally bought at shops called 'off-licences'. They also sell petrol and some items traditionally found in chemists and newsagents.

However, this trend has not gone as far as it has in some other European countries. For example, few supermarkets sell clothes, shoes, kitchen utensils or electrical goods. They still concentrate mainly on everyday needs. An exception is the first warehouse shopping club in Europe, opened in 1993 in Essex by the American company Costco. Here, 'members' (who have paid a small fee) can find almost everything that a shopper could ever want to buy – at a reduced price. Shopping clubs of this kind have spread rapidly all over the USA. At the time of writing, it is too early to say whether they will do so in Britain. The move out of town, however, is already well established, with many of the country's chain stores following the supermarkets into specially built shopping centres, most of them covered. (Britain has some of the largest covered shopping areas in Europe.) In 1980 only 5% of shop sales took place in these locations. In 1994 this figure had jumped to 25%.

The area in town where the local shops are concentrated is known as the high street (the American equivalent is 'Main Street'). British high streets have suffered from the move towards out-of-town shopping. In the worst-affected towns, as many as a quarter of the shops in the high street are vacant. But high streets have often survived by adapting. In larger towns, shops have tended to become either more specialized or to sell especially cheap goods (for people who are too poor to own a car and drive out of town). Many have become charity shops (selling second-hand items and staffed by volunteers) and discount stores. Many of the central streets are now reserved for pedestrians, so that they are more pleasant to be in.

Even most small high streets still manage to have at least one representative of the various kinds of conventional food shop (such as butcher, grocer, fishmonger, greengrocer), which do well by selling more expensive luxury items. (Although the middle classes use them, supermarkets have never been regarded as 'smart' or fashionable places in which to shop.)

The survival of the high street has been helped by the fact that department stores have been comparatively slow to move out of town. Almost every large town or suburb has at least one of these. They are usually not chain stores and each company runs a maximum of a few branches in the same region.

Shop opening hours

The normal time for shops to open is nine in the morning. Large out-of-town supermarkets stay open all day until about eight o'clock. Most small shops stay open all day (some take a break for lunch, usually between one and two) and then close at half-past five or a bit later. In some towns there is an 'early closing day' when the shops shut at midday and do not open again. However, this is becoming rarer. In fact, over the last twenty-five years, shop opening hours have become more varied. Regulations have been relaxed. It is now much easier than it used to be to find shops open after six. In some areas the local authorities are encouraging high street shops to

▶ The corner shop

A shop by itself in a residential area is often referred to as 'the corner shop'. These sometimes sell various kinds of food, but they are not always general grocers. Usually their main business is in newspapers, magazines, sweets and tobacco products. It is from these that most 'paper rounds' (see chapter 16) are organized. Only in corner shops do shopkeepers know their customers personally. Only in them is the interaction across the counter often social as well as transactional. People working in other shops are often very helpful, but the conversation usually has some clear purpose.

In the last few decades, many corner shops have been taken over by people from southern Asia who have delighted the neighbourhood by staying open very long hours.

A 'corner shop'

Some well-known names

The best known supermarket chains are Sainsbury and Tesco, although there are others. Asda is the best known of many discount stores.

There is only one department store with a large number of branches. This is Marks & Spencer. It is so well-known that it is often referred to as 'Marks and Sparks' or just 'M and S'. To the British, clothes at M and S are typical of the middle range: they are neither cheap nor expensive, fairly good quality and rather conservative. Unlike most other department stores, M and S also has a 'food hall', where items are more expensive than they are in supermarkets.

In a category all by itself is Woolworth's, which used to have a branch in almost every high street in the country. It sells mostly sweets, music, toys and children's clothes of the cheaper kind.

stay open very late on some evenings as a way of putting new life into their 'dead' town centres.

But the most significant change in recent years has been with regard to Sundays. By the early 1990s many shops, including chain stores, were opening on some Sundays, especially in the period before Christmas. In doing this they were taking a risk with the law. Sometimes they were taken to court, sometimes not. The rules were so old and confused that nobody really knew what was and what wasn't legal. It was agreed that something had to be done. On one side were the 'Keep Sunday Special' lobby, a group of people from various Christian churches and trade unions. They argued that Sunday should be special, a day of rest, a day for all the family to be together. They also feared that Sunday-opening would mean that shop workers would be forced to work too many hours. On the other side were a number of lobbies, especially people from women's and consumer groups. They argued that working women needed more than one day (Saturday) in which to rush around doing the shopping. In any case, they argued, shopping was also something that the whole family could do together. In 1993 Parliament voted on the matter. By a small majority, the idea of a complete 'free-for-all' was defeated. Small shops are allowed to open on Sundays for as long as they like, but large shops and supermarkets can only open for a maximum of six hours.

QUESTIONS

1 What are the differences (if any) between the present role of trade unions in Britain and their role in your country?

2 How can banking be such an important part of the British economy when some British people don't even have bank accounts?

3 Here is an extract from a book written by a Frenchman who has spent a long time living in England:

> *Continentals are always disconcerted by the English attitude to work. They appear neither to view it as a heavy burden imposed by fate, nor to embrace it as a sacred obligation. Effort is a matter of personal choice, and payment simply a quid pro quo.*

(from *Les Anglais* by Phillipe Daudy)

Do you find the British attitude to work confusing? In your country, do people see work as a 'heavy burden' or a 'sacred obligation' (or something else)?

4 In your country, do shops stay open for more or fewer hours a week than they do in Britain? Do you think the de-regulation of shop opening hours is a good thing?

16
The media

British people watch a lot of television. They are also reported to be the world's most dedicated home-video users. But this does not mean that they have given up reading. They are the world's third biggest newspaper buyers; only the Japanese and the Swedes buy more.

The importance of the national press

Newspaper publication is dominated by the national press, which is an indication of the comparative weakness of regional identity in Britain (see chapter 4). Nearly 80% of all households buy a copy of one of the main national papers every day. There are more than eighty local and regional daily papers; but the total circulation of all of them together is much less than the combined circulation of the national 'dailies'. The only non-national papers with significant circulations are published in the evenings, when they do not compete with the national papers, which always appear in the mornings.

Most local papers do not appear on Sundays, so on that day the dominance of the national press is absolute. The 'Sunday papers' are so-called because that is the only day on which they appear. Some of them are sisters of a daily (published by the same company) but employing separate editors and journalists.

The morning newspaper is a British household institution; such an important one that, until the laws were relaxed in the early 1990s, newsagents were the only shops that were allowed to open on Sundays. People could not be expected to do without their newspapers for even one day, especially a day when there was more free time to read them. The Sunday papers sell slightly more copies than the national dailies and are thicker. Some of them have six or more sections making up a total of well over 200 pages.

Another indication of the importance of 'the papers' is the morning 'paper round'. Most newsagents organize these, and more than half of the country's readers get their morning paper delivered to their door by a teenager who gets up at around half-past five every day in order to earn a bit of extra pocket money.

▶ The national papers and Scotland

There is an exception to the dominance of the national press throughout Britain. This is in Scotland, where one paper, the *Sunday Post*, sells well over a million copies. Another weekly, *Scotland on Sunday*, also has a large circulation. There are three other notable 'Scotland only' papers, but two of these, the *Glasgow Herald* and the *Scotsman*, are quality papers (see page 152) with small circulations and the other, the *Daily Record*, is actually the sister paper of the (London) *Daily Mirror*. The other national British papers are all sold in Scotland, although sometimes in special Scottish editions.

Different approaches, different subjects

Here are some details of the front pages of some national dailies for one date (25 March 1993). For each paper, the first line is the main headline and the figures in brackets are the height of the letters used for it.

- **The Sun**
  I'VE MESSED UP MY LIFE (5.4 cm high)
  Topic: an interview with the Duchess of York
  Total text on page: 155 words (one article)

- **The Daily Mirror**
  £5m FERGIE'S HIJACKED OUR CHARITY (3.5 cm)
  Topic: the activities of the Duchess of York
  Total text on page: 240 + words (two articles)

- **The Daily Express**
  MINISTER URGES SCHOOL CONDOMS (3 cm)
  Topic: government campaign to reduce teenage pregnancies
  Total text on page: 260 + words (three articles)

- **The Times**
  South Africa had nuclear bombs, admits de Klerk (1.7 cm)
  Total text on page: 1,900 + words (five articles)

- **The Guardian**
  Serb shelling halts UN airlift (1.7 cm)
  Topic: the war in the former Yugoslavia
  Total text on page: 1,900 + words (four articles)

- **The Daily Telegraph**
  Tory Maastricht revolt is beaten off (1.5 cm)
  Topic: discussion of the Maastricht Treaty in Parliament
  Total text on page: 2,100 + words (five articles)

The two types of national newspaper

Each of the national papers can be characterized as belonging to one of two distinct categories. The 'quality papers', or 'broadsheets', cater for the better educated readers. The 'popular papers', or 'tabloids', sell to a much larger readership. They contain far less print than the broadsheets and far more pictures. They use larger headlines and write in a simpler style of English. While the broadsheets devote much space to politics and other 'serious' news, the tabloids concentrate on 'human interest' stories, which often means sex and scandal!

However, the broadsheets do not completely ignore sex and scandal or any other aspect of public life. Both types of paper devote equal amounts of attention to sport. The difference between them is in the treatment of the topics they cover, and in which topics are given the most prominence (▷ *Different approaches, different subjects*).

The reason that the quality newspapers are called broadsheets and the popular ones tabloids is because they are different shapes. The broadsheets are twice as large as the tabloids. It is a mystery why, in Britain, reading intelligent papers should need highly-developed skills of paper-folding! But it certainly seems to be the rule. In 1989 a new paper was published, the *Sunday Correspondent*, advertising itself as the country's first 'quality tabloid'. It closed after one year.

▶ How many do they sell?

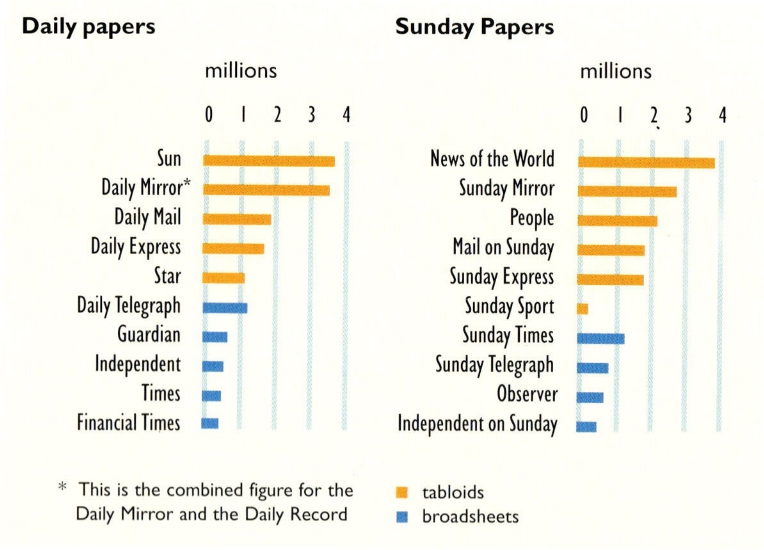

The graphs above show the approximate average daily circulation figures for national newspapers in the early 1990s. You can see that the tabloids sell about six times as many copies as the broadsheets. This, however, is an improvement on past decades. In 1950, for example, they sold twenty times as many. Education seems to be having an effect on people's reading habits.

The characteristics of the national press: politics

The way politics is presented in the national newspapers reflects the fact that British political parties are essentially parliamentary organizations (see chapter 6). Although different papers have differing political outlooks, none of the large newspapers is an organ of a political party. Many are often obviously in favour of the policies of this or that party (and even more obviously against the policies of another party), but none of them would ever use 'we' or 'us' to refer to a certain party (▷ *Papers and politics*).

What counts for the newspaper publishers is business. All of them are in the business first and foremost to make money. Their primary concern is to sell as many copies as possible and to attract as much advertising as possible. They normally put selling copies ahead of political integrity. The abrupt turnabout in the stance of the Scottish edition of the *Sun* in early 1991 is a good example. It had previously, along with the Conservative party which it normally supports, vigorously opposed any idea of Scottish independence or home rule; but when it saw the opinion polls in early 1991 (and bearing in mind its comparatively low sales in Scotland), it decided to change its mind completely (see chapter 12).

The British press is controlled by a rather small number of extremely large multinational companies. This fact helps to explain two notable features. One of these is its freedom from interference from government influence, which is virtually absolute. The press is so powerful in this respect that it is sometimes referred to as 'the fourth estate' (the other three being the Commons, the Lords and the monarch). This freedom is ensured because there is a general

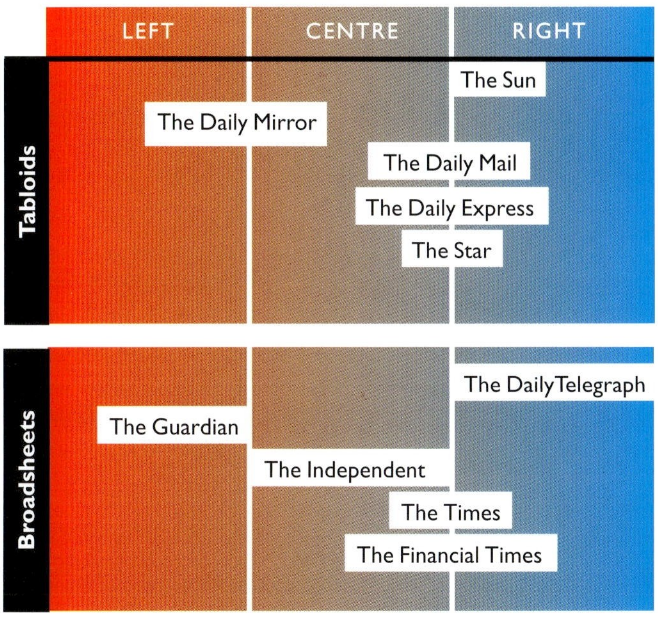

▶ Papers and politics

None of the big national newspapers 'belongs' to a political party. However, each paper has an idea of what kind of reader it is appealing to and a fairly predictable political outlook. Each can therefore be seen, rather simplistically, as occupying a certain position on the right–left spectrum.

As you can see, the right seems to be heavily over-represented in the national press. This is not because such a large majority of British people hold right-wing views. It is partly because the press tends to be owned by Conservative party supporters. In any case, a large number of readers are not very interested in the political coverage of a paper. They buy it for the sport, or the human interest stories, or for some other reason.

feeling in the country that 'freedom of speech' is a basic constitutional right. A striking example of the importance of freedom of speech occurred during the Second World War. During this time, the country had a coalition government of Conservative and Labour politicians, so that there was really no opposition in Parliament at all. At one time, the cabinet wanted to use a special wartime regulation to temporarily ban the *Daily Mirror*, which had been consistently critical of the government. The Labour party, which until then had been completely loyal to the government, immediately demanded a debate on the matter, and the other national papers, although they disagreed with the opinions of the *Mirror*, all leapt to its defence and opposed the ban. The government was forced to back down and the *Mirror* continued to appear throughout the war.

The characteristics of the national press: sex and scandal

The other feature of the national press which is partially the result of the commercial interests of its owners is its shallowness. Few other European countries have a popular press which is so 'low'. Some of the tabloids have almost given up even the pretence of dealing with serious matters. Apart from sport, their pages are full of little except stories about the private lives of famous people. Sometimes their 'stories' are not articles at all, they are just excuses to show pictures of almost naked women. During the 1980s, page three of the *Sun* became infamous in this respect and the women who posed for its photographs became known as 'page three girls'.

The desire to attract more readers at all costs has meant that, these days, even the broadsheets in Britain can look rather 'popular' when compared to equivalent 'quality' papers in some other countries. They are still serious newspapers containing high-quality articles whose presentation of factual information is usually reliable. But even they now give a lot of coverage to news with a 'human interest' angle when they have the opportunity. (The treatment by *The Sunday Times* of Prince Charles and Princess Diana is an example – see chapter 7.)

This emphasis on revealing the details of people's private lives has led to discussion about the possible need to restrict the freedom of the press. This is because, in behaving this way, the press has found itself in conflict with another British principle which is as strongly felt as that of freedom of speech – the right to privacy. Many journalists now appear to spend their time trying to discover the most sensational secrets of well-known personalities, or even of ordinary people who, by chance, find themselves connected with some newsworthy situation. There is a widespread feeling that, in doing so, they behave too intrusively.

Complaints regarding invasions of privacy are dealt with by the Press Complaints Commission (PCC). This organization is made up

▶ **Sex and scandal**

Sex and scandal sell newspapers. In September 1992, when there were plenty of such stories around involving famous people and royalty, sales of tabloids went up by 122,000. But in October, when stories of this kind had dried up, they fell by more than 200,000. Even the quality *Observer* got in on the act. On 11 October 1992, its magazine section featured nine pages of photos of the pop-star Madonna taken from *Sex* (her best-selling book). That week, its sales were 74,000 greater than usual. The next Sunday, without Madonna, they were exactly 74,000 less than they had been the week before.

of newspaper editors and journalists. In other words, the press is supposed to regulate itself. It follows a Code of Practice which sets limits on the extent to which newspapers should publish details of people's private lives. Many people are not happy with this arrangement and various governments have tried to formulate laws on the matter. However, against the right to privacy the press has successfully been able to oppose the concept of the public's 'right to know'.

Of course, Britain is not the only country where the press is controlled by large companies with the same single aim of making profits. So why is the British press more frivolous? The answer may lie in the function of the British press for its readers. British adults never read comics. These publications, which consist entirely of picture stories, are read only by children. It would be embarrassing for an adult to be seen reading one. Adults who want to read something very simple, with plenty of pictures to help them, have almost nowhere to go but the national press. Most people don't use newspapers for 'serious' news. For this, they turn to another source – broadcasting.

Examples of some well-known weekly magazines

▶ The rest of the press

If you go into any well-stocked newsagent's in Britain, you will not only find newspapers. You will also see rows and rows of magazines catering for almost every imaginable taste and specializing in almost every imaginable pastime. Among these publications there are a few weeklies dealing with news and current affairs. Partly because the national press is so predictable (and often so trivial), some of these periodicals manage to achieve a circulation of more than a hundred thousand.

The Economist is of the same type as *Time*, *Newsweek*, *Der Spiegel* and *L'Express*. Its analyses, however, are generally more thorough. It is fairly obviously right-wing in its views, but the writing is of very high-quality and that is why it has the reputation of being one of the best weeklies in the world.

The *New Statesman and Society* is the left-wing equivalent of *The Economist* and is equally serious and well-written.

Private Eye is a satirical magazine which makes fun of all parties and politicians, and also makes fun of the mainstream press. It specializes in political scandal and, as a result, is forever defending itself in legal actions. It is so outrageous that some chains of newsagents sometimes refuse to sell it. Although its humour is often very 'schoolboyish', it is also well-written and it is said that no politician can resist reading it.

The country's bestselling magazine is the *Radio Times*, which, as well as listing all the television and radio programmes for the coming week, contains some fifty pages of articles. (Note the typically British appeal to continuity in the name 'Radio Times'. The magazine was first published before television existed and has never bothered to update its title.)

The BBC

Broadcasting House, headquarters of the BBC

Just as the British Parliament has the reputation for being 'the mother of parliaments', so the BBC might be said to be 'the mother of information services'. Its reputation for impartiality and objectivity in news reporting is, at least when compared to news broadcasting in many other countries, largely justified. Whenever it is accused of bias by one side of the political spectrum, it can always point out that the other side has complained of the same thing at some other time, so the complaints are evenly balanced. In fact, the BBC has often shown itself to be rather proud of the fact that it gets complaints from both sides of the political divide, because this testifies not only to its impartiality but also to its independence.

Interestingly, though, this independence is as much the result of habit and common agreement as it is the result of its legal status. It is true that it depends neither on advertising nor (directly) on the government for its income. It gets this from the licence fee which everybody who uses a television set has to pay. However, the government decides how much this fee is going to be, appoints the BBC's board of governors and its director general, has the right to veto any

▶ High ideals and independence

The reference to one man in the inscription on the right, which is found in the entrance to Broadcasting House (headquarters of the BBC), is appropriate. British politicians were slow to appreciate the social significance of 'the wireless' (this is what the radio was generally known as until the 1960s). Moreover, being British, they did not like the idea of having to debate culture in Parliament. They were only too happy to leave the matter to a suitable organization and its director general, John (later Lord) Reith.

Reith was a man with a mission. He saw in radio an opportunity for 'education' and initiation into 'high culture' for the masses. He included light entertainment in the programming, but only as a way of capturing an audience for the more 'important' programmes of classical music and drama, and the discussions of various topics by famous academics and authors whom Reith had persuaded to take part.

THIS TEMPLE TO THE ARTS AND MUSES
IS DEDICATED
TO ALMIGHTY GOD
BY THE FIRST GOVERNORS
IN THE YEAR OF OUR LORD 1931
JOHN REITH BEING DIRECTOR-GENERAL
AND THEY PRAY THAT THE GOOD SEED SOWN
MAY BRING FORTH GOOD HARVESTS
THAT ALL THINGS FOUL OR HOSTILE TO PEACE
MAY BE BANISHED HENCE
AND THAT THE PEOPLE INCLINING THEIR EAR
TO WHATSOEVER THINGS ARE LOVELY AND HONEST
WHATSOEVER THINGS ARE OF GOOD REPORT
MAY TREAD THE PATH OF VIRTUE
AND OF WISDOM

BBC programme before it has been transmitted and even has the right to take away the BBC's licence to broadcast. In theory, therefore, it would be easy for a government to influence what the BBC does.

Nevertheless, partly by historical accident (▷ *High ideals and independence*), the BBC began, right from the start, to establish its effective independence and its reputation for impartiality. This first occurred through the medium of radio broadcasts to people in Britain. Then, in 1932 the BBC World Service was set up, with a licence to broadcast first to the empire and then to other parts of the world. During the Second World War it became identified with the principles of democracy and free speech. In this way the BBC's fame became international. Today, the World Service still broadcasts around the globe, in English and in several other languages. In 1986 the Prime Minister of India, Mrs Indhira Ghandi, was assassinated. When her son Rajiv first heard reports that she had been attacked, he immediately tuned to the BBC World Service to get details that he could rely on. The BBC also runs five national radio stations inside Britain and several local ones (▷ *BBC radio*).

Television: organization

In terms of the size of its audience, television has long since taken over from radio as the most significant form of broadcasting in Britain. Its independence from government interference is largely a matter of tacit agreement. There have been occasions when the government has successfully persuaded the BBC not to show something. But there have also been many occasions when the BBC has refused to bow to government pressure. Most recent cases have involved Northern Ireland. For a brief period starting in the late 1980s, the government broke with the convention of non-interference and banned the transmission of interviews with members of outlawed organizations such as the IRA on television. The BBC's response was to make a mockery of this law by showing such interviews on the screen with an actor's voice (with just the right accent) dubbed over the moving mouth of the interviewee!

There is no advertising on the BBC. But Independent Television (ITV), which started in 1954, gets its money from the advertisements it screens. It consists of a number of privately owned companies, each of which is responsible for programming in different parts of the country on the single channel given to it. In practice, these companies cannot afford to make all their own programmes, and so they generally share those they make. As a result, it is common for exactly the same programme to be showing on the ITV channel throughout the country.

When commercial television began, it was feared that advertisers would have too much control over programming and that the new channel would exhibit all the worst features of tabloid journalism. The Labour party, in opposition at the time of its introduction, was

▶ BBC radio

Radio 1 began broadcasting in 1967. Devoted almost entirely to pop music, its birth was a signal that popular youth culture could no longer be ignored by the country's established institutions. In spite of recent competition from independent commercial radio stations, it still has over ten million listeners.

Radio 2 broadcasts mainly light music and chat shows.

Radio 3 is devoted to classical music.

Radio 4 broadcasts a variety of programmes, from plays and comedy shows to consumer advice programmes and in-depth news coverage. It has a small but dedicated following.

Radio 5 is largely given over to sports coverage and news.

Two particular radio programmes should be mentioned. Soap operas are normally associated with television, but *The Archers* is actually the longest-running soap in the world. It describes itself as 'an everyday story of country folk'. Its audience, which is mainly middle-class with a large proportion of elderly people, cannot compare in size with the television soaps, but it has become so famous that everybody in Britain knows about it and tourist attractions have been designed to capitalize on its fame.

Another radio 'institution' is the live commentary of cricket Test Matches in the summer (see chapter 21).

absolutely against it. So were a number of Conservative and Liberal politicians. Over the years, however, these fears have proved to be unfounded. Commercial television in Britain has not developed the habit of showing programmes sponsored by manufacturers. There has recently been some relaxation of this policy, but advertisers have never had the influence over programming that they have had in the USA.

Most importantly for the structure of commercial television, ITV news programmes are not made by individual television companies. Independent Television News (ITN) is owned jointly by all of them. For this and other reasons, it has always been protected from com-

▶ The four channels

These are the channels which all viewers in the country receive.

<table>
<tr><th></th><th>BBC1</th><th>ITV</th><th>BBC2</th><th>Channel 4</th></tr>
<tr><td></td><td>Started 1936</td><td>Started 1954</td><td>Started 1964</td><td>Started 1982</td></tr>
<tr><td>Advertising</td><td>No</td><td>Yes</td><td>No</td><td>Yes</td></tr>
<tr><td>Early weekday mornings</td><td colspan="2">A rather relaxed style of news magazine punctuated with more formal news summaries</td><td>Open University programmes</td><td>A very informal breakfast show</td></tr>
<tr><td>Mornings and early afternoons</td><td colspan="2">Popular discussion programmes, quizzes, soaps and a relaxed type of magazine programme, usually with a male-female pair of presenters</td><td colspan="2">Educational programmes, some aimed at schools and others with a more general educational purpose</td></tr>
<tr><td>Late afternoons</td><td colspan="2">Children's programmes, which vary greatly in style and content</td><td colspan="2">General documentary and features</td></tr>
<tr><td>Evenings</td><td colspan="2">News (including regional news programmes) and the most popular soaps, dramas, comedies, films and various programmes of light entertainment and general interest</td><td colspan="2">Documentaries and programmes appealing to minority interests; drama and 'alternative' comedy; comparatively serious and 'in-depth' news programmes</td></tr>
<tr><td></td><td colspan="2"></td><td>Open University (late at night)</td><td></td></tr>
<tr><td>Weekends</td><td colspan="4">Much of weekend afternoons are devoted to sport. Saturday evenings include the most popular live variety shows.</td></tr>
</table>

Channel 5 Started in 1997. It is a commercial channel (it gets its money from advertising) which is received by about two-thirds of British households. Its emphasis is on entertainment (for example, it screens a film every night at peak viewing time). However, it makes all other types of programme too. Of particular note is its unconventional presentation of the news, which is designed to appeal to younger adults.

There is also a Welsh language channel for viewers in Wales.

mercial influence. There is no significant difference between the style and content of the news on ITV and that on the BBC.

The same fears about the quality of television programmes that were expressed when ITV started are now heard with regard to satellite and cable television. This time the fears may be more justified, as the companies that run satellite and cable television channels are in a similar commercial and legal position to those which own the big newspapers (and in some cases are actually the same companies). However, only about a third of households receive satellite and/or cable, and so far these channels have not significantly reduced the viewing figures for the main national channels.

Television: style

Although the advent of ITV did not affect television coverage of news and current affairs, it did cause a change in the style and content of other programmes shown on television. The amount of money that a television company can charge an advertiser depends on the expected number of viewers at the time when the advertisement is to be shown. Therefore, there was pressure on ITV from the start to make its output popular. In its early years ITV captured nearly three-quarters of the BBC's audience. The BBC then responded by making its own programmes equally accessible to a mass audience. Ever since then, there has been little significant difference in what is shown on the BBC and commercial television. Both BBC1 and ITV (and also the more recent Channel 5) show a wide variety of programmes. They are in constant competition with each other to attract the largest audience (this is known as the ratings war). But they do not each try to show a more popular type of programme than the other. They try instead to do the same type of programme 'better'.

Of particular importance in the ratings war is the performance of the channels' various soap operas. The two most popular and long-running of these, which are shown at least twice a week, are not glamorous American productions showing rich and powerful people (although series such as *Dallas* and *Dynasty* are sometimes shown). They are ITV's *Coronation Street*, which is set in a working-class area near Manchester, and BBC1's *EastEnders*, which is set in a working-class area of London. They, and other British-made soaps and popular comedies, certainly do not paint an idealized picture of life. Nor are they very sensational or dramatic. They depict (relatively) ordinary lives in relatively ordinary circumstances. So why are they popular? The answer seems to be that their viewers can see themselves and other people they know in the characters and, even more so, in the things that happen to these characters.

The British prefer this kind of pseudo-realism in their soaps. In the early 1990s, the BBC spent a lot of money filming a new soap called *Eldorado*, set in a small Spanish village which was home to a large number of expatriate British people. Although the BBC used its most

▶ **Glued to the goggle box**

As long ago as 1953, it was estimated that twenty million viewers watched the BBC's coverage of the coronation of Queen Elizabeth II. By 1970, 94% of British households had a television set (known colloquially as a 'goggle box'), mostly rented rather than bought. Now, 99% of households own or rent a television and the most popular programmes are watched by as many people as claim to read the *Sun* and the *Daily Mirror* combined.

Television broadcasting in Britain has expanded to fill every part of every day of the week. One of the four channels (ITV) never takes a break (it broadcasts for twenty-four hours) and the others broadcast from around six in the morning until after midnight. A survey reported in early 1994 that 40% of British people watched more than three hours of television every day; and 16% watched seven hours or more! Television news is watched every day by more than half of the population. As a result, its presenters are among the best-known names and faces in the whole country – one of them once boasted that he was more famous than royalty!

▶ The ratings: a typical week

The ratings are dominated by the soaps (*Coronation Street*, *EastEnders*, *Neighbours* and *Emmerdale*) and soap-style dramas (*Casualty*, which is set in a hospital, and *The Bill*, which is about the police). Light-entertainment talk shows also feature prominently (e.g. *This Is Your Life*, *Barrymore* and *Noel's House Party*) and quiz shows are sometimes very popular (e.g. *Countdown*). It is unusual that only one comedy programme appears below (*Red Dwarf*). Certain cinema films can also get high ratings (marked ** below). Science fiction remains a popular genre; *Quantum Leap* and *Red Dwarf* are both long-running series. Sports programmes appear in the top ten when they feature a particular sporting occasion. This happens frequently. There is one example in the list below (*The Big Fight Live*).

The list includes just one representative of 'high culture': the dramatization of the novel *Middlemarch*, by the nineteenth century author George Eliot. There are two documentaries, a travel series (*Great Railway Journeys*) and a science series (*Horizon*).

The Antiques Roadshow comes from a different location in the country every week. In it, local people bring along objects from their houses and ask experts how much they are worth.

Apart from the films, there is only one American programme in the list below (*Quantum Leap*).

Characters from 'Coronation Street'

The top twenty television programmes in the first week of February 1994

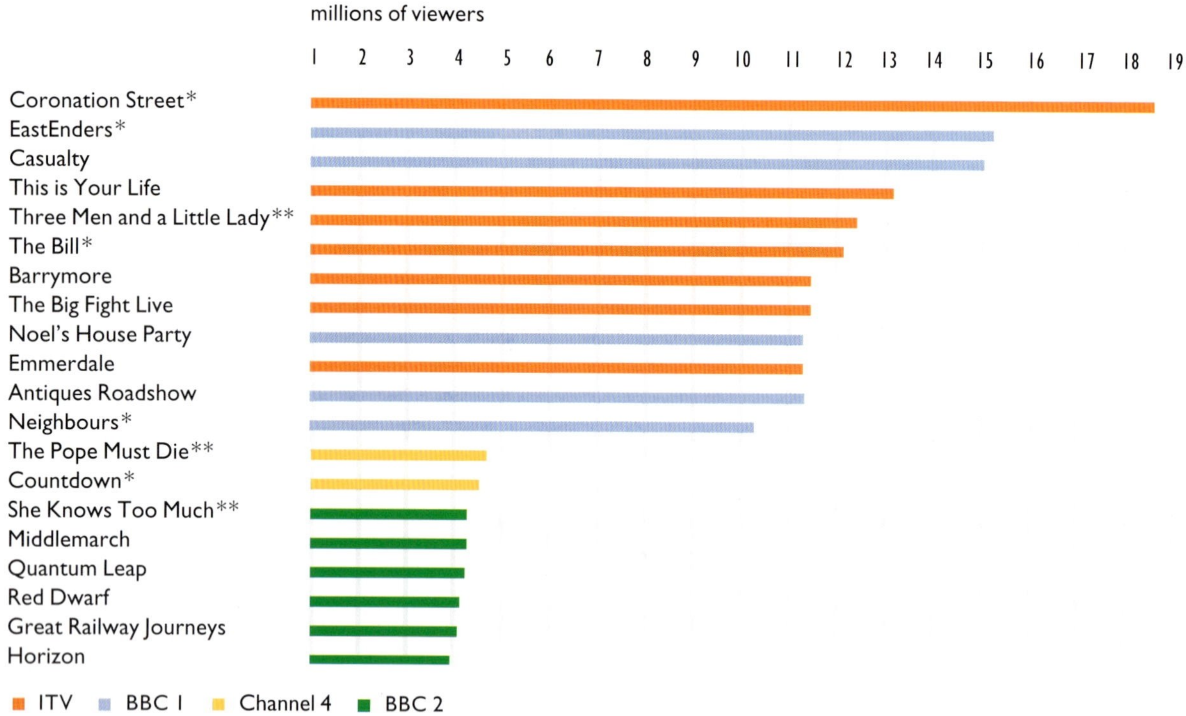

* Average for the week (programmes shown more than once a week)
** Film
Source: BARB (Broadcasters' Audience Research Board Ltd)

successful soap producers and directors, it was a complete failure. Viewers found the complicated storylines and the Spanish accents too difficult to follow, and could not identify with the situations in which the characters found themselves. It was all just too glamorous for them. It was abandoned after only a year.

It became obvious in the early 1960s that the popularity of soap operas and light entertainment shows meant that there was less room for programmes which lived up to the original educational aims of television. Since 1982 Britain has had two channels (BBC2 and Channel 4) which act as the main promoters of learning and 'culture'. Both have been successful in presenting programmes on serious and weighty topics which are nevertheless attractive to quite large audiences. BBC2 is famous for its highly acclaimed dramatizations of great works of literature and for certain documentary series that have become world-famous 'classics' (the art history series *Civilisation* and the natural history series *Life On Earth* are examples). Another thing that these channels do well, particularly Channel 4, is to show a wide variety of programmes catering to minority intersts – including, even, subtitled foreign soap operas!

QUESTIONS

1 It is easy to tell by the size and shape of British newspapers what kinds of readers they are aimed at. What are the two main types called, and who reads them? What other differences are there between newspapers? Are there similarly clear distinctions between types of newspaper in your country?

2 The dominant force in British Broadcasting is the BBC. What enabled it to achieve its position, and how does it maintain this? Can you describe some of the characteristics which give the BBC its special position in Britain and in the rest of the world?

3 There is one aspect of newspaper publishing which, in the 1980s and 1990s, received a lot of public and parliamentary criticism. People felt that the invasion of privacy of private individuals and public figures (such as members of the royal family) had reached unacceptable levels. Legislation was drafted, but there was no new law passed to control the press's activities. What problems are there in Britain with getting legislation like this approved? What arguments can be put forward in favour of keeping the status quo? How is the press controlled in your country?

4 What does the television ratings chart tell you about British viewing habits? Does this tell you anything about the British? What are the most popular television programmes in your country? What does this reveal, if anything, about your nation?

SUGGESTIONS

- Have a look at a couple of examples of each type of national newspaper. Try to get hold of examples from the same day.
- If you don't already do so, listen to the BBC World Service if you can.

17 Transport

The British are enthusiastic about mobility. They regard the opportunity to travel far and frequently as a right. Some commuters spend up to two or three hours each day getting to work in London or some other big city and back home to their suburban or country homes in the evening. Most people do not spend quite so long each day travelling, but it is taken for granted that few people live near enough to their work or secondary school to get there on foot.

As elsewhere in Europe, transport in modern Britain is dominated by the motor car and there are the attendant problems of traffic congestion and pollution. These problems are, in fact, more acute than they are in many other countries both because Britain is densely populated and also because a very high proportion of goods are transported by road. There is an additional reason for congestion in Britain. While the British want the freedom to move around easily, they do not like living near big roads or railways. Any proposed new road or rail project leads to 'housing blight'. The value of houses along or near the proposed route goes down. Every such project is attended by an energetic campaign to stop construction. Partly for this reason, Britain has, in proportion to its population, fewer kilometres of main road and railway than any other country in northern Europe.

Transport policy is a matter of continual debate. During the 1980s the government's attitude was that public transport should pay for itself (and should not be given subsidies) and road building was given priority. However, the opposite point of view, which argues in favour of public transport, has become stronger during the 1990s, partly as a result of pressure from environmental groups. It is now generally accepted that transport policy should attempt to more than merely accommodate the predicted doubling in the number of cars in the next thirty years, but should consider wider issues.

On the road

Nearly three-quarters of households in Britain have regular use of a car and about a quarter have more than one car. The widespread enthusiasm for cars is, as elsewhere, partly a result of people using them to project an image of themselves. Apart from the obvious status indicators such as size and speed, the British system of vehicle regis-

▶ The romance of travel: the steam engine

Perhaps because they were the first means of mass transportation, perhaps because they go through the heart of the countryside, there is an aura of romance attached to trains in Britain. Many thousands of people are enthusiastic 'train spotters' who spend an astonishing amount of time at stations and along the sides of railway lines trying to 'spot' as many different engines as possible. Steam trains, symbolizing the country's lost industrial power, have the greatest romance of all. Many enthusiasts spend their free time keeping them in operation and finance this by offering rides to tourists. In 1993 more than 10 million journeys were taken on steam trains in Europe. More than 80% of those journeys were taken in Britain.

▶ The AA and the RAC

These are the initials of the Automobile Association and the Royal Automobile Club. A driver who joins either of them (by paying a subscription) can get emergency help when his or her car breaks down. The fact that both organizations are very well-known is an indication of the importance of the car in modern British life.

RAC AA

tration introduces another. Registration plates, known as 'number plates', give a clear indication of the age of cars. Up to 1999 there was a different letter of the alphabet for each year and in summer there were a lot of advertisements for cars on television and in the newspapers because the new registration 'year' began in August.

Another possible reason for the British being so attached to their cars is the opportunity which they provide to indulge the national passion for privacy. Being in a car is like taking your 'castle' with you wherever you go (see chapter 19). Perhaps this is why the occasional attempts to persuade people to 'car pool' (to share the use of a car to and from work) have met with little success.

The privacy factor may also be the reason why British drivers are less 'communicative' than the drivers of many other countries. They use their horns very little, are not in the habit of signalling their displeasure at the behaviour of other road users with their hands and are a little more tolerant of both other drivers and pedestrians. They are also a little more safety conscious. Britain has the best road safety record in Europe. The speed limit on motorways is a little lower than in most other countries (70 mph = 112 kph) and people go over this limit to a somewhat lesser extent. In addition, there are frequent and costly government campaigns to encourage road safety. Before Christmas 1992, for instance, £2.3 million was spent on such a campaign.

Another indication that the car is perceived as a private space is that Britain was one of the last countries in western Europe to introduce the compulsory wearing of seat belts (in spite of British concern for safety). This measure was, and still is, considered by many to be a bit of an infringement of personal liberty.

The British are not very keen on mopeds or motorcycles. They exist, of course, but they are not private enough for British tastes. Every year twenty times as many new cars as two-wheeled motor vehicles are registered. Millions of bicycles are used, especially by younger people, but except in certain university towns such as Oxford and Cambridge, they are not as common as they are in other parts of north-western Europe. Britain has been rather slow to organize special cycle lanes. The comparative safety of the roads means that parents are not too worried about their children cycling on the road along with cars and lorries.

Public transport in towns and cities

Public transport services in urban areas, as elsewhere in Europe, suffer from the fact that there is so much private traffic on the roads that they are not as cheap, as frequent or as fast as they otherwise could be. They also stop running inconveniently early at night. Efforts have been made to speed up journey times by reserving certain lanes for buses, but so far there has been no widespread attempt to give priority to public transport vehicles at traffic lights.

▶ The decline of the lollipop lady

In 1953 most schoolchildren walked to school. For this reason, school crossing patrols were introduced. A 'patrol' consists of an adult wearing a bright waterproof coat and carrying a red-and-white stick with a circular sign at the top which reads STOP, CHILDREN. Armed with this 'lollipop', the adult walks out into the middle of the road, stops the traffic and allows children to cross. 'Lollipop ladies' (80% of them are women) are a familiar part of the British landscape. But since the 1980s, they have become a species in decline. So many children are now driven to school by car that local authorities are less willing to spend money on them. However, because there are more cars than there used to be, those children who are not driven to school need them more than ever. The modern lollipop lady has survived by going commercial! In 1993 Volkswagen signed a deal to dress London's 1,000 lollipop ladies in coats which bear the company's logo. Many other local authorities in the country arranged similar deals.

A lollipop lady at a zebra crossing

An interesting modern development is that trams, which disappeared from the country's towns during the 1950s and 1960s, are now making a comeback. Research has shown that people seem to have more confidence in the reliability of a service which runs on tracks, and are therefore readier to use a tram than they would be to use an ordinary bus.

Britain is one of the few countries in Europe where double-decker buses (i.e. with two floors) are a common sight. Although single-deckers have also been in use since the 1960s, London still has more than 3,000 double-deckers in operation. In their original form they were 'hop-on, hop-off' buses. That is, there were no doors, just an opening at the back to the outside. There was a conductor who walked around collecting fares while the bus was moving. However, most buses these days, including double-deckers, have separate doors for getting on and off and no conductor (fares are paid to the driver).

The famous London Underground, known as 'the tube', is feeling the effects of its age (it was first opened in 1863). It is now one of the dirtiest and least efficient of all such systems in European cities. However, it is still heavily used because it provides excellent connections with the main line train stations and with the suburbs surrounding the city.

Another symbol of London is the distinctive black taxi (in fact, they are not all black these days, nor are they confined to London).

A traffic warden giving a parking ticket to a motorist

Traffic cones on the M1 motorway

▶ The road to hell

The M25 is the motorway which circles London. Its history exemplifies the transport crisis in Britain. When the first section was opened in 1963 it was seen as the answer to the area's traffic problems. But by the early 1990s the congestion on it was so bad that traffic jams had become an everyday occurrence. A rock song of the time called it 'the road to hell'. In an effort to relieve the congestion, the government announced plans to widen some parts of it to fourteen lanes – and thus to import from America what would have been Europe's first 'super highways'. This plan provoked widespread opposition.

▶ What the British motorist hates most

Traffic wardens are not police officers, but they have the force of law behind them as they walk around leaving parking tickets on the windscreens of cars that are illegally parked. By convention, they are widely feared and disliked by British motorists. Every year there are nearly a hundred serious attacks on them. In 1993 government advisers decided that their image should change. They were officially renamed 'parking attendants' (although everyone still calls them traffic wardens).

Traffic cones are orange and white, about a metre tall and made of plastic. Their appearance signals that some part of the road ahead (the part marked out by the cones) is being repaired and therefore out of use, and that therefore there is probably going to be a long delay. Workers placing them in position have had eggs thrown at them and lorry drivers have been accused by police of holding competitions to run them down. On any one day at least 100,000 of them are in use on the country's roads.

According to the traditional stereotype, the owner-drivers of London taxis, known as cabbies, are friendly Cockneys (see chapter 4) who never stop talking. While it may not be true that they are all like this, they all have to demonstrate, in a difficult examination, detailed familiarity with London's streets and buildings before they are given their licence. (This familiarity is known simply as 'the knowledge'.) Normally, these traditional taxis cannot be hired by phone. You simply have to find one on the street. But there are also many taxi companies who get most of their business over the phone. Their taxis are known as 'minicabs'. They tend to have a reputation, not always justified, for unreliability as well as for charging unsuspecting tourists outrageous prices (in common with taxis all over the world). However, taxis and minicabs are expensive and most British people rarely use them, except, perhaps, when going home late at night after public transport has stopped running, especially if they have been drinking alcohol.

Queueing

An Englishman, even if he is alone, forms an orderly queue of one.

GEORGE MIKES

Waiting for buses allows the British to indulge their supposed passion for queueing. Whether this really signifies civilized patience is debatable (see chapter 5). But queueing is certainly taken seriously. When buses serving several different numbered routes stop at the same bus stop, instructions on it sometimes tell people to queue on one side for some of the buses and on the other side for others. And yes, people *do* get offended if anybody tries to 'jump the queue'.

Public transport between towns and cities

It is possible to travel on public transport between large towns or cities by road or rail. Coach services are generally slower than trains but are also much cheaper. In some parts of the country, particularly the south-east of England, there is a dense suburban rail network, but the most commercially successful trains are the Inter-City services that run between London and the thirty or so largest cities in the country.

The difference between certain trains is a fascinating reflection of British insularity. Elsewhere in Europe, the fastest and smartest trains are the international ones. But in Britain, they are the Inter-City trains. The international trains from London to the Channel ports of Newhaven, Dover and Ramsgate are often uncomfortable commuter trains stopping at several different stations.

The numbers of trains and train routes were slowly but continuously reduced over the last forty years of the twentieth century. In October 1993 the national train timetable scheduled 10,000 fewer trains than in the previous October. The changes led to many complaints. The people of Lincoln in eastern England, for example, were worried about their tourist trade. This town, which previously had fifteen trains arriving on a Sunday from four different directions, found that it had only four, all arriving from the same direction. The Ramblers' Association (for people who like to go walking in the countryside) were also furious because the ten trains on a Sunday from Derby to Matlock, near the highest mountains in England, had all been cancelled. At the time, however, the government wanted very much to privatize the railways. Therefore, it had to make them look financially attractive to investors, and the way to do this was to cancel as many unprofitable services as possible.

The dominance of London

The arrangement of the country's transport network illustrates the dominance of London. London is at the centre of the network, with a 'web' of roads and railways coming from it. Britain's road-numbering system, (M for motorways, then A, B and C class roads) is based on the direction out of London that roads take.

It is notable that the names of the main London railway stations are known to almost everybody in the country, whereas the names of stations in other cities are only known to those who use them regularly or live nearby. The names of the London stations are: Charing Cross, Euston, King's Cross, Liverpool Street, Paddington, St Pancras, Victoria, Waterloo. Each runs trains only in a certain direction out of London. If your journey takes you through London, you have to use the Underground to get from one of these stations to another.

▶ Le compromise

One small but remarkable success of the chunnel (the Channel tunnel) enterprise seems to be linguistic. You might think that there would have been some argument. Which language would be used to talk about the chunnel and things connected with it? English or French? No problem! A working compromise was soon established, in which English nouns are combined with French words of other grammatical classes. For example, the company that built the chunnel is called *Transmanche Link* (*la Manche* is the French name for the Channel), and the train which carries vehicles through the tunnel is officially called *Le Shuttle*.

This linguistic mixing quickly became popular in Britain. On 12 February 1994, hundred of volunteers walked the 50 kilometres through the chunnel to raise money for charity. The *Daily Mail*, the British newspaper that organized the event, publicized it as 'Le walk', and the British media reported on the progress of 'Les walkers'.

The story of the chunnel

On Friday 6 May 1994, Queen Elizabeth II of Britain and President Mitterand of France travelled ceremonially under the sea that separates their two countries and opened the Channel tunnel (often known as 'the chunnel') between Calais and Folkestone. For the first time ever, people were able to travel between Britain and the continent without taking their feet off solid ground.

The chunnel was by far the biggest building project in which Britain was involved in the twentieth century. The history of this project, however, was not a happy one. Several workers were killed during construction, the price of construction turned out to be more than double the £4.5 billion first estimated and the start of regular services was repeatedly postponed, the last time even after tickets had gone on sale. On top of all that, the public showed little enthusiasm. On the day that tickets went on sale, only 138 were sold in Britain (and in France, only 12!). On the next day, an informal telephone poll found that only 5% of those calling said that they would use the chunnel.

There were several reasons for this lack of enthusiasm. At first the chunnel was open only to those with private transport. For them, the small saving in travel time did not compensate for the comparative discomfort of travelling on a train with no windows and no facilities other than toilets on board, especially as the competing ferry companies had made their ships cleaner and more luxurious. In addition, some people felt it was unnatural and frightening to travel under all that water. There were also fears about terrorist attacks. However unrealistic such fears were, they certainly interested Hollywood. Every major studio was soon planning a chunnel disaster movie!

The public attitude is becoming more positive, although very slowly. The direct train services between Paris and London and Brussels and London seem to offer a significant reduction of travel time when compared to travel over the sea, and this enterprise has been more of a success. At the time of writing, however, the high-speed rail link to take passengers between the British end of the chunnel and London has not been completed.

Air and water

A very small minority, of mostly business people, travel within Britain by air. International air travel, however, is very important economically to Britain. Heathrow, on the western edge of London, is the world's busiest airport. Every year, its four separate terminals are used by more than 30 million passengers. In addition, Gatwick Airport, to the south of London, is the fourth busiest passenger airport in Europe. There are two other fairly large airports close to London (Stansted and Luton) which deal mainly with charter flights, and there is also the small City Airport, which caters mainly for business travellers between London and north-western Europe.

There are plans for a fifth terminal at Heathrow, bigger than the other four combined. The aim is to double the capacity of Heathrow by the year 2015. However, while some British people may be proud at the prospect of Heathrow retaining its world number-one position, others are not so pleased. The problem is the noise (which British people tend to regard as an invasion of their privacy). Local farmers and the hundreds of thousands of people who live under Heathrow's flight path are objecting to the idea. The airport planners are arguing that the next generation of planes will be much quieter than present-day ones. Nevertheless, the plan is going to have to win a tough fight before it goes ahead.

Modern Britain makes surprisingly little use of its many inland were busy thoroughfares, and the profession of 'waterman', the river equivalent of the London cabbie, was well-known. In the last hundred years transport by land has almost completely taken over. A few barges still go up and down the Thames through London, but are used mostly by tourists. Several attempts have been made to set up a regular service for commuters, but none has been a success so far. There is no obvious practical reason for this failure. It just seems that British people have lost the habit of travelling this way.

The story of goods transport by water is the same. In the nineteenth century, the network of canals used for this purpose was vital to the country's economy and as extensive as the modern motorway network. The vast majority of these canals are no longer used in this way. Recently the leisure industry has found a use for the country's waterways with the increasing popularity of boating holidays.

▶ **Monster jumbos**

British Airways is one of the biggest airlines in the world. Its ambitious plans for the future include operating an enormous new kind of jumbo aircraft. This will not travel any faster than today's aircraft, but will be big enough for passengers to move around inside in rather the same way as they do on a ship. There will be no duty-free trolleys or meals coming round; instead, passengers will go to the bar, café or shop to get what they want. First class travellers will have sleeping cabins and a fully-equipped business area. But how many airports will be able to accomodate the new monsters of the sky?

QUESTIONS

1. The car is the preferred means of transport for most people in Britain. The same is probably true in your country. What effects has this had, in Britain and in your country?
2. Many people in Britain are beginning to realize that other means of transport, apart from the car, should be used. What kinds of presently under-used means of transport are being revived in Britain, and where do people argue that money should be spent by the government instead of on building more new roads?
3. Although freedom of movement (usually by car) is dear to the hearts of most British people, there is something even more dear to their hearts which makes the building of new roads a slow and difficult process. What is this? Does the objection to new roads, rail links and even airport terminals surprise you?
4. British individualism shows itself in many ways in the area of transport. Can you find examples in this chapter?

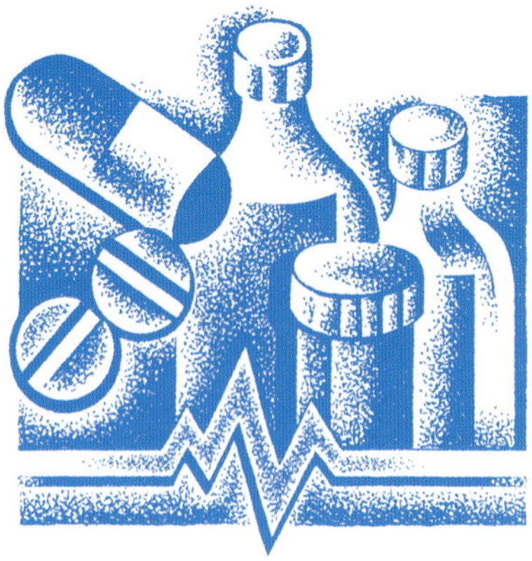

18 Welfare

▶ **The origins of the welfare state in Britain**

Before the twentieth century, welfare was considered to be the responsibility of local communities. The 'care' provided was often very poor. An especially hated institution in the nineteenth century was the workhouse, where the old, the sick, the mentally handicapped and orphans were sent. People were often treated very harshly in workhouses, or given as virtual slaves to equally harsh employers.

During the first half of the twentieth century a number of welfare benefits were introduced. These were a small old-age pension scheme (1908), partial sickness and unemployment insurance (1912) and unemployment benefits conditional on regular contributions and proof of need (1934). The real impetus for the welfare state came in 1942 from a government commission, headed by William Beveridge, and its report on 'social insurance and allied services'. In 1948 the National Health Act turned the report's recommendations into law and the National Health Service was set up.

The mass rush for free treatment caused the government health bill to swell enormously. In response to this, the first payment within the NHS (a small fixed charge for medicines) was introduced in 1951. Other charges (such as that for dental treatment in 1952) followed.

Britain can claim to have been the first large country in the world to have accepted that it is part of the job of government to help any citizen in need and to have set up what is generally known as a 'welfare state'.

The benefits system

The most straightforward way in which people are helped is by direct payments of government money. Any adult who cannot find paid work, or any family whose total income is not enough for its basic needs, is entitled to financial help. This help comes in various ways and is usually paid by the Department of Social Security.

Anyone below the retirement age of sixty-five who has previously worked for a certain minimum period of time can receive unemployment benefit (known colloquially as 'the dole'). This is organized by the Department of Employment.

All retired people are entitled to the standard old-age pension, provided that they have paid their national insurance contributions for most of their working lives. After a certain age, even people who are still earning can receive their pension (though at a slightly reduced rate). Pensions account for the greatest proportion of the money which the government spends on benefits.

The government pension, however, is not very high. Many people therefore make arrangements during their working lives to have some additional form of income after they retire. They may, for instance, contribute to a pension fund (also called a 'superannuation scheme'). These are usually organized by employers and both employer and employee make regular contributions to them. A life insurance policy can also be used as a form of saving. A lump sum is paid out by the insurance company at around the age of retirement.

Some people are entitled to neither pension nor unemployment benefit (because they have not previously worked for long enough or because they have been unemployed for a long time). These people can apply for income support (previously called supplementary benefit) and if they have no significant savings, they will receive it. Income support is also sometimes paid to those with paid work but who need extra money, for instance because they have a particularly large family or because their earnings are especially low.

A wide range of other benefits exist. For example, child benefit is a small weekly payment for each child, usually paid direct to mothers. Other examples are housing benefit (distributed by the local authority, to help with rent payments), sickness benefit, maternity benefit and death grants (to cover funeral expenses).

The system, of course, has its imperfections. On the one hand, there are people who are entitled to various benefits but who do not receive them. They may not understand the complicated system and not know what they are entitled to, or they may be too proud to apply. Unlike pensions and unemployment benefit, claiming income support involves subjecting oneself to a 'means test'. This is an official investigation into a person's financial circumstances which some people feel is too much of an invasion of their privacy. On the other hand, there are people who have realized that they can have a higher income (through claiming the dole and other benefits) when not working than they can when they are employed.

The whole social security system is coming under increasing pressure because of the rising numbers of both unemployed people and pensioners. It is believed that if everybody actually claimed the benefits to which they are entitled, the system would reach breaking point. It has long been a principle of the system that most benefits are available to everybody who qualifies for them. You don't have to be poor in order to receive your pension or your dole money or your child benefit. It is argued by some people that this blanket distribution of benefits should be modified and that only those people who really need them should get them. However, this brings up the possibility of constant means tests for millions of households, which is a very unpopular idea (and would in itself be very expensive to administer).

▸ The language of benefits

With the gradually increasing level of unemployment in the last quarter of the twentieth century, many aspects of unemployed life have become well-known in society at large. Receiving unemployment benefit is known as being 'on the dole' and the money itself is often referred to as 'dole money'. In order to get this money, people have to regularly present their UB40s (the name of the government form on which their lack of employment is recorded) at the local social security office and 'sign on' (to prove that they don't have work). They will then get (either directly or through the post) a cheque which they can cash at a post office. This cheque is often referred to as a 'giro'.

Social services and charities

As well as giving financial help, the government also takes a more active role in looking after people's welfare. Services are run either directly or indirectly (through 'contracting out' to private companies) by local government. Examples are the building and running of old people's homes and the provision of 'home helps' for people who are disabled.

Professional social workers have the task of identifying and helping members of the community in need. These include the old, the mentally handicapped and children suffering from neglect or from maltreatment. Social workers do a great deal of valuable work. But their task is often a thankless one. For example, they are often blamed for not acting to protect children from violent parents. But they are also sometimes blamed for exactly the opposite – for taking children away from their families unnecessarily. There seems to be a conflict of values in modern Britain. On the one hand, there is the traditional

A poster advertising the Samaritans (see below)

respect for privacy and the importance placed by successive governments on 'family values'; on the other hand, there is the modern expectation that public agencies will intervene in people's private lives and their legal ability to do so.

Before the welfare state was established and the concept of 'social services' came into being, the poor and needy in Britain turned to the many charitable organizations for help. These organizations were (and still are) staffed mostly by unpaid volunteers, especially women, and relied (and still do rely) on voluntary contributions from the public. There are more than 150,000 registered charities in the country today. Taken together, they have an income of more than £15 billion. Most of them are charities only in the legal sense (they are non-profit-making and so do not pay income tax) and have never had any relevance to the poor and needy. However, there are still today a large number which offer help to large sections of the public in various ways (▷ *Some well-known charities*).

Charities and the social services departments of local authorities sometimes co-operate. One example is the 'meals-on-wheels' system, whereby food is cooked by local government staff and then distributed by volunteers to the homes of people who cannot cook for themselves. Another example is the Citizens Advice Bureau (CAB), which has a network of offices throughout the country offering free information and advice. The CAB is funded by local authorities and the Department of Trade and Industry, but the offices are staffed by volunteers.

The national health service

The NHS (the national health service is commonly referred to by this abbreviation) is generally regarded as the jewel in the crown of the welfare state. Interestingly, it is very 'un-British' in the uniformity and comprehensiveness of its organization. When it was set up it did not, as was done in so many other areas of British public life, accommodate itself to what had already come into existence. Instead of entering into a partnership with the hundreds of existing hospitals run by charities, it simply took most of them over. The system is organized centrally and there is little interaction with the private sector. For instance, there is no working together with health insurance companies and so there is no choice for the public regarding which health insurance scheme they join. Medical insurance is organized by the government and is compulsory.

However, in another respect the NHS is very typically British. This is in its avoidance of bureaucracy. The system, from the public's point of view, is beautifully simple. There are no forms to fill in and no payments to be made which are later refunded. All that anybody has to do to be assured the full benefits of the system is to register with a local NHS doctor. Most doctors in the country are General Practitioners (GPs) and they are at the heart of the system. A visit to

▶ Some well-known charities

The Samaritans organization offers free counselling by phone, with anonymity guaranteed, to anybody who is in despair and thinking of committing suicide.

The Salvation Army is organized on military lines and grew out of Christian missionary work in the slums of London in the nineteenth century. It offers help to the most desperate and needy, for example, overnight accommodation in hostels for the homeless.

Barnado's, also founded in the nineteenth century, used to provide homes for orphaned children and still helps children in need.

MENCAP is a charity for the mentally handicapped and campaigns on their behalf.

▶ Getting medicine on the NHS

When medicine is needed, the doctor writes out a prescription which the patient then takes to a chemist's (that is, a pharmacy, but this word is used only by medical professionals). There is a charge for each prescription, which is the same regardless of the real cost of the medicine, although many categories of people are exempt.

the GP is the first step towards getting any kind of treatment. The GP then arranges for whatever tests, surgery, specialist consultation or medicine are considered necessary. Only if it is an emergency or if the patient is away from home can treatment be obtained in some other way.

As in most other European countries, the exceptions to free medical care are teeth and eyes. Even here, large numbers of people (for example, children) do not have to pay and patients pay less than the real cost of dental treatment because it is subsidized.

The modern difficulties of the NHS are the same as those faced by equivalent systems in other countries. The potential of medical treatment has increased so dramatically, and the number of old people needing medical care has grown so large, that costs have rocketed. The NHS employs well over a million people, making it the largest single employer in the country. Medical practitioners frequently have to decide which patients should get the limited resources available and which will have to wait, possibly to die as a result.

In the last few decades, the British government has implemented reforms in an attempt to make the NHS more cost-efficient. One of these is that hospitals have to use external companies for duties such as cooking and cleaning if the cost is lower this way. Another is that hospitals can 'opt out' of local authority control and become self-governing 'trusts' (i.e. registered charities). Similarly, GPs who have more than a certain number of patients on their books can choose to control their own budgets. Together these two reforms mean that some GPs now 'shop around' for the best-value treatment for their patients among various hospitals.

These changes have led to fears that commercial considerations will take precedence over medical ones and that the NHS system is being broken down in favour of private health care. And certainly, although pride and confidence in the NHS is still fairly strong, it is decreasing. There has been a steady rise in the number of people paying for private medical insurance (▷ *Private medical care*) in addition to the state insurance contribution which, by law, all employed people must pay.

In fact, though, Britain's health system can already claim cost-efficiency. The country spends less money per person on health care than any other country in the western world. One possible reason for this is the way that GPs are paid. The money which they get from the government does not depend on the number of consultations they perform. Instead, it depends on the number of registered patients they have – they get a 'capitation' allowance for each one. Therefore, they have no incentive to arrange more consultations than are necessary. It is in their interest that their patients remain as healthy as possible and come to see them as little as possible, so that they can have more patients on their books. The other possible reason is the British 'stiff upper lip'. In general, people do not like to make a big drama out of being ill. If the doctor tells them that there is nothing

▶ Private medical care

People with private medical insurance

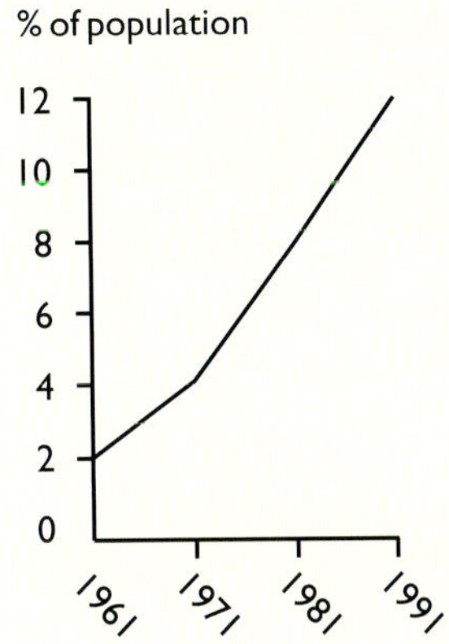

There are a number of private medical insurance schemes in the country. The biggest is BUPA. As you can see, such schemes are becoming increasingly popular. This is not because people believe that private treatment is any better than NHS treatment from a purely medical point of view. But it is widely recognized as being more convenient. NHS patients who need a non-urgent operation often have to wait more than a year, and even those who need a relatively urgent operation sometimes have to wait more than a month. Under private schemes, people can choose to have their operation whenever, and as soon as, they want. It is this which is their main attraction. The length of 'waiting lists' for operations within the NHS is one of the most hotly discussed public issues. Private patients sometimes use 'pay beds' in NHS hospitals, which are usually in a separate room (NHS patients are usually accommodated in wards containing ten to twenty beds). There are also some hospitals and clinics which are completely private. These are sometimes called 'nursing homes'.

▶ Nurses' uniforms

One of the most instantly recognizable uniforms in Britain is that conventionally worn by female nurses.

For years it has been widely criticized as out-of-date and sexist, promoting the image of nurses as brainless, sexy girls. The annual conference of the Royal College of Nursing always passes a resolution calling for the introduction of trousers. Skirts are said to result in back pain (and thousands of lost working days every year) as nurses struggle to keep their dignity while lifting heavy patients. The hat is also criticized as impractical.

It is probable that change is at last on the way.

A nurse wearing the traditional uniform

▶ The emergency services

From anywhere in Britain, a person who needs emergency help can call '999' free of charge. The operator connects the caller to the fire service, the ambulance service, or the police.

to worry about, they are likely to accept this diagnosis. Partly as a result of this, British GPs prescribe significantly less medicine for their patients than doctors in other countries in Europe do.

When it was set up, the NHS was intended to take the financial hardship out of sickness – to offer people medical insurance 'from the womb to the tomb'. In this respect, despite the introduction of charges for some kinds of treatment, it can still claim to be largely successful.

The medical profession

Doctors generally have the same very high status in Britain that they have throughout the world. Specialist doctors have greater prestige than ordinary GPs, with hospital consultants ranking highest. These specialists are allowed to work part-time for the NHS and spend the rest of their time earning big fees from private patients. Some have a surgery in Harley Street in London, conventionally the sign that a doctor is one of the best. However, the difference in status between specialists and ordinary GPs is not as marked as it is in most other countries. At medical school, it is not automatically assumed that a brilliant student will become a specialist. GPs are not in any way regarded as second-class. The idea of the family doctor with personal knowledge of the circumstances of his or her patients was established in the days when only rich people could afford to pay for the services of a doctor. But the NHS capitation system (see above) has encouraged this idea to spread to the population as a whole.

Most GPs work in a 'group practice'. That is, they work in the same building as several other GPs. This allows them to share facilities such as waiting rooms and receptionists. Each patient is registered with just one doctor in the practice, but this system means that, when his or her doctor is unavailable, the patient can be seen by one of the doctor's colleagues.

The status of nurses in Britain may be traced to their origins in the nineteenth century. The Victorian reformer Florence Nightingale became a national heroine for her organization of nursing and hospital facilities during the Crimean War in the 1850s. Because of her, nurses have an almost saintly image in the minds of the British public, being widely admired for their caring work. However, this image suggests that they are doing their work out of the goodness of their hearts rather than to earn a living wage. As a result, the nursing profession has always been rather badly paid and there is a very high turnover of nursing staff. Most nurses, the vast majority of whom are still women, give up their jobs after only a few years. The style of the British nursing profession can also be traced back to its origins. Born at a time of war, it is distinctively military in its uniforms, its clear-cut separation of ranks, its insistence on rigid procedural rules and its tendency to place a high value on group loyalty.

A shop selling 'alternative medicine'

▶ Alternative medicine

One reason why the British are, per person, prescribed the fewest drugs in Europe is possibly the common feeling that many orthodox medicines are dangerous and should only be taken when absolutely necessary. An increasing number of people regard them as actually bad for you. These people, and others, are turning instead to some of the forms of treatment which generally go under the name of 'alternative medicine'. A great variety of these are available (reflecting, perhaps, British individualism). However, the medical 'establishment' (as represented, for example, by the British Medical Association) has been slow to consider the possible advantages of such treatments and the majority of the population still tends to regard them with suspicion. Homeopathic medicine, for example, is not as widely available in chemists as it is in some other countries in north-western Europe. One of the few alternative treatments to have originated in Britain are the Bach flower remedies.

QUESTIONS

1 In Britain, the only people who can choose whether or not to pay national insurance contributions are the self-employed. More and more of them are choosing not to do so. Why do you think this is?

2 Would you say that the balance in Britain between welfare provided by the state and welfare offered by charities is different from that in your country? In Britain, does the balance appear to be a stable one, or is it shifting in favour of one or the other? Is the same true in your country?

3 From your reading of this chapter do you think that the British welfare state is successful in giving help to everybody who needs it? How many and what kinds of people do you think 'slip through the net' of care?

4 What, according to this chapter, are the main problems of the welfare state in modern Britain? Are similar problems encountered in your country? What solutions have been suggested or tried in Britain? Do you think they are the right ones?

5 How does the general status and public image of nurses in Britain compare with that of nurses in your country?

19 Housing

Almost everybody in Britain dreams of living in a detached house; that is, a house which is a separate building. The saying, 'An Englishman's home is his castle' is well-known. It illustrates the desire for privacy and the importance attached to ownership which seem to be at the heart of the British attitude to housing.

Houses, not flats

A large, detached house not only ensures privacy. It is also a status symbol. At the extreme end of the scale there is the aristocratic 'stately home' set in acres of garden. Of course, such a house is an unrealistic dream for most people. But even a small detached house, surrounded by garden, gives the required suggestion of rural life which is dear to the hearts of many British people. Most people would be happy to live in a cottage, and if this is a thatched cottage, reminiscent of a pre-industrial age, so much the better.

Most people try to avoid living in blocks of flats (what the Americans call 'apartment blocks'). Flats, they feel, provide the least amount of privacy. With a few exceptions, mostly in certain locations in central London, flats are the cheapest kind of home. The people who live in them are those who cannot afford to live anywhere else.

The dislike of living in flats is very strong. In the 1950s millions of poorer people lived in old, cold, uncomfortable nineteenth century houses, often with only an outside toilet and no bathroom. During the next twenty years many of them were given smart new 'high rise' blocks of flats to live in which, with central heating and bathrooms, were much more comfortable and were surrounded by grassy open spaces. But people hated their new homes. They said they felt cut off from the world all those floors up. They missed the neighbourliness. They couldn't keep a watchful eye on their children playing down there in those lovely green spaces. The new high-rise blocks quickly deteriorated. The lifts broke down. The lights in the corridors didn't work. Windows got broken and were not repaired. There was graffiti all over the walls.

A thatched cottage: an idealized country retreat

In theory (and except for the difficulty with supervising children), there is no objective reason why these high-rise blocks (also known as 'tower blocks') could not have been a success. In other countries millions of people live reasonably happily in flats. But in Britain they were a failure because they do not suit British attitudes. The failure has been generally recognized for several years now. No more high rises are being built. At the present time, only 4% of the population live in one. Only 20% of the country's households live in flats of any kind.

The most desirable home: a detached house

The photo is from a builder's advertisement. Notice:

- the 'traditional' building materials of brick (the walls) and slate (the roof);
- the irregular, 'non-classical', shape, with all those little corners, making the house feel 'cosy' (see main text);
- the suggestion of a large front garden with a tree and bushes, evoking not only the countryside but also giving greater privacy;
- that the garage (on the left) is hidden discretely away, so that it is not too obvious and doesn't spoil the rural feeling;
- that the front door is not even in the picture (the privacy criterion at work again).

A detached house

Second best: a semi-detached

Unless they are located in the remotest parts of the country, detached houses are too expensive for most people. So this is what a very large proportion of people live in: one building with two separate households. Each house is the mirror of the other, inside and out. These houses can be found, street after street, in the suburbs of cities and the outskirts of towns all over Britain. Notice the separate front garden for each house. At the sides, there is access to the back, where there will also be two gardens. The most common building material is brick. The typical semi-detached has two floors and three bedrooms.

An exception: the town house

These houses, which can be found in the inner areas of most cities, are an exception to the general pattern. There is great variety regarding both design and use. They often have three or more floors, perhaps including a basement or semi-basement. Although they are usually terraced, those that are well-preserved and in a 'good' area may be thought highly desirable. Many have been broken up into flats or rooms for rent. Most of the comparatively small number of people who rent from private owners live in flats of this kind. Sometimes, these are 'self-contained' flats (they have washing and cooking facilities and it is not necessary to walk through anybody else's flat to get to your own); sometimes, they are 'bedsits' (i.e. bed-sitting rooms; residents have one room to themselves and share washing and cooking facilities with other residents).

Less desirable: a terraced house

This kind of house usually has no way through to the back except through the house itself. Each house in the row is joined to the next one. (Houses at the end of the row are a bit more desirable – they are the most like a semi-detached). They usually have two floors, with two bedrooms upstairs. Some have gardens back and front, others only at the back and others no garden at all. Before the 1960s, Britain had millions of terraced houses, most with no inside toilet or bathroom. Many of these were then knocked down, but in some areas those that have survived have become quite desirable – after repairs and building work have been carried out.

The least desirable: a flat

Not having a separate entrance to the outside world does not suit British tastes. Although it is densely populated, Britain has the second lowest proportion of flat-dwellers in the EU (the lowest of all is in Ireland).

Private property and public property

The image of a home as a castle implies a clear demarcation between private property and the public domain. This is very clear in the case of a detached house. Flats, on the other hand, involve uncertainties. You share the corridor outside your front door, but who with? The other residents on the same floor, or all the residents in the building? What about the foyer downstairs? Is this only for the use of the people who live in the block, or for the public in general? These uncertainties perhaps explain why the 'communal' living expected of flat-dwellers has been unsuccessful in most of Britain.

Law and custom seem to support a clear separation between what is public and what is private. For example, people have no general right to reserve the road directly outside their house for their own cars. The castle puts limits on the domain of its owner as well as keeping out others. It also limits responsibility. It is comparatively rare, for example, for people to attempt to keep the bit of pavement outside their house clean and tidy. That is not their job. It is outside their domain.

To emphasize this clear division, people prefer to live in houses a little bit set back from the road. This way, they can have a front garden or yard as a kind of buffer zone between them and the world. These areas are not normally very big. But they allow residents to have low fences, walls or hedges around them. Usually, these barriers do not physically prevent even a two-year old child from entering, but they have psychological force. They announce to the world exactly where the private property begins. Even in the depths of the countryside, where there may be no road immediately outside, the same phenomenon can be seen.

The importance of 'home'

Despite the reverence they tend to feel for 'home', British people have little deep-rooted attachment to their house as an object, or to the land on which it stands. It is the abstract idea of 'home' which is important, not the building. This will be sold when the time and price is right and its occupiers will move into some other house which they will then turn into 'home' – a home which they will love just as much as they did the previous one.

But the houses themselves are just investments. An illustration of this lack of attachment to mere houses (as opposed to homes) is that two-thirds of all inherited houses are immediately sold by the people who inherit them, even if these people have lived there themselves at some time in their lives. Another is the fact that it is extremely rare for people to commission the building of their own houses. (Most houses are commissioned either by local government authorities – for poorer people to live in – or, more frequently, by private companies known as 'property developers' who sell them on the open market.)

▶ The stately home

There is one exception to the rule that 'homes' are more important than 'houses'. This is among the aristocracy. Many of these families own fine old country houses, often with a great deal of land attached, in which they have lived for hundreds of years. They have a very great emotional investment in their houses – and are prepared to try very hard to stay in them. This can be very difficult in modern times, partly because of death duties (very high taxes which the inheritor of a large property has to pay).

So, in order to stay in their houses, many aristocrats live lives which are less physically comfortable than those of most people (they may not, for example, have central heating). Many have also turned their houses and land into tourist attractions. These are popular not only with foreign tourists. British visitors are also happy to be able to walk around in rural surroundings as they inspect a part of their country's history.

This attitude is so dominant that it leads to a strange approach towards house prices. Whenever these fall, it is generally regarded as a 'bad thing'. You might think that it would be a good thing, because people can then find somewhere to live more cheaply. After all, it is *rising* prices that are usually regarded as bad. But with houses it is the other way around. Falling prices mean that most people cannot afford to sell their house. They have borrowed a lot of money to buy it (sometimes more than its present value). They are stuck! To most British people, such immobility is a *terrible* misfortune.

Individuality and conformity

Flats are not unpopular just because they do not give enough privacy. It is also because they do not allow enough scope for the expression of individuality. People like to choose the colour of their own front door and window frames, and also to choose what they are going to do with a little bit of outside territory, however small that may be.

The opportunity which it affords for individual self-expression is another advantage of the front garden. In any one street, some are paved, some are full of flowerbeds with paths in between, others are just patches of grass, others are a mixture of these. Some are demarcated by walls, others by fences, others by privet hedges and some have no barrier at all. The possibilities for variety are almost endless!

However, not everything about housing in Britain displays individuality. Because most houses are built by organizations, not individuals, they are not usually built one at a time. Instead, whole streets, even neighbourhoods (often called 'estates'), are built at the same time. For reasons of economy, all the houses on an estate are usually built to the same design. Viewed from the air, adjacent streets in British towns often seem to be full of houses that are identical (▷ *Similar, but not the same*). Indeed, they are so similar that when a building company advertises a new estate, it often invites people to its 'show home'. This is just one of the houses, but by looking around it, people can get a fairly accurate impression of any house on the estate.

But if, later, you walked down the same streets that you saw from the air, every single house would seem different. The residents will have made sure of that! In an attempt to achieve extra individuality, some people even give their house a name (although others regard this as pretentious). In suburbs and towns, there is a constant battle going on between the individualistic desires of the householder and the necessity for some element of regimentation in a densely populated area. This contest is illustrated by the fact that anybody who wants to build an extension to their house, or even a garden shed, must (if it is over a certain size) first get 'planning permission' from the local authorities.

▸ **Similar, but not the same**

A typical suburban district. You might think that living in one of these streets would be much the same as living in the one next to it. But an attempt at individuality is found here too. In Britain, there are an enormous number of words which are used in place of the word 'street' (such as *avenue, close, crescent, drive, lane* and *park*). It is quite common to find three streets next to each other named, for example, 'Pownall Close', 'Pownall Gardens' and 'Pownall Crescent'. The idea here is that one street is different from a neighbouring street not just because it has a different name – it is a different kind of place!

Interiors: the importance of cosiness

British houses have a reputation for being the coldest in Europe. Moreover, to many people from other countries, British people seem to be ridiculously keen on 'fresh air'. This reputation is exaggerated. It is partly the result of the fact that houses in Britain are, on average, older than they are in other countries and are not so well insulated. In fact, about three-quarters now have central heating. However, there is a grain of truth in it. Windows, for example, are designed so that they can be conveniently opened to a great variety of degrees – instead of, as in many other countries, either being completely shut or fully open. This way, air can be let into the house in winter without freezing its inhabitants.

Just as the British idea of home is a mental concept as much as a physical reality, so is their idea of domestic comfort. The important thing is to feel cosy – that is, to create an atmosphere which seems warm even if it isn't really warm. This desire usually has priority over aesthetic concerns, which is why the British also have a reputation for bad taste. Most people would rather buy several items of cheap, mass-produced furniture, with chairs and sofas covered in synthetic material, than one more beautiful and more physically comfortable item. The same is true with regard to ornaments – if you want to be cosy, you have to fill the room up.

To many, tradition is part of cosiness, and this can be suggested by being surrounded by old items of furniture. And if you cannot have furniture which is old, you can always have other things that suggest age. The open fire is an example. In Britain, it is regarded by many as very desirable to have a 'real fire' (as it is often called). It is the perfect traditional symbol of warmth because it is what most people used in the past to keep warm. So strong is the attraction of a 'real fire' that many houses have an imitation open fire, complete with plastic coal which glows red when it is switched on. Bad taste? So what!

Most older houses, even very small ones, have not one but two general living rooms (which estate agents call 'reception rooms'). This arrangement maintains privacy (which is linked to cosiness). It allows the front room to be kept for comparatively formal visits, while family members and close friends can spend their time, safely hidden from public view, in the back room. Most modern smaller houses are built with just one living room (and in some older houses the two reception rooms have been converted into one). However, privacy must be preserved so these houses normally have a 'hall' onto which the front door opens. It is rare for it to open straight onto the living room. Some houses also have a tiny 'porch', with its own door, through which people pass before getting to the hall – an extra line of defence! The same concern can be seen where there is both a front door and a back door. Even if both can be reached from the street, the back door is for family and close friends only.

▶ Rooms: uses and names

It is difficult to generalize about how British people use the various rooms in their houses. They may like the idea of tradition, but they are too individualistic to follow the same traditional habits. The only safe generalization is that, in a house with two floors, the rooms upstairs are the ones used as bedrooms. The toilet (often separate) and bathroom are also usually upstairs. The living room(s) and kitchen are downstairs. The latter is usually small, but those who can afford the space often like to have a 'farmhouse kitchen', big enough for the family to eat in.

Class divisions are sometimes involved in the names used for rooms. With living rooms, for example, the terms 'sitting room' and 'drawing room' are regarded as upper-middle class, while 'lounge' is regarded as lower class. 'Front room' and 'back room' are also sometimes looked down on.

Owning and renting

Most British people do not 'belong' to a particular place (see chapter 4), nor are they usually brought up in a long-established family house to which they can always return. Perhaps this is why they are not usually content to rent their accommodation. Wherever they are, they like to put down roots.

The desire to own the place where you live is almost universal in Britain. However, house prices are high. This dilemma is overcome by the mortgage system, which is probably a more established aspect of everyday life than it is anywhere else in the world. About 70% of all the houses in the country are occupied by their owners and almost all of these were bought with a mortgage. At any one time, half of these are owned by people who have borrowed 80% (or even more) of their price and are now paying this money back month by month. The normal arrangement is for the borrower to pay back the money over a period of twenty to twenty-five years. The financial institutions known as 'building societies' were originally set up to provide mortgages. In the 1980s, however, regulations were relaxed, so that banks now offer mortgages as well.

People are happy to take out mortgages because house prices normally increase a bit faster than the general cost of living. Therefore, most people can make a profit when they sell their house. So strong is this expectation that phrases such as 'first-time buyer' and 'second-time buyer' are well-known. The former can only afford one of the cheaper houses available. But around ten years later, when some of their mortgage has been paid off, they can become the latter. They sell their houses at a profit and move into a more expensive house.

Although nearly everybody wants to own their house, it was only at the end of the twentieth century that a majority of people began to do so. Before that time, most working-class people lived in rented accommodation. At one time, most of them rented from private landlords, some of whom exploited them badly. In the 1950s and 1960s, however, millions of homes were built by local government authorities. By 1977, two-thirds of all tenants lived in these 'council houses' (or, in some cases, flats). Council rents are subsidized, so they are low. Each local council keeps a waiting list of households who want to move into a council property. The order of preference is worked out by a complicated set of priorities. Once they are given a council house, tenants have security; that is, they do not have to move out even if they become rich.

From 1950 to 1980 the proportion of 'owner-occupiers' gradually increased. The ambition to own was made easier by policies of 'tax relief'. Some of the interest which people paid on their mortgage could be subtracted from the income tax they had to pay and people selling their houses did not have to pay 'capital gains tax' on any profit. With both owner-occupiers and council tenants increasing in numbers, the percentage of people who rented from private landlords

▶ **Owning and renting: modern developments**

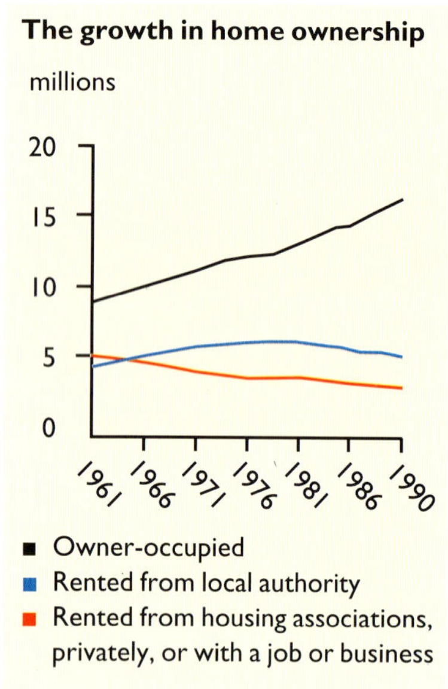

Source: Department of the Environment

This graph shows how home-ownership has increased in the second half of the twentieth century. Britain now has a percentage of owner-occupied households which is well above the European average.

Who owns? Who rents?

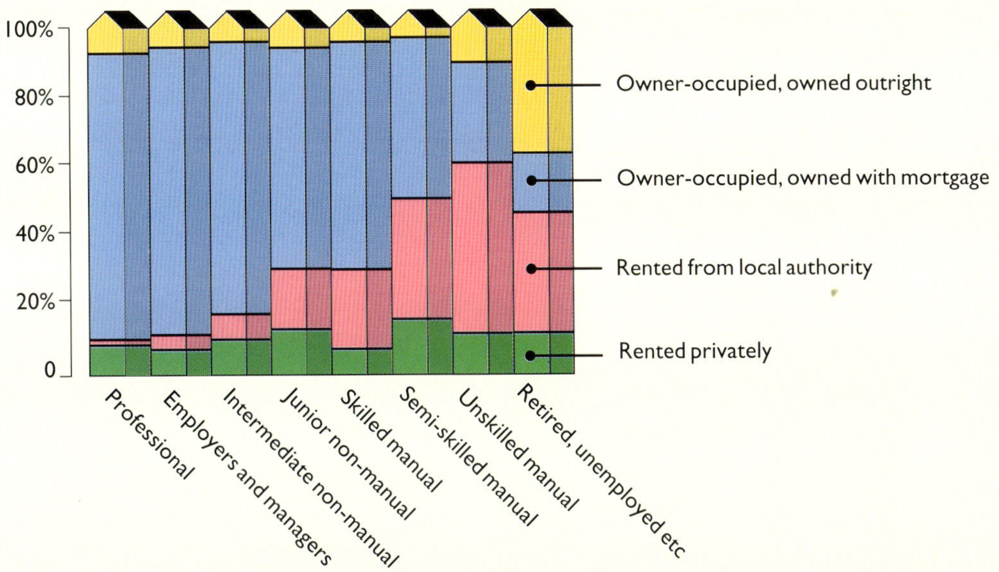

Source: General Household Survey (1989–90)

became one of the lowest in the world – and continues to be so.

Then during the 1980s, the number of owner-occupiers increased more sharply. A major part of the philosophy of Thatcherism (under Prime Minister Margaret Thatcher) was the idea of the 'property-owning democracy'. Council tenants were allowed to buy their council houses and were given financial incentives to do so. The de-regulation of mortgage-lending (see above) also encouraged house-buying. So did an increase in the financial help given to owners who wanted to make improvements to their property. At the same time, local councils were severely limited in the number of properties which they could build and were also encouraged to sell their properties to private 'housing associations'. As a result, the number of council tenants actually decreased.

By the mid 1990s, the trends of the previous decade seemed to have halted. Fewer council-house tenants were buying their houses and tax relief on mortgages was being phased out. The policy of selling off council houses had been discredited by the 'homes-for-votes' scandal. In the early 1990s it became clear that a few local councils run by the Conservative party had decided to keep their properties empty, instead of renting them to families who needed them, until they found buyers for them. The idea was that the buyers would probably vote Conservative – while people who could only afford to rent would probably not.

▶ Owning and renting: class

In the middle years of the twentieth century, whether you owned or rented a house was a marker of class. If you owned your house, you were middle class; if you lived in a council house, you were working class. However, the graph above shows that this is no longer true. A clear majority of skilled manual workers are owner-occupiers, as are 40% of even unskilled manual workers. Notice the small proportion of people (of any category) who own their house 'outright' (i.e. they have finished paying off the mortgage) or rent privately. Only among those with higher-status jobs are there more private tenants than council tenants.

Finding somewhere to live

If you want to buy a house, it is very rare to deal directly with the person selling. Instead, you go to an estate agent. These companies exist solely to act as 'go-betweens' for people buying and selling houses. They help with the various procedures – and take a fat commission! If you are interested in one of the houses 'on their books', they will arrange a 'viewing'. You can also spot houses for sale by the 'For sale' signs which are put up on wooden posts outside the houses concerned.

If you want to rent somewhere from a private landlord (not a council), the usual place to look is in the local newspaper. Estate agents do not often deal with places for rent, although there are special lettings agencies.

Another possible way of finding somewhere to live is to 'squat'. Squatters are people who occupy empty houses without paying rent. If you do not cause any damage when moving in to an empty house, you have not broken the law. If the owner wants to get you out, he or she has to get an order from the court to have you evicted.

Alternatively, you could become a 'New Age Traveller' and live in a bus, coach or van, moving from place to place.

New Age Travellers

Homelessness

In 1993 it was estimated that there were half a million homeless people in Britain – that's one of the highest proportions of the population in all the countries of Europe. The supply of council housing is limited, and has decreased since the 1980s because of the sale of council houses and the lack of money available for building new ones. In addition, many council houses and flats were badly built and are now uninhabitable. Laws passed in the 1970s to increase the security of tenants renting from private landlords made it less profitable for people to let out their houses, so the supply of private accommodation for rent has also gone down. There are large numbers of people who can't afford to rent somewhere to live privately, who are not eligible for council accommodation (and who would probably be at the end of a long waiting list if they were) and who certainly can't afford to buy a house or flat. Finally, as elsewhere in western Europe, the average size of households has become smaller, so that, although the population is increasing only very slowly, more places to live are still needed.

In the early 1990s many people who previously thought that they were secure in their own homes suddenly faced the prospect of homelessness. They had taken out large mortgages to buy their homes at a time when the country was going through an economic boom and house prices were rising (and looked as if they would continue to rise). Many of these people lost their jobs in the recession and so could no longer afford the monthly mortgage payments. To make matters worse, the value of houses, unusually, fell sharply at this time. They had to sell their homes, often for less than they bought them, and so were in debt as well as homeless.

Most homeless families are provided with temporary accommodation in boarding houses (small privately run guest houses or 'bed and breakfasts') by their local council. It is the duty of local authorities to house homeless families. Some families, and many single people, find even more temporary shelter in hostels for the homeless which are run by charitable organizations. Thousands of single people simply live on the streets, where they 'sleep rough'. The phrase 'cardboard city' became well-known in the 1980s to describe areas of big cities, particularly London, where large numbers of homeless people camped out, protected from the weather only by cardboard boxes.

Solving the problem of homelessness is not a political priority for the British government, partly because the level of public awareness of the situation is low (in spite of the efforts of charities such as Shelter, who give advice to the homeless and who campaign on their behalf). In many cases, the homeless are those with personal problems which make it difficult for them to settle down. In some cases, they are people who simply don't want to 'settle down' and who wouldn't class themselves as homeless. There are, for example, several thousand 'travellers' in the country, both traditional gypsies who have led a nomadic life for generations, and more recent converts to this lifestyle (often known as 'New Age Travellers' – see chapter 13 for an explanation of 'New Age'). Their homes are the vehicles in which they move from place to place, and they are often persecuted by unsympathetic authorities. For these people, the problem is not that they are 'homeless' but in the official attitude towards their way of life.

QUESTIONS

1 British people living in flats in other parts of Europe have sometimes been absolutely horrified when they realize that they are supposed to have the same colour flowers on their balconies as all the other flats in the block. Why are they so horrified?

2 How do you explain the popularity of the different types of dwelling in Britain? Are the same types popular in your country?

3 Even in a small town in Britain, several offices and shops will be occupied by companies called 'estate agents', whose only role is to help people buy and sell their houses. In the same town, however, there may be no housebuilding companies at all to which people could go. Why do you think this is? Is the same true in your country?

4 In modern Britain there is no widespread feeling of resentment against aristocrats who live in large, beautiful country houses. Why not?

5 In 1933 George Orwell wrote a book called *Down and Out in Paris and London*, recounting his experiences mixing with homeless people in these two cities. In the book, he compares the laissez-faire attitude towards homeless people in Paris with the rigid attitude in London:

> *In Paris, if you had no money and could not find a public bench, you would sit on the pavement. Heaven knows what sitting on the pavement would lead to in London – prison probably.*

It has been observed that the contrast is now the other way around. It is now in Paris, not London, that homeless people, if they want to avoid being taken away by the police, need to make sure that they don't bring attention to themselves. Can you think why this change has occurred? How does the present British attitude to homelessness compare with that in your country?

SUGGESTIONS

- Shelter, the organization dedicated to bringing the plight of the homeless to the attention of the British government and to giving help and advice to homeless people (or people with housing problems), will send out an information pack on request. Because it is a charity, Shelter would like a self-addressed envelope and the cost of postage to be included with requests. The address of Shelter is 88 Old Street, London EC1V 9HU.

20
Food and drink

On the Continent people have good food; in England people have good table manners.

GEORGE MIKES

Britain and good food are two things which are not commonly associated. Visitors to Britain have widely varying opinions about all sorts of aspects of the country, but most of them seem to agree that the food is terrible. Why? One reason could simply be that British tastes are different from everybody else's. However, the most common complaint is not so much that British food has a strange, unpleasant taste, but rather that it has very little taste at all. The vegetables, for example, are overcooked. It is all too bland.

Another explanation may be that most visitors to Britain do not get the opportunity to sample home cooking. They either eat the food cooked in an institution, such as a university canteen, or they 'eat out' a lot, usually in rather cheap restaurants and cafés. These places are definitely *not* where to find good British food. Typical British cooking, which involves a lot of roasting, does not suit the larger scale production or the quick preparation which is required in such places. For one thing, food should, according to British people, be eaten hot, which is difficult to arrange when feeding large numbers of people. In addition, the British have not got into the habit of preparing sauces with grilled food in order to make it tastier.

Attitudes to food

The explanations above can only serve as a partial excuse for the unfortunate reputation of British cuisine. Even in fast food restaurants and everyday cafés, the quality seems to be lower than it is in equivalent places in other countries. It seems that British people simply don't care enough to bother.

The country has neither a widespread 'restaurant culture' nor a 'café society'. In the middle of the day, people just want to eat up quickly and are not interested much in quality (the lunch break is an hour at most). Young people and families with children who eat at fast food places are similarly not interested in quality. Little effort is made to make the hamburgers tasty because nobody expects them to be. The coffee is horrible not because British people prefer it that way but because they don't go to a café for a delicious, slow cup of coffee – they go there because they need the caffeine.

Even at home, food and drink is given relatively little attention. The coffee is often just as bad as it is in the cafés. British supermarkets sell far more instant coffee than what the few people who drink it often call 'real' coffee. Instant coffee is less trouble. Meals tend to be eaten quickly and the table cleared. Parties and celebrations are not normally centred around food. For example, if a British person expresses a liking for barbecues, this does not necessarily mean that he or she likes barbecued food – it is understood to mean that he or she enjoys the typical barbecue atmosphere.

When the British do pay attention to food, it is most frequently not to appreciate it but to notice what they don't like about it. Food hits the headlines only in the context of its dangers: for example in 1993, when it was discovered that 100 tonnes of six-year-old beef had been allowed to go on sale; or when a government minister announced that the country's eggs were infected with salmonella. In the early 1990s, everybody in the country knew about 'mad cow disease' (a disease affecting the brains of infected cattle). There are quite a large number of vegetarians in Britain and an even larger number who are aware of the implications for their health of what they eat. 'Health food shops' are as abundant in the country's high streets as delicatessens.

British people have been mostly urban, having little contact with 'the land', for longer than the people of other countries. Perhaps this is why the range of plants and animals which they will eat is rather narrow. There are plenty of enthusiastic British carnivores who feel quite sick at the thought of eating horsemeat. To most people, the idea of going out to pick wild plants for the table is exotic. It is perhaps significant that when the British want to refer to the people of another country insultingly, they often allude to their eating habits. Because of the strange things they do with cabbage, for example, the Germans are 'krauts'. Because of their outrageous taste for frog's legs, the French are 'frogs'.

However, the picture is not entirely negative. While the British are conservative about ingredients, they are no longer conservative about the way they are served. In the 1960s, it was reported that the first British package tourists in Spain not only insisted on eating (traditionally British) fish and chips all the time but also on having them, as was traditional, wrapped up in specially imported British newspaper! By now, however, the British are extremely open to the cuisine of other countries. The country's supermarket shelves are full of the spices and sauces needed for cooking dishes from all over the world (the increasingly multicultural nature of the population has helped in this respect). In addition, there is increasing interest in the pure enjoyment of eating and drinking.

▶ What British people eat

A 'fry-up' is a phrase used informally for several items fried together. The most common items are eggs, bacon, sausages, tomatoes, mushrooms, and even bread. It is not always accompanied by 'chips' (the normal British word for french fried potatoes). The British eat rather a lot of fried food.

Although it is sometimes poetically referred to as 'the staff of life', bread is *not* an accompaniment to every meal. It is not even normally on the table at either lunch or the evening meal. It is most commonly eaten, with butter and almost anything else, for a snack, either as a sandwich or as toast (a British household regards toasting facilities as a basic necessity). On the other hand, the British use a lot of flour for making pastry dishes, both savoury and sweet, normally called 'pies', and for making cakes.

Eggs are a basic part of most people's diet. They are either fried, soft-boiled and eaten out of an 'egg cup', hard-boiled (so that they can be eaten with the fingers or put into sandwiches) or poached (steamed).

Cold meats are not very popular. To many British people, preserved meats are typically 'Continental'.

It is common in most households for a family meal to finish with a prepared sweet dish. This is called either 'pudding', 'sweet' or 'dessert' (class distinctions are involved here). There is a great variety of well-known dishes for this purpose, many of which are served hot (often a pie of some sort).

The British are the world's biggest consumers of sugar – more than five kilograms per person per year. It is present in almost every tinned food item and they also love 'sweets' (which means both all kinds of chocolate and also what the Americans call 'candy').

Eating out

Although it is far less unusual than it used to be, going to a restaurant is still a comparatively rare event for most British people. Regular restaurant-going is confined mostly to the richest section of society. Partly for this reason, there is an element of snobbery associated with it. Merely being in an expensive restaurant sometimes seems to be more important to people than the food eaten in it. For example, in 1992 a survey by experts found that most of the caviar in top London restaurants was not what it claimed to be (the most prized beluga variety) and was often stale or going bad. The experts commented that restaurants used the mystique of caviar to hide the low quality of what they served because 'the majority of people . . . don't really know what they're eating.'

Another expression of snobbery in the more expensive restaurants is in the menus. In a country where few public notices appear in any language other than English, these are a unique phenomenon – all the dishes have non-English names, most commonly French (reflecting the high regard for French cuisine). It also makes the food sound more exotic and therefore more exciting. Many customers of these restaurants have little idea of what actually goes in to the dish they have chosen. But when, in 1991, the government suggested that menus should give details of ingredients in dishes, all the country's chefs and restaurateurs were outraged. They argued this would take the fun out of eating out. The assumption behind this argument is that going to a restaurant is a time to be adventurous. This 'adventure' concept is undoubtedly widespread. It helps to explain why so few restaurants in Britain are actually British. Because they do it so rarely, when people go out for a meal in the evening, they want to be served something they don't usually eat. Every town in the country has at least one Indian restaurant and probably a Chinese one too. Larger towns and cities have restaurants representing cuisine from all over the world.

Eating places which serve British food are used only for more everyday purposes. Apart from pubs, there are two types, both of which are comparatively cheap. One is used during the day, most typically by manual workers, and is therefore sometimes described as a 'workman's cafe' (pronounced 'caff'). But it is also used by anybody else who wants a filling meal, likes the informal atmosphere and is not over-worried about cleanliness. It offers mostly fried food of the 'English breakfast' type (see chapter 5) and for this reason it is also sometimes jokingly called a 'greasy spoon'. Many of them are 'transport cafes' at the sides of main roads. In 1991 Prime Minister John Major deliberately and publicly ate at one of these in order to prove that he was 'a man of the people'. The other type is the fish-and-chip shop, used in the evening for 'take-away' meals. Again, the fish is (deep) fried.

▶ When people eat what: meals

Again, generalizations are dangerous. Below is described what everybody knows about – but this is not necessarily what everybody does!

Breakfast is usually a packeted 'cereal' (e.g. cornflakes) and/or toast and marmalade. It isn't usually a 'traditional' British breakfast (see chapter 5).

'Elevenses' is, conventionally, a cup of tea or coffee and some biscuits at around eleven o'clock. In fact, people drink tea or coffee whenever they feel like it. This is usually quite often.

Lunch is typically at one o'clock (any shops which close for lunch close from one to two). But it is often a bit earlier for schoolchildren and those who start work at eight o'clock.

For the urban working class (and a wider section of the population in Scotland and Ireland) tea is the evening meal, eaten as soon as people get home from work (at around six o'clock). For other classes, it means a cup of tea and a snack at around four o'clock.

'Supper' is the usual word for the evening meal among most people who do not call it 'tea'.

'Dinner' is also sometimes used for the evening meal. It suggests something rather grander and eaten comparatively late (at around eight o'clock). It is associated with relative formality (many people talk about 'Christmas dinner', even if they have it in the middle of the day). It is also sometimes used to refer to the midday meal in schools.

Inside a 'greasy spoon' cafe

Fast food outlets are now more common in Britain than they are in most other countries. Cynics might claim this is because the British have no sense of taste. However, their popularity is probably better explained sociologically. Other types of eating place in Britain tend to have class associations. As a result, large sections of society feel unable to relax in them. But a fast food restaurant does not have such strong associations of this kind. Although there is sometimes local middle-class protest when a new one appears in their area, people from almost any class background can feel comfortable in them.

Alcohol

The attitude to alcohol in Britain is ambivalent. On the one hand, it is accepted and welcomed as an integral part of British culture. The local pub plays an important role in almost every neighbourhood – and pubs, it should be noted, are predominantly for the drinking of beer and spirits. The nearest pub is commonly referred to as 'the local' and people who go there often are known as 'regulars'. The action in both the country's most popular television soaps (see chapter 18) revolves around a pub. Even a certain level of drunkenness is acceptable. Provided this does not lead to violence, there is no shame attached to it.

On the other hand, the puritan tradition has led to the widespread view that drinking is something potentially dangerous which should therefore be restricted, in terms of both who can do it and where it can be done. Most people, including regular drinkers, consider that it would be wrong to give a child even half a glass of beer. When, in 1993, research was published showing that nearly 70% of fifteen-year-old children in the country drank some alcohol in an average week, it was generally agreed that this was a serious 'social problem'. People cannot be served in pubs until the age of eighteen and they are not even allowed inside one (unless it has a special children's certificate) until they are fourteen. For many people, drinking is

▶ What people drink

As well as large amounts of hot drinks such as tea, coffee and cocoa, British people – especially children – drink squash (a sweetened fruit concentrate that has to be diluted with water) and brand-name 'soft' (non-alcoholic) drinks. They also expect to be able to drink water straight from the tap.

Before the 1960s, wine was drunk only by the higher social classes and was associated in most people's minds with expensive restaurants. Since that time, it has increased enormously in popularity.

Beer is still the most popular alcoholic drink. The most popular pub beer is 'bitter', which is draught (i.e. from the barrel), has no gas in it and is conventionally, as are all British beers, drunk at room temperature. A sweeter, darker version of bitter is 'mild'. These beers have a comparatively low alcoholic content. This is one reason why people are able to drink so much of them! In most pubs, several kinds of bottled beer, usually known as 'ales', are also available.

Beer which has gas in it and is closer to continental varieties is known as 'lager'. During the 1980s strong lager became popular among some young people. Because these people were used to drinking weaker traditional beer, they sometimes drank too much of it and became aggressive and even violent. They therefore became known as 'lager louts'.

In some pubs, cider is available on draught, and in some parts of Britain, most typically in the English west country, it is this, and not beer, which is the most common pub drink.

Shandy is half beer and half fizzy lemonade. It has the reputation of being very good for quenching the thirst.

Returning from a trip across the Channel with cheap beer

confined to pubs. Wine or beer is not as much a part of home life as it is in some other European countries. Most cafés are not allowed to serve even beer.

For most of the twentieth century, pubs operated under strict laws which limited their opening hours. These have recently been relaxed. Moreover, many more types of shop now sell alcohol than previously. However, this lessening of the negative attitude to alcohol has been balanced by increasing concerns about its impact on health and safety. There are government-sponsored guidelines which state the maximum amount of alcohol it is advisable for people to drink in a week without endangering their health. Although millions of people pay little attention to these, the general feeling that alcohol can be bad for you has increased. Moreover, the laws against drinking and driving have been strengthened and are fairly strictly observed.

Nevertheless, alcohol, especially beer, is an important part of the lives of many people. Notice, for example, the mass rush across the Channel after customs duties were changed in 1992. Beer was much cheaper in France and people were allowed to bring back almost as much as they liked. It was calculated that in that first year the single European market cost the British government about £250 million in lost taxes on alcohol.

Pubs

The British pub (short for 'public house') is unique. This is not just because it is different in character from bars or cafés in other countries. It is also because it is different from any other public place in Britain itself. Without pubs, Britain would be a less sociable country. The pub is the only indoor place where the average person can comfortably meet others, even strangers, and get into prolonged conversation with them. In cafés and fast food restaurants, people are expected to drink their coffee and get out. The atmosphere in other eating places is often rather formal. But pubs, like fast food restaurants, are classless. A pub with forty customers in it is nearly always much noisier than a café or restaurant with the same number of people in it.

As with so many other aspects of British life, pubs have become a bit less distinctive in the last few decades. They used to serve almost nothing but beer and spirits. These days, you can get wine, coffee and some hot food at most of them as well. This has helped to widen their appeal. At one time, it was unusual for women to go to pubs. These days, only a few pubs exist where it is surprising for a woman to walk in.

Nevertheless, pubs have retained their special character. One of their notable aspects is that there is no waiter service. If you want something, you have to go and ask for it at the bar. This may not seem very welcoming and a strange way of making people feel comfortable and relaxed. But to British people it is precisely this. To be

▶ The meanings of 'bar' in British English

1. The area in a hotel or other public place where alcoholic drinks can be drunk.
2. The different rooms in a pub. Although pubs have always been used by all social classes, there used to be an informal class division. The 'public bar' was used by the working class. This is where a dart board and other pub games could be found. The 'saloon bar', on the other hand, was used by the middle classes. Here there was a carpet on the floor and the drinks were a little more expensive. Some pubs also had a 'private bar', which was even more exclusive. Of course, nobody had to demonstrate class membership before entering this or that bar. These days, most pubs do not bother with the distinction. In some, the walls between the bars have been knocked down and in others the beer costs the same in any of the bars.
3. The counter in a pub where you go to get your drinks.

Inside a pub

served at a table is discomforting for many people. It makes them feel they have to be on their best behaviour. But because in pubs you have to go and fetch your drinks yourself, it is more informal. You can get up and walk around whenever you want – it is like being in your own house. This 'home from home' atmosphere is enhanced by the relationship between customers and those who work in pubs. Unlike in any other eating or drinking place in Britain, the staff are expected to know the regular customers personally, to know what their usual drink is and to chat with them when they are not serving someone. It is also helped by the availability of pub games (most typically darts) and, frequently, a television.

Another notable aspect of pubs is their appeal to the idea of tradition. For example, each has its own name, proclaimed on a sign hanging outside, always with old-fashioned associations. Many are called by the name of an aristocrat (for example, 'The Duke of Cambridge') or after a monarch; others take their names from some traditional occupation (such as 'The Bricklayer's Arms'); they often have rural associations (for example, 'The Sheep Shearers' or 'The Bull'). It would certainly be surprising to see a pub called 'The Computer Programmers' or 'The Ford Escort'. For the same reason, the person who runs a pub is referred to as the 'landlord' (he is nearly always a man) – even though he is, in reality, the exact opposite. He is a tenant. Nearly all pubs are owned by a brewery. The 'landlord' is simply employed by the brewery as its manager. But the word is used because it evokes earlier times when all pubs were privately owned 'inns' where travellers could find a bed for the night. The few pubs that really are privately owned proudly advertise themselves as 'free houses'. The practical significance of this for the customer is that a much wider variety of beers can usually be found inside.

▶ The pub

This photograph of a pub shows several typical features. First, notice that it looks old. Most pubs are like this. It is part of their appeal to tradition. Even a newly built pub is often designed to look, inside and out, as if it were several hundred years old. Second, notice the windows. They are small because, unlike the large plate-glass windows of cafés, they help to make the pub feel homely. But notice also that it is difficult to see inside the pub from the outside. The Victorians thought that it was somehow not proper for people to be seen drinking. That is why very few pubs have tables outside. Instead, many have a garden at the back. Because children are only allowed inside a pub if the pub has a children's certificate, a garden can be an important feature for some customers.

▶ How to shut the pub

Although pubs can now stay open longer than they were allowed to previously, they still have to close at their advertised closing time. Therefore, the traditions of 'closing time' have remained in place. Several phrases are connected with this process which are well-known to everybody in the country.

A few minutes before the official closing time, the landlord or barman shouts 'last orders, please', which means that anybody who wants to buy another drink should do so at once.

When closing time arrives, the barman shouts 'Time, ladies and gentlemen, please', and, as with his first shout, possibly accompanies this with the ringing of a bell.

However, customers do not have to leave immediately. They still have 'drinking-up time'. This is a concept which is recognized in law and is assumed to last about ten minutes.

▶ Nostalgia

A 'ploughman's lunch' (consisting of crusty bread, butter, cheese and pickle) is a well-known pub snack. Like other traditional food in pubs (such as 'shepherd's pie'), its name evokes traditional rural life. Pubs never use symbols of modernity. But modern agriculture is, of course, not at all traditional. This is the point of the cartoon. A cattle inseminator is a person who makes cows pregnant by injecting them with sperm! Notice his white laboratory coat (very non-traditional and non-rural).

"A pint please, and a cattle inseminator's lunch . . ."

QUESTIONS

1. In what kind of place(s) are you most likely to find good British cooking?
2. Why are Indian restaurants popular in Britain? Think of as many reasons as you can why British people prefer to eat food from other countries when they go out to eat.
3. What are the differences (if any) between laws relating to the consumption of alcohol in Britain and those in your country? What possible reasons are there for these differences?
4. The text mentions the rush across the channel to buy cheap alcohol in 1992. What effect do you think this started to have on traditional British drinking habits (with respect to both what people drink and where they drink)? Why were some people (even some of the people rushing across the Channel!) worried about this trend?
5. In what ways are British pubs different from typical cafés and bars in your country?

SUGGESTIONS

- Delia Smith is probably the most popular and well-known cookery writer and broadcaster in Britain. Her *Complete Cookery Course* for example, published by BBC Books, gives a good idea of the kind of food British people cook (or would like to cook) at home.
- There are lots of hotel, restaurant and pub guides which are published annually and which describe the kind of food and other facilities available at British eating and drinking places. For example, *The Good Food Guide* published by Which Books and the *Good Pub Guide* published by Vermilion.

21
Sport and competition

Think of your favourite sport. Whatever it is, there is a good chance that it was first played in Britain, and an even better chance that its modern rules were first codified in Britain. The public schools (see chapter 14) of the Victorian era believed that organized competitive games had many psychological benefits. These games appealed to, and developed, the British sense of 'fair play'. This concept went far beyond abiding by the written rules of a game. It also meant observing its unwritten rules, which governed behaviour before, during and after the game. You had to be a 'good loser'. To be a cheat was shameful, but to lose was just 'part of the game'. Team games were best, because they developed 'team spirit'.

Modern sport in Britain is very different. 'Winning isn't everything' and 'it's only a game' are still well-known sayings which reflect the amateur approach of the past. But to modern professionals, sport is clearly not just a game. These days, top players in any sport talk about having a 'professional attitude' and doing their 'job' well, even if, officially, their sport is still an amateur one. Nevertheless, the public-school enthusiasm for sport and the importance placed on simply taking part has had a lasting influence on the nature and role of sport in Britain today.

Gentlemen and players

The middle-class origins of much British sport means that it began as an amateur pastime – a leisure-time activity which nobody was paid for taking part in. Even in football, which has been played on a professional basis since 1885, one of the first teams to win the FA (Football Association) Cup was a team of amateur players (the Corinthians). In many other sports there has been resistance to professionalism. People thought it would spoil the sporting spirit. Not until 1968 were tennis professionals allowed to compete at Wimbledon. In cricket there was, until 1962, a rigid distinction between 'gentlemen' (amateurs) and 'players' (professionals), even when the two played together in the same team. These days, all 'first class' cricketers are professionals.

A national passion

Sport probably plays a more important part in people's lives in Britain than it does in most other countries. For a very large number, and this is especially true for men, it is their main form of entertainment. Millions take part in some kind of sport at least once a week. Many millions more are regular spectators and follow one or more sports. There are hours of televised sport each week. Every newspaper, national or local, quality or popular, devotes several pages entirely to sport.

The British are only rarely the best in the world at particular sports in modern times. However, they are *one* of the best in the world in a much larger number of different sports than any other country (British individualism at work again). This chapter looks at the most publicized sports with the largest followings. But it should be noted that hundreds of other sports are played in Britain, each with its own small but enthusiastic following. Some of these may not be seen as a sport at all by many people. For most people with large gardens, for example, croquet is just an agreeable social pastime for a sunny afternoon. But to a few, it is a deadly serious competition. The same is true of other games such as indoor bowling, darts or snooker. Even board games, the kind you buy in a toy shop, have their national champions. Think of any pastime, however trivial, which involves some element of competition and, somewhere in Britain, there is probably a 'national association' for it which organizes contests.

The British are so fond of competition that they even introduce it into gardening. Many people indulge in an informal rivalry with their neighbours as to who can grow the better flowers or vegetables. But the rivalry is sometimes formalized. Through the country, there are competitions in which gardeners enter their cabbages, leeks, onions, carrots or whatever in the hope that they will be judged 'the best'. There is a similar situation with animals. There are hundreds of dog and cat shows throughout the country at which owners hope that their pet will win a prize.

A gardener with his prize-winning onion

The social importance of sport

The importance of participation in sport has legal recognition in Britain. Every local authority has a duty to provide and maintain playing fields and other facilities, which are usually very cheap to use and sometimes even free. Spectator sport is also a matter of official public concern. For example, there is a law which prevents the television rights to the most famous annual sporting occasions, such as the Cup Final and the Derby (▷ *The sporting calendar*), being sold exclusively to satellite channels, which most people cannot receive. In these cases it seems to be the event, rather than the sport itself, which is important. Every year the Boat Race and the Grand National are watched on television by millions of people who have no great interest in rowing or horse-racing. Over time, some events have developed a mystique which gives them a higher status than the standard at which they are played deserves. In modern times, for example, the standard of rugby at the annual Varsity Match has been rather low – and yet it is always shown live on television.

Sometimes the traditions which accompany an event can seem as important as the actual sporting contest. Wimbledon, for instance, is not just a tennis tournament. It means summer fashions, strawberries and cream, garden parties and long, warm English summer evenings. This reputation created a problem for the event's organizers in 1993, when it was felt that security for players had to be tightened. Because Wimbledon is essentially a middle-class event, British tennis fans would never allow themselves to be treated like football fans. Wimbledon with security fences, policemen on horses and other measures to keep fans off the court? It just wouldn't be Wimbledon!

The long history of such events has meant that many of them, and

▶ Trophies: real and imaginary

Quite often, sporting contests in Britain have a prize attached to them which gives them a special significance.

The Calcutta Cup
The annual rugby union match between England and Scotland is only rarely the decisive one in the Five Nations Championship (▷ *The sporting calendar*). But it is important because it is played for the Calcutta Cup, an ornate silver trophy made in India in the 1870s.

The Ashes
When England and Australia play a series of cricket matches, they are said to be competing for the Ashes. In 1882, after a heavy defeat by Australia, the 'ashes' of English cricket (actually a burnt piece of cricketing equipment) were placed inside an urn as a symbol of the 'death' of English cricket. In fact, the urn never leaves Lord's cricket ground.

The Triple Crown
In rugby union, if one of the four nations of the British Isles beats all the other three nations in the same year, they are recorded as having won the Triple Crown, even though a physical object called 'the Triple Crown' does not exist!

their venues, have become world-famous. Therefore, it is not only the British who tune in to watch. The Grand National, for example, attracts a television audience of 300 million. This worldwide enthusiasm has little to do with the standard of British sport. The cup finals of other countries often have better quality and more entertaining football on view – but more Europeans watch the English Cup Final than any other. The standard of British tennis is poor, and Wimbledon is only one of the world's major tournaments. But if you ask any top tennis player, you find that Wimbledon is the one they really want to win. Every footballer in the world dreams of playing at Wembley, every cricketer in the world of playing at Lord's. Wimbledon, Wembley and Lord's (▷ *Famous sporting venues*) are the 'spiritual homes' of their respective sports. Sport is a British export!

Cricket

Judging by the numbers of people who play it and watch it (▷ *Spectator attendance at major sports*), cricket is definitely *not* the national sport of Britain. In Scotland, Wales and Northern Ireland, interest in it is largely confined to the middle classes. Only in England and a small part of Wales is it played at top level. And even in England, where its enthusiasts come from all classes, the majority of the population do not understand its rules. Moreover, it is rare for the English national team to be the best in the world.

When people refer to cricket as the English national game, they are not thinking so much of its level of popularity or of the standard of

▶ Famous sporting venues in Britain

Football
Wembley (London)
Hampden Park (Glasgow)

Rugby union
Twickenham (London)
Cardiff Arms Park (Wales)
Murrayfield (Edinburgh)
Lansdowne Road (Dublin)

Horse-racing
Flat: *Ascot, Epsom, Newmarket*
National hunt: *Aintree, Cheltenham*

Cricket
Lord's (London)
The Oval (London)
Old Trafford (Manchester)
Headingley (Leeds)
Trent Bridge (Nottingham)
Edgbaston (Birmingham)

Golf
St Andrew's (Scotland)

Motor racing
Silverstone (Northampton)
Brands Hatch (Rochester)

▶ Sporting language

The central place of sport in Britain is indicated by the very large number of sporting expressions and metaphors which have entered the everyday language. Here are some of them.

From cricket
on a sticky wicket: in a difficult situation
on an easy wicket: in a fortunate situation
stumped: at a loss for an answer to a question or solution to a problem
hit something for six: dismiss something emphatically
play with a straight bat: do something in an honest and straightforward way
it's not cricket: it is not the proper or fair way of doing something (cricket is supposed to be the perfect example of the concept of 'fair play')
have a good innings: have a large or adequate amount of time in a certain post; have a long life
off one's own bat: without help from anyone else

From boxing
saved by the bell: saved from a bad or dangerous situation by a sudden event
on the ropes: in a weak position; close to defeat or failure
floored: defeated or confused in an argument or discussion
throw in the towel: admit defeat

From horse-racing and riding
first past the post: the winner
have the bit between the teeth: determined
to be given free rein: to be allowed to do exactly what one wants, without restrictions
in the saddle: in control (in modern times, the expression 'in the driving seat' is often used instead)

From other sports or sport in general
team player: somebody who is good at co-operating with other people in groups
run with the pack: have no individual principles but just blindly follow the majority
win hands down: win easily
go to the dogs: start to lead an aimless and self-destructive life
in the final straight/on the last lap: in the last stage of some process
a safe pair of hands: a reliable person

▶ Notes on cricket

- Eleven players in each team.
- Test matches between national teams can last up to five days of six hours each. Top club teams play matches lasting between two and four days. There are also one-day matches lasting about seven hours.
- Played at top level in Australia, England, India, New Zealand, Pakistan, South Africa, Sri Lanka, the West Indies (those places in the Caribbean which once belonged to the British empire). Can be considered the 'national sport' in India and the West Indies. The team most frequently regarded as 'the best' is the West Indies.

A cricket match in progress

English players but more of the very English associations that it carries with it. Cricket is much more than just a sport; it symbolizes a way of life – a slow and peaceful rural way of life. Cricket is associated with long sunny summer afternoons, the smell of new-mown grass and the sound of leather (the ball) connecting with willow (the wood from which cricket bats are made). Cricket is special because it combines competition with the British dream of rural life. Cricket is what the village green is for! As if to emphasize the rural connection, 'first class' cricket teams in England, unlike teams in other sports, do not bear the names of towns but of counties (Essex and Yorkshire, for example).

Cricket is, therefore, the national English game in a symbolic sense. However, to some people cricket is more than just a symbol. The comparatively low attendance at top class matches does not give a true picture of the level of interest in the country. One game of cricket takes a terribly long time (▷ *Notes on cricket*), which a lot of people simply don't have to spare. In fact there are millions of people in the country who don't just enjoy cricket but are passionate about it! These people spend up to thirty days each summer tuned to the live radio commentary of 'Test' (= international) Matches. When they get the chance, they watch a bit of the live television coverage. Some people even do both at the same time (they turn the sound down on the television and listen to the radio). To these people, the commentators become well-loved figures. When, in 1994, one famous commentator died, the Prime Minister lamented that 'summers will never be the same again'. And if cricket fans are too busy to listen to the radio commentary, they can always phone a special number to be given the latest score!

Football

The full official name of 'soccer' (as it is called in the USA and sometimes in Britain) is 'association football'. This distinguishes it from other kinds such as rugby football (almost always called simply 'rugby'), Gaelic football, Australian football and American football. However, most people in Britain call it simply 'football'. This is indicative of its dominant role. Everywhere in the country except south Wales, it is easily the most popular spectator sport, the most-played sport in the country's state schools and one of the most popular participatory sports for adults. In terms of numbers, football, not cricket, is the national sport, just as it is everywhere else in Europe.

British football has traditionally drawn its main following from the working class. In general, the intelligentsia ignored it. But in the last two decades of the twentieth century, it started to attract wider interest. The appearance of fanzines is an indication of this. Fanzines are magazines written in an informal but often highly intelligent and witty style, published by the fans of some of the clubs. One or two books of literary merit have been written which focus not only on players, teams and tactics but also on the wider social aspects of the game. Light-hearted football programmes have appeared on television which similarly give attention to 'off-the-field' matters. There has also been much academic interest. At the 1990 World Cup there was a joke among English fans that it was impossible to find a hotel room because they had all been taken by sociologists!

Many team sports in Britain, but especially football, tend to be men-only, 'tribal' affairs. In the USA, the whole family goes to watch the baseball. Similarly, the whole family goes along to cheer the Irish national football team. But in Britain, only a handful of children or women go to football matches. Perhaps this is why active support for local teams has had a tendency to become violent. During the 1970s and 1980s football hooliganism was a major problem in England. In the 1990s, however, it seemed to be on the decline. English fans visiting Europe are now no worse in their behaviour than the fans of many other countries.

Attendances at British club matches have been falling for several decades (▷ *Spectator attendance at major sports*). Many stadiums are very old, uncomfortable and sometimes dangerous. Accidents at professional football matches led to the decision to turn the grounds of first division and premiership clubs into 'all-seater' stadiums. Fans can no longer stand, jump, shout and sway on the cheap 'terraces' behind the goals (there have been emotional farewells at many grounds to this traditional 'way of life'). It is assumed that being seated makes fans more well-behaved. It remains to be seen whether this development will turn football matches into events for the whole family.

▶ **Spectator attendance at major sports**

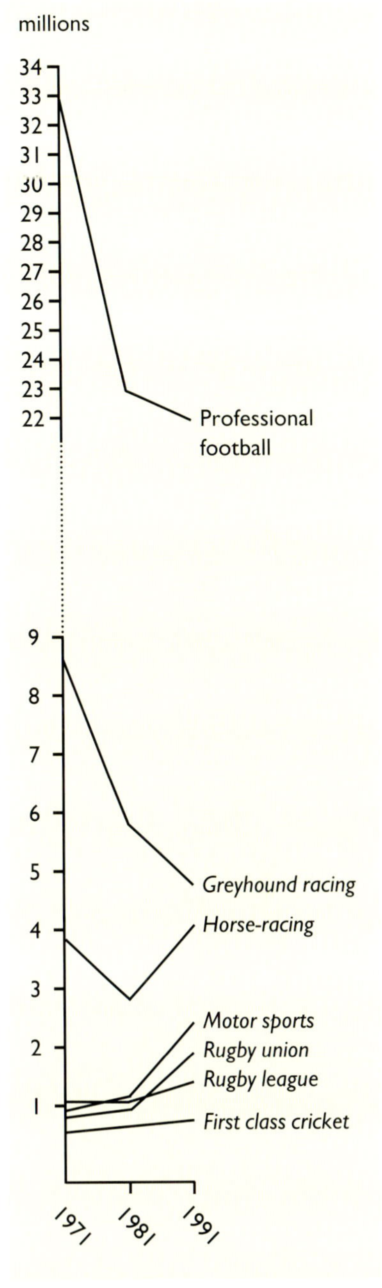

Source: Key Data

▶ Notes on rugby

- Similar to American football in the ball it uses (egg-shaped) and its aim (to carry the ball over the opposing team's line). But very different in details – most notably, you cannot interfere with a player who does not have the ball. Also different in that, like all British sports, there are no 'time-outs' and players do not wear body armour.
- Fifteen players per team in rugby union and thirteen in rugby league.
- Playing time is eighty minutes.
- Rugby union is played at top level in the British Isles, France, Australia, South Africa and New Zealand. Also to a high level in North America, Argentina, Romania and some Pacific islands. Can be considered the 'national sport' of Wales, New Zealand, Fiji, Western Samoa and Tonga, and of South African whites. The teams most frequently regarded as the best are from the southern hemisphere.
- Rugby league is played at top level in Britain, Australia and New Zealand.

A rugby match in progress

Rugby

There are two versions of this fast and aggressive ball game: rugby union and rugby league. They are so similar that somebody who is good at one of them can quickly learn to become good at the other. The real difference between them is a matter of social history. Rugby union is the older of the two. In the nineteenth century it was enthusiastically taken up by most of Britain's public schools. Rugby league split off from rugby union at the end of the century. Although it has now spread to many of the same places in the world where rugby union is played (▷ *Notes on rugby*), its traditional home is among the working class of the north of England, where it was a way for miners and factory workers to make a little bit of extra money from their sporting talents. Unlike rugby union, it has always been a professional sport.

Because of these social origins, rugby league in Britain is seen as a working class sport, while rugby union is mainly for the middle classes. Except in south Wales. There, rugby union is a sport for all classes, and more popular than football. In Wales, the phrase 'international day' means only one thing – that the national rugby team are playing. In the 1970s and 1980s some of the best Welsh players were persuaded to 'change codes'. They were 'bought' by one of the big rugby league clubs, where they could make a lot of money. Whenever this happened it was seen as a national disaster among the Welsh.

Rugby union has had some success in recent years in selling itself to a wider audience. As a result, just as football has become less exclusively working class in character, rugby union has become less exclusively middle class. In 1995 it finally abandoned amateurism. In fact, the amateur status of top rugby union players had already become meaningless. They didn't get paid a salary or fee for playing, but they received large 'expenses' as well as various publicity contracts and paid speaking engagements.

Animals in sport

Traditionally, the favourite sports of the British upper class are hunting, shooting and fishing. The most widespread form of hunting is foxhunting – indeed, that is what the word 'hunting' usually means in Britain (▷ Foxhunting). This is a popular pastime among some members of the higher social classes and a few people from lower social classes, who often see their participation as a mark of newly won status.

Killing birds with guns is known as 'shooting' in Britain. It is a minority pastime confined largely to the higher social classes; there are more than three times as many licensed guns for this purpose in France as there are in Britain. The birds which people try to shoot (such as grouse) may only be shot during certain specified times of the year. The upper classes often organize 'shooting parties' during the 'season'.

The only kind of hunting which is associated with the working class is hare-coursing, in which greyhound dogs chase hares. However, because the vast majority of people in Britain are urban dwellers, this too is a minority activity.

The one kind of 'hunting' which is popular among all social classes is fishing. In fact, this is the most popular participatory sport of all in Britain. Between four and five million people go fishing regularly. When fishing is done competitively, it is called 'angling'.

Apart from being hunted, another way in which animals are used in sport is when they race. Horse-racing is a long-established and popular sport in Britain, both 'flat racing' and 'national hunt' racing (where there are jumps for the horses), sometimes known as 'steeplechase'. The former became known as 'the sport of kings' in the seventeenth century, and modern British royalty has close connections with sport involving horses. Some members of the royal family own racehorses and attend certain annual race meetings (Ascot, for example); some are also active participants in the sports of polo and show-jumping (both of which involve riding a horse).

The chief attraction of horse-racing for most people is the opportunity it provides for gambling (see below). Greyhound racing, although declining, is still popular for the same reason. In this sport, the dogs chase a mechanical hare round a racetrack. It is easier to organize than horse-racing and 'the dogs' has the reputation of being the 'poor man's racing'.

▶ Foxhunting

Foxhunting works like this. A group of people on horses, dressed in eighteenth century riding clothes, ride around with a pack of dogs. When the dogs pick up the scent of a fox, somebody blows a horn and then dogs, horses and riders all chase the fox. Often the fox gets away, but if not, the dogs get to it before the hunters and tear it to pieces. As you might guess in a country of animal-lovers, where most people have little experience of the harsher realities of nature, foxhunting is strongly opposed by some people. The League Against Cruel Sports wants it made illegal and the campaign has been steadily intensifying. There are sometimes violent encounters between foxhunters and protestors (whom the hunters call 'saboteurs').

Hunters and saboteurs clashing during a foxhunt

Other sports

Almost every sport which exists is played in Britain. As well as the sports already mentioned, hockey (mostly on a field but also on ice) is quite popular, and both basketball (for men) and netball (for women) are growing in popularity. So too is the ancient game of rounders (▷ *Rounders*).

The British have a preference for team games. Individual sports such as athletics, cycling, gymnastics and swimming have comparatively small followings. Large numbers of people become interested in them only when British competitors do well in international events. The more popular individual sports are those in which socializing is an important aspect (such as tennis, golf, sailing and snooker). It is notable in this context that, apart from international competitions, the only athletics event which generates a lot of enthusiasm is the annual London Marathon. Most of the tens of thousands of participants in this race are 'fun runners' who are merely trying to complete it, sometimes in outrageous costumes, and so collect money for charity.

There seem to be two main exceptions to this tendency to prefer team games. One is boxing, where some of the attraction lies in the opportunity for gambling. But while boxing is declining in popularity, the other exception, motor sports, is becoming more popular.

▶ Rounders

This sport is rather similar to American baseball, but it certainly does not have the same image. It has a long history in England as something that people (young and old, male and female) can play together at village fêtes. It is often seen as not being a proper 'sport'.

However, despite this image, it has recently become the second most popular sport for state schools in Britain. More traditional sports such as cricket and rugby are being abandoned in favour of rounders, which is much easier to organize. Rounders requires less special equipment, less money and boys and girls can play it together. It also takes up less time. It is especially attractive for state schools with little money and time to spare. More than a quarter of all state-school sports fields are now used for rounders. Only football, which is played on nearly half of all state-school fields, is more popular.

Gambling

Even if they are not taking part or watching, British people like to be involved in sport. They can do this by placing bets on future results. Gambling is widespread throughout all social classes. It is so basic to sport that the word 'sportsman' used to be a synonym for 'gambler'.

When, in 1993, the starting procedure for the Grand National did not work properly, so that the race could not take place, it was widely regarded as a national disaster. The £70 million which had been gambled on the result (that's more than a pound for each man, woman and child in the country!) all had to be given back.

Every year, billions of pounds are bet on horse races. So well-known is this activity that everybody in the country, even those with no interest in horse-racing, would understand the meaning of a question such as 'who won the 2.30 at Chester?' (Which horse won the race that was scheduled to take place at half past two today at the Chester racecourse? The questioner probably wants to know because he or she has gambled some money on the result.) The central role of horse-racing in gambling is also shown by one of the names used to denote companies and individuals whose business it is to take bets. Although these are generally known as 'bookmakers', they sometimes call themselves 'turf accountants' ('turf' is a word for ground where grass grows).

▶ A nation of gamblers

In 1993 a total of £12.7 billion was wagered by the British – that's £289 for every adult in the country. £9.5 billion was won. The government took just over £1 billion in taxes. The rest was kept by the bookmakers. About half of all the money bet in 1993 was on horses or greyhounds. 74% of all adults gambled at least once during the year.

At least once every two weeks:

- 39% did the football pools;
- 20% played on gaming and fruit machines;
- 18% played bingo;
- 14% put money on the horses.

In Britain in 1993, there was one betting shop for every 3,000 adults. There were also:

- 120 casinos;
- 120,000 fruit machines;
- 1,000 bingo clubs;
- 1,000 lotteries;
- 59 racetracks;
- 37 greyhound stadiums.

▶ The sporting calendar

This chart shows the seasons for Britain's most popular spectator sports and some of the most important sporting events which take place every year. There are other, less regular, events which can be very important and other annual events in particular sports which are more important for followers of those sports. However, these are the ones that are well-known to the general public.

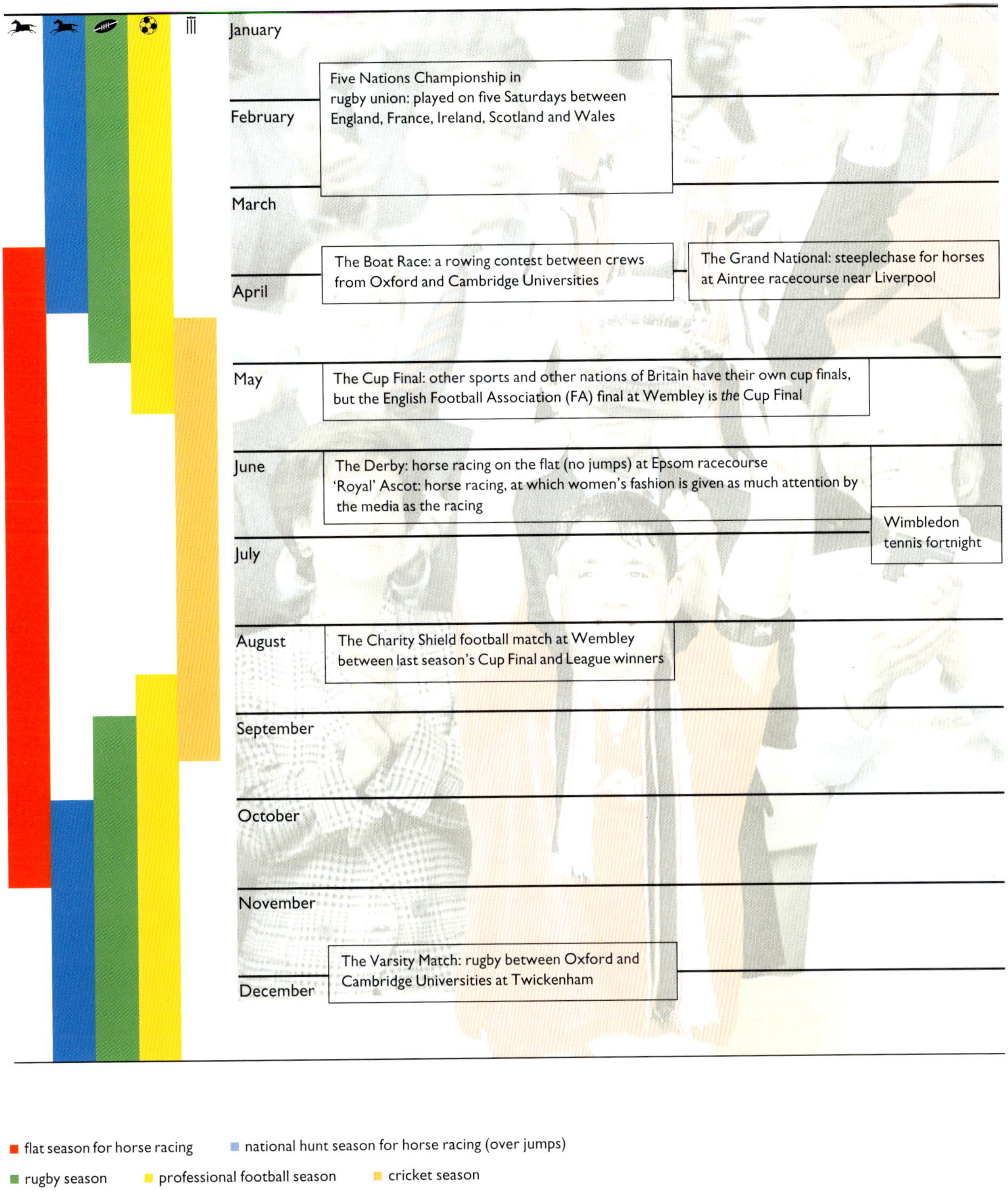

Apart from the horses and the dogs, the most popular form of gambling connected with sports is the football pools. Every week, more than ten million people stake a small sum on the results of Saturday's professional matches. Another popular type of gambling, sterotypically for middle-aged working class women, is bingo.

Nonconformist religious groups (see chapter 13) traditionally frown upon gambling and their disapproval has had some influence. Perhaps this is why Britain did not have a national lottery until 1994. But if people want to gamble, then they will. For instance, before the national lottery started, the British gambled £250,000 on which company would be given the licence to run it! The country's big bookmakers are willing to offer odds on almost anything at all if asked. Who will be the next Labour party leader? Will it rain during the Wimbledon tennis tournament? Will it snow on Christmas Day? All of these offer opportunities for 'a flutter'.

QUESTIONS

1 The manager of Liverpool Football Club during the 1970s once said: 'Football is not a matter of life and death to me – it's more important than that!' Do you think his comment is typical of the British attitude to sport (the traditional one, the modern one, both or neither)?

2 Cricket's great drawback is that it cannot be played during or immediately after rain because the grass is too wet. In the early 1990s it was suggested that first-class cricket should be played on plastic surfaces so that play could begin again as soon as the rain had stopped. English cricket enthusiasts were horrified by this suggestion. One member of the MCC (Marylebone Cricket Club, the club which partly controls the sport in England) commented, 'The man must have been drunk when he thought of it'. How do you explain this extreme reaction?

3 In 1993 Roddy Doyle, a winner of the literary Booker Prize (see chapter 22) made regular appearances on a television football programme. In terms of the history of football in Britain, how was this significant? Are the sociological associations of football in your country different from those in Britain?

4 For about three months each year, the British spend millions of pounds betting on the results of Australian football – a sport which the vast majority have no interest in (and no understanding of)! Why do you think they do this? What does it tell us about British attitudes to sport and gambling? Are the chief forms of gambling in Britain the same as those in your country?

SUGGESTIONS

- Copies of football club fanzines can be bought from Sports Pages, Caxton Walk, 94–96 Charing Cross Road, London WC2H 0JG. There is a general football fanzine called *When Saturday Comes* which is available from the same address or from 4th Floor, 2 Pear Tree Court, London EC1R 0DS. This includes details of most of the individual club fanzines available.

22
The arts

The arts in society

Interest in the arts in Britain used to be largely confined to a small élite. Compared with fifty years ago, far more people today read books, visit art galleries, go to the theatre and attend concerts. Nevertheless, the fact remains that most British people prefer their sport, their television and videos (▷ *Videos*), and their other free-time activities to anything 'cultural'.

The arts in Britain are met with a mixture of public apathy and private enthusiasm. Publicly, the arts are accepted and tolerated but not actively encouraged. As a proportion of its total expenditure, government financial support for the arts is one of the lowest of any western country. During the 1980s it was the lowest of all. One of the principles of Thatcherism was that the arts should be driven by 'market forces'. The government reduced the money it gave to the Arts Council, the organization which allocates funds to projects in the arts. It was politically acceptable to do this because of the widespread view that 'culture' is of interest to a small section of the rich only. Therefore, the government's action was seen as democratic – it was refusing to subsidize the tastes of the wealthy. The counter-argument, that such an attitude is undemocratic because it makes 'culture' too expensive for the ordinary person, is not one that carries much weight in Britain. In schools, subjects such as art and music, though always available, tend to be pushed to the sidelines. In the national curriculum (see chapter 14), they are the only two 'core' subjects which pupils at the age of fourteen are allowed to drop completely.

In addition, the arts are not normally given a very high level of publicity. Television programmes on 'cultural' subjects are usually shown late at night. Each summer, many high-quality arts festivals take place around the country (▷ *Annual arts festivals*), but the vast majority of people do not even know of their existence. London has some of the finest collections of painting and sculpture in the world, but tourist brochures give little space to this aspect of the city. Except for the most famous, artists themselves have comparatively little public recognition. Some British artists have international reputations, and yet most people in Britain don't even know their names.

▶ What are 'the arts'?

The arts is an 'umbrella' term for literature, music, painting, sculpture, crafts, theatre, opera, ballet, film etc. It usually implies seriousness, so that particular examples of these activities which are regarded as 'light' may be referred to simply as 'entertainment' instead.

Art, or *fine arts*, is often used to refer to those arts which use space, but not time, for their appreciation (such as painting and sculpture). This, for example, is what is covered by the subject 'art' in schools.

The word *artist* can sometimes refer to a person working in the fine arts, and sometimes to a person working in any field of the arts. In this chapter, it is used in this latter sense.

▶ What is 'culture'?

The word *culture* has two meanings. In this book, it is used in its anthropological sense to mean 'way of life'. But many people also use it as a synonym for 'the arts'. When it is used this way in this chapter, it has inverted commas around it.

▶ Videos

Every year, more than £1 billion worth of videos are sold or rented in Britain. More than 60% of all households in the country own a video cassette recorder. Every year, these households hire an average of about twenty-five videos each and buy an average of about five videos each. Here is a graph showing the types of video that people watched in 1993.

Videos for sale and rent
% of current market

Sale

1	Children's/Disney	31
2	Films	30
3	TV/others	22
4	Music	9
5	Fitness/sport	8

Rental

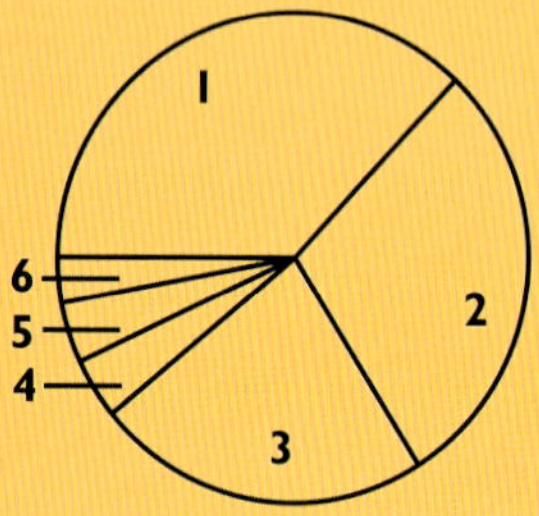

1	Dramas/thrillers	37
2	Action/adventure	29
3	Comedy	23
4	Children/family	4
5	Science fiction	4
6	Horror	3

An amateur theatrical production

It is very rare, for example, for any British artist to use his or her fame in the arts as a springboard onto the political stage. If you were to ask the average person to name some famous painters, composers, opera singers and ballet dancers, you would probably be given very few British names – or even none at all.

It is almost as if the British are keen to present themselves as a nation of philistines. And yet, hundreds of thousands of people are enthusiastically involved in one or other of the arts, but (in typically British fashion) with a more-or-less amateur or part-time status. For example, every town in the country has at least one 'amateur dramatics' society, which regularly gives performances and charges no more than enough to cover its costs. All over the country, thousands of people learn handicrafts (such as pottery) in their free time, and sometimes sell their work in local craft shops. Similarly, there are thousands of musicians of every kind, performing around the country for very little money and making their own recordings in very difficult circumstances. Some amateur British choirs, such as the Bach Choir of London and King's College Chapel Choir in Cambridge, are well-known throughout the world.

The characteristics of British arts and letters

If there is one characteristic of British work in the arts that seems to stand out, it is its lack of identification with wider intellectual trends. It is not usually ideologically committed, nor associated with particular political movements. Playwrights and directors, for instance, can be left-wing in their political outlook, but the plays which they produce rarely convey a straightforward political message. The same is largely true of British novelists and poets. Their writing is typically naturalistic and is not connected with particular intellectual movements. They tend to be individualistic, exploring emotions rather than ideas, the personal rather than the political. Whatever the critics say, it is quite common for British playwrights and novelists to claim that they just record 'what they see' and that they do not consciously intend any social or symbolic message. Similarly, British work in the arts also tends to be individualistic within its own field. That is, artists do not usually consider themselves to belong to this or that 'movement'. In any field of the arts, even those in which British artists have strong international reputations, it is difficult to identify a 'British school'.

The style of the arts also tends to be conventional. The avant-garde exists, of course, but, with the possible exception of painting and sculpture, it is not through such work that British artists become famous. In the 1980s, Peter Brook was a highly successful theatre director. But when he occasionally directed avant-garde productions, he staged them in Paris!

In these features of the work of British artists (lonely individualism expressing itself within conventional formats), it is perhaps possible to find an explanation for the apparent contradiction between, on the one hand, the low level of public support for the arts and, on the other hand, the high level of enthusiasm on the part of individuals. There appears to be a general assumption in Britain that artistic creation is a personal affair, not a social one, and that therefore the flowering of artistic talent cannot be engineered. Either it happens, or it doesn't. It is not something for which society should feel responsible.

Theatre and cinema

The theatre has always been very strong in Britain. Its centre is, of course, London, where successful plays can sometimes run without a break for many years (▷*They ran and ran!*). But every large town in the country has its theatres. Even small towns often have 'repertory' theatres, where different plays are performed for short periods by the same group of professional actors (a repertory company).

It seems that the conventional format of the theatrical play gives the undemonstrative British people a safe opportunity to look behind the mask of accepted social behaviour. The country's most successful and respected playwrights are usually those who explore the darker side of the personality and of personal relationships (albeit often through comedy).

British theatre has such a fine acting tradition that Hollywood is forever raiding its talent for people to star in films. British television does the same thing. Moreover, Broadway, when looking for its next blockbuster musical, pays close attention to London productions. In short, British theatre is much admired. As a consequence, it is something that British actors are proud of. Many of the most well-known television actors, though they might make most of their money in this latter medium, continue to see themselves as first and foremost theatre actors.

▶ Annual arts festivals

There are many festivals throughout Britain during the year, but these are perhaps the most well-known.

Aldeburgh
June. East Anglia. Classical music. Relatively informal atmosphere.

Edinburgh International Festival
August. All the performing arts, including avant-garde. More than ten different performances every day around the city. World famous.

The Proms
July–September. London. Classical music. 'Proms' is short for 'promenades', so-called because most of the seats are taken out of the Albert Hall, where the concerts take place, and the audience stands or walks around instead.

Glyndebourne
All summer. In the grounds of a large country house in Sussex. Opera.

Royal National Eisteddfod
July. Wales. Music, poetry and dance from many different countries. Mostly in the form of competitions, with special categories for Welsh performing arts.

Glastonbury and Reading
Probably the two most well-established rock music festivals. The **Bradford** and **Cambridge** festivals emphasize folk music.

▶ They ran and ran!

In the second half of the twentieth century, the two longest-running theatrical productions have been *The Mousetrap* (from a novel by Agatha Christie) and the comedy *No Sex Please, We're British*. Both played continuously for more than fifteen years.

In contrast, the cinema in Britain is often regarded as not quite part of 'the arts' at all – it is simply entertainment. Partly for this reason, Britain is unique among the large European countries in giving almost no financial help to its film industry. Therefore, although cinema-going is a regular habit for a much larger number of people than is theatre-going, British film directors often have to go to Hollywood because the resources they need are not available in Britain. As a result, comparatively few films of quality are made in the country. This is not because expertise in film making does not exist. It does. American productions often use studios and technical facilities in Britain. Moreover, some of the films which Britain does manage to make become highly respected around the world (▷ *British films*). But even these films often make a financial loss.

Music

Classical music in Britain is a minority interest. Few classical musicians, whether British or foreign, become well known to the general public. When they do, it is usually because of circumstances which have nothing to do with their music. For example, the Italian tenor Pavarotti became famous in the country when an aria sung by him was used by the BBC to introduce its 1990 football World Cup coverage. Despite this low profile, thousands of British people are dedicated musicians and many public libraries have a well-stocked music section. Several British orchestras, soloists, singers, choirs, opera companies and ballet companies, and also certain annual musical events, have international reputations.

In the 1960s, British artists had a great influence on the development of music in the modern, or 'pop' idiom. The Beatles and other British groups were responsible for several innovations which were then adopted by popular musicians in the USA and the rest of the world. These included the writing of words and music by the performers themselves, and more active audience participation. The words of their songs also helped to liberate the pop idiom from its

The last night of the proms (▷ Annual arts festivals)

▶ British films

Here are some of the most successful and/or respected British films of the 1980s and 1990s:

Chariots of Fire (1981)
Gregory's Girl (1981)
Gandhi (1982)
A Letter to Brezhnev (1985)
My Beautiful Launderette (1985)
A Room with a View (1985)
A Fish Called Wanda (1988)
Shirley Valentine (1989)
Henry V (1989)
Howard's End (1992)
The Crying Game (1992)
Much Ado About Nothing (1993)
Four Weddings and a Funeral (1994)
The Full Monty (1997)
Notting Hill (1999)

▶ Some well-known arts venues

The Shakespeare Memorial Theatre in Stratford is the home of the Royal Shakespeare Company (RSC). All the other venues mentioned here are in London.

Theatres include the Old Vic (the home of the National Theatre Company), the Mermaid, the Royal Court and the Barbican (where the RSC also performs).

For opera and ballet, there is the Royal Opera House at Covent Garden and the Coliseum, where the Sadler's Wells Company performs.

The South Bank area has several concert halls (notably the Royal Festival Hall) and the National Theatre.

former limitation to the topics of love and teenage affection. Other British artists in groups such as Pink Floyd and Cream played a major part in making the musical structure of pop music similarly more sophisticated.

Since the 1960s, popular music in Britain has been an enormous and profitable industry. The Beatles were awarded the honour (see chapter 7) of MBE (Member of the British Empire) for their services to British exports. Within Britain the total sales of the various kinds of musical recording are more than 200 million every year – and the vast majority of them are of popular music. Many worldwide trends have come out of Britain and British 'pop' artists have been active in attempting to cross the boundaries between popular music, folk music and classical music.

Literature

Although the British are comparatively uninterested in formal education, and although they watch a lot of television, they are nonetheless enthusiastic readers.

Many people in the literary world say that British literature lost its way at the end of the twentieth century. The last British author to win the Nobel Prize for literature was William Golding, in 1983. Many others disagree with this opinion. But what is not in doubt is that a lot of the exciting new literature written in English and published in Britain in recent years has been written by people from outside Britain. The Booker Prize is the most important prize in Britain for a work of fiction. Starting with Salman Rushdie in 1981, nine of its next fourteen winners were writers from former British colonies such as Canada, India, Ireland and Nigeria.

Although many of the best 'serious' British writers manage to be popular as well as profound, the vast majority of the books that are read in Britain could not be classified as 'serious' literature. Britain is the home of what might be called 'middlebrow' literature. (That is, mid-way between serious, or 'highbrow' literature and popular, or 'pulp' fiction.) For example, the distinctly British genre of detective fiction (the work of writers like Agatha Christie and Ruth Rendell) is regarded as entertainment rather than literature – but it is entertainment for intelligent readers. There are many British authors, mostly female (for example, Norah Lofts and Rummer Godden), who write novels which are sometimes classified as 'romances' but which are actually deeper and more serious than that term often implies. They are neither popular 'blockbusters' nor the sort of books which are reviewed in the serious literary press. And yet they continue to be read, year after year after year, by hundreds of thousands of people.

In 1993 more than half of the hundred most-borrowed books from Britain's public libraries were romantic novels. Many were of the middlebrow type. The rest were more simplistic stories about romance (she is young and pretty, he is tall, dark and handsome

▶ The arts and television

There are now only a quarter of the number of cinema seats in Britain as there were in 1965. This decline is generally assumed to be the result of the popularity of television. In fact, television has taken an increasingly important supporting role in the arts. The making of some high-quality British films has only been possible because of the financial help of Channel 4. The BBC regularly commissions new works of music for the proms. Television drama and comedy help to keep hundreds of actors in work.

Moreover, television can actually help to promote other art forms. When a book is dramatized on television, its sales often rocket. The most spectacular example of this occurred in the late 1960s. *The Forsyte Saga*, a series of novels by John Galsworthy, had been out of print for several decades. When an adaptation was shown on the BBC, half a million copies of the books were sold!

▶ Mountains of books!

For the really scholarly reader, the British Library (a department of the British Museum) has more than 10 million volumes, occupying 320 kilometres of shelf space. At present, the library is obliged to house a copy of every book published in the country. This obligation, however, will probably disappear in the future. It is just too difficult to organize. By 1993, its collection was expanding at the rate of 150 centimetres of books per hour. It possesses more than 6,000 different editions of Shakespeare's plays and more than 100 different editions of most novels by Charles Dickens. The result of all this is that it can take up to two days to find a particular book!

A child could do that!

British people often complain about modern abstract painting by saying, 'It doesn't look very special to me. A child of four could do that'. Well, in 1993 a child of four *did* do it.

One of the paintings offered to the Manchester Academy of Fine Arts for its annual exhibition was a work called *Rhythm of the Trees*. The Academy's experts liked it and included it in the exhibition. Only later did they discover that its creator, Carly Johnson, was four years old (the title was her grandfather's idea).

The news of this discovery was greatly enjoyed by the whole of Britain. Everybody loves it when experts are made to look like fools, especially when they are experts about something that most people don't understand. It did not occur to many people to think that perhaps a child genius had been discovered. Somebody else must have liked Carly's painting too – it sold for £295.

with a very firm jaw; whatever happens during the story, they end up in each other's arms – forever). The British publisher which sells more books than any other is Mills & Boon, whose books are exclusively of this type.

It is more than 200 years since poetry stopped being the normal mode of literary self-expression. And yet, poetry at the end of the twentieth century is surprisingly, and increasingly, popular in Britain. Books of poetry sell in comparatively large numbers. Their sales are not nearly as large as sales of novels, but they are large enough for a few small publishers to survive entirely on publishing poetry. Many poets are asked to do readings of their work on radio and at arts festivals. Many of these poets are not academics and their writing is accessible to non-specialists. Perhaps the 'pop' idiom and the easy availability of sound recording have made more people comfortable with spoken verse then they were fifty years ago.

The fine arts

Painting and sculpture are not as widely popular as music is in Britain. There is a general feeling that you have to be a specialist to appreciate them, especially if they are contemporary. Small private art galleries, where people might look at paintings with a view to buying them, are rare. Nevertheless, London is one of the main centres of the international collector's world. The two major auction houses of Sotheby's and Christie's are world-famous.

Until the 1980s, the country's major museums and galleries charged nothing for admission. Most of them now do so, although sometimes payment is voluntary. This has caused a lot of complaint that a great tradition of free education has been lost.

Modern art at the Tate Gallery

Museums and art galleries

The major museums in London are the British Museum (the national collection of antiquities), the Victoria and Albert Museum, which houses the world's largest display of the decorative arts, the Natural History Museum and the Science Museum. There are numerous other small, specialist museums in London and throughout the rest of the country, usually with an emphasis on history and British 'heritage'. There has been a move to make museums come alive with appropriate sounds and even smells.

Art galleries in London which house permanent collections include the National Gallery, the adjoining National Portrait Gallery, and the Tate Gallery, which is the nation's gallery of British art and the national museum of modern art. These galleries also hold special temporary exhibitions. The Hayward Gallery and the Royal Academy put on a series of shows, some of which are extremely popular. The Royal Academy is famous for its annual Summer Exhibition. Outside London there is the Burrell Collection near Glasgow and the Tate Galleries in Liverpool and St Ives. Most major towns and cities have their own museums and art galleries.

QUESTIONS

1 How does the British government justify its policy of low spending on the arts? Does the government in your country subsidize the arts and encourage artistic endeavor in schools and elsewhere?

2 What evidence can you find in this chapter to support the view that the arts are of interest to a small minority of British people only? What evidence can you find to support the opposite view – that interest in the arts is widespread? How is it that there can be an element of truth in both of these opinions?

3 Which areas of the arts seem to be particularly appreciated and valued in Britain and which seem to be ignored or under-valued? In what ways does the appreciation of the different aspects of the arts vary in your country?

4 The British are very conscious of the distinction between high art or 'culture' and light 'entertainment'. In what area of the arts have they succeeded in establishing a widely accepted and approved compromise which appeals to a broad range of people from different social backgrounds and with varying levels of education?

SUGGESTIONS

- Most of the major museums publish guides to their collections, pointing out their most highly-prized exhibits, which are often illustrated in the guides.
- Any biography of any of the major British theatrical figures of this century, such as Sir Laurence Olivier (there is one published by Fontana, written by Donald Spoto) would reveal a lot about the history of the theatre in Britain and about British theatre in general.

23 Holidays and special occasions

Britain is a country governed by routine. It has fewer public holidays than any other country in Europe and fewer than North America. (Northern Ireland has two extra ones, however). Even New Year's Day was not an official public holiday in England and Wales until quite recently (but so many people gave themselves a holiday anyway that it was thought it might as well become official!). There are almost no semi-official holidays either. Most official holidays occur either just before or just after a weekend, so that the practice of making a 'bridge' is almost unknown. Moreover, there are no traditional extra local holidays in particular places. Although the origin of the word 'holiday' is 'holy day', not all public holidays (usually known as 'bank holidays') are connected with religious celebrations.

The British also seem to do comparatively badly with regard to annual holidays. These are not as long as they are in many other countries. Although the average employee gets four weeks' paid holiday a year, in no town or city in the country would a visitor ever get the impression that the place had 'shut down' for the summer break. (In fact, about 40% of the population do not go away anywhere for their holidays.)

Traditional seaside holidays

The British upper class started the fashion for seaside holidays in the late eighteenth century. The middle classes soon followed them and when they were given the opportunity (around the beginning of the twentieth century), so did the working classes. It soon became normal for families to spend a week or two every year at one of the seaside resort towns which sprang up to cater for this new mass market. The most well-known of these are close to the larger towns and cities (▷ *Holiday resorts in England*).

These seaside towns quickly developed certain characteristics that are now regarded as typical of the 'traditional' English holiday resort. They have some hotels where richer people stay, but most families stay at boarding houses. These are small family businesses, offering either 'bed and breakfast' or, more rarely, 'full board' (meaning that all meals are provided). Some streets in seaside resorts are full of nothing but boarding houses. The food in these, and in local restaurants, is cheap and conventional with an emphasis on fish and chips.

Stereotypically, daytime entertainment in sunny weather centres around the beach, where the children make sandcastles, buy ice-creams and sometimes go for donkey rides. Older adults often do not bother to go swimming. They are happy just to sit in their deck chairs and occasionally go for a paddle with their skirts or trouser-legs hitched up. The water is always cold and, despite efforts to clean it up, sometimes very dirty. But for adults who swim, some resorts have wooden huts on or near the beach, known as 'beach cabins', 'beach huts' or 'bathing huts', in which people can change into their swimming costumes. Swimming and sunbathing without any clothing is rare. All resorts have various other kinds of attraction, including more-or-less permanent funfairs.

For the evenings, and when it is raining, there are amusement arcades, bingo halls, dance halls, discos, theatres, bowling alleys and so on, many of these situated on the pier. This unique British architectural structure is a platform extending out into the sea. The large resorts have decorations which light up at night. The 'Blackpool illuminations', for example, are famous.

Another traditional holiday destination, which was very popular in Britain in the 1950s and 1960s, is the holiday camp, where visitors stay in chalets in self-contained villages with all food and entertainment organized for them. Butlin's and Pontin's, the companies which own most of these, are well-known names in Britain. The enforced good-humour, strict meal-times and events such as 'knobbly knees' competitions and beauty contests that were characteristic of these camps have now given way to a more relaxed atmosphere.

▶ Rock

There is one kind of sweet associated with holiday resorts. This is 'rock', a hard thick stick of sugar. Each resort has the letters of its name appearing throughout the stick, so that one hears of 'Brighton Rock', 'Blackpool Rock' and so on.

A shop selling rock

Blackpool beach

▶ Seaside postcards

Humorous postcards like the one below can still be bought at seaside resorts. The joke always has an element of sexual innuendo in it. The traditional seaside holiday in the first half of the twentieth century represented a relaxing of Victorian restrictions on overt reference to sex. These days, of course, no such restrictions exist, so these postcards are mainly enjoyed in a spirit of nostalgia for the past.

A traditional seaside postcard by Donald McGill

Modern holidays

Both of the traditional types of holiday have become less popular in the last quarter of the twentieth century. The increase in car ownership has encouraged many people to take caravan holidays. But the greatest cause of the decline of the traditional holiday is foreign tourism. Before the 1960s, only the rich took holidays abroad. By 1971, the British were taking 7 million foreign holidays and by 1987, 20 million. These days, millions of British people take their cars across the channel every year and nearly half of all the nights spent on holidays away from home are spent abroad.

Most foreign holidays are package holidays, in which transport and accommodation are booked and paid for through a travel agent. These holidays are often booked a long time in advance. In the middle of winter the television companies run programmes which give information about the packages being offered. People need cheering up at this time of the year! In many British homes it has become traditional to get the holiday brochures out and start talking about where to go in the summer on Boxing Day (▷*Calendar of special occasions*). Spain is by far the most popular package-holiday destination.

Half of all the holidays taken within Britain are now for three days or less. Every bank-holiday weekend there are long traffic jams along the routes to the most popular holiday areas. The traditional seaside resorts have survived by adjusting themselves to this trend. (Only the rich have second houses or cottages in the countryside to which they can escape at weekends.) But there are also many other types of holiday. Hiking in the country and sleeping at youth hostels has long been popular (see chapter 5) and so, among an enthusiastic minority, has pot-holing (the exploration of underground caves). There are also a wide range of 'activity' holidays available, giving full expression to British individualism. You can, for example, take part in a 'murder weekend', and find yourself living out the plot of detective story.

An increasing number of people now go on 'working' holidays, during which they might help to repair an ancient stone wall or take part in an archaeological dig. This is an echo of another traditional type of 'holiday' – fruit picking. It used to be the habit of poor people from the east end of London, for example, to go to Kent at the end of the summer to help with the hop harvest (hops are used for making beer).

Christmas and New Year

Christmas is the one occasion in modern Britain when a large number of customs are enthusiastically observed by most ordinary people within the family. The slow decrease in participation in organized religion (see chapter 13), and the fact that Christmas in modern times is as much a secular feast as a religious one, has had little effect on these traditions. Even people who consider themselves to be anti-religious quite happily wish each other a 'Happy Christmas' or a 'Merry Christmas'. They do not (as in some other countries) self-consciously wish each other a 'Happy New Year' instead.

Indeed, the 'commercialization' of Christmas has itself become part of tradition. Every November in Oxford Street (one of the main shopping streets in the centre of London), a famous personality ceremoniously switches on the 'Christmas lights' (decorations) thus 'officially' marking the start of the period of frantic Christmas shopping. And it certainly is frantic. Between that time and the middle of January, most shops do nearly half of their total business for the year (most have 'sales' in early January when prices are reduced). Most people buy presents for the other members of their household and also for other relatives, especially children. Some people also buy presents for their close friends. And to a wider circle of friends and relatives, and sometimes also to working associates and neighbours, they send Christmas cards (▷ *Christmas cards*). Some people even send such greetings to people whom they have not seen for many years, often using the excuse of this tradition to include a letter passing on the year's news.

Christmas cards

▶ Christmas cards

Many people send cards at Christmas time depicting some aspect of the birth of Christ. Most people, however, do not. Christmas is an opportunity for the British to indulge their dreams about a vanished rural past. You can see this on many typical Christmas cards. They often show scenes from either the nineteenth or eighteenth centuries and may be set in the countryside, very frequently covered with snow. (In fact, snow at Christmas is rare in most parts of Britain).

People also buy Christmas trees (a tradition imported from Germany in the nineteenth century). Almost every household has a tree decorated in a different way (in many cases, with coloured lights). Most people also put up other decorations around the house. Exactly what these are varies a great deal, but certain symbols of Christmas, such as bits of the holly and mistletoe plants, are very common, and the Christmas cards which the household has received are usually displayed. A 'crib', which is a model depicting the birth of Christ, also sometimes forms part of the Christmas decorations. In December, as Christmas gets closer, carols (usually, but not always, with a religious theme) are sung in churches and schools, often at special concerts, and also, though less often than in the past, by groups of people who go from house to house collecting money for charitable causes.

The role of Father Christmas (or Santa Claus) and the customs associated with the giving of gifts vary from family to family. Most households with children tell them that Father Christmas comes down the chimney on the night of Christmas Eve (even though most houses no longer have a working chimney!). Many children lay out a Christmas stocking at the foot of their beds, which they expect to see filled when they wake up on Christmas morning. Most families put wrapped presents around or on the Christmas tree and these are opened at some time on Christmas Day.

Other activities on Christmas Day may include the eating of Christmas dinner (▷ *Christmas dinner*) and listening to the Queen's Christmas message. This ten-minute television broadcast is normally the only time in the year when the monarch speaks directly to 'her' people on television. (When, in 1993, a national newspaper published the text of her speech a few days beforehand, it was a national scandal.)

The general feeling is that Christmas is a time for families. Many of the gatherings in houses on Christmas Day and Boxing Day consist of extended families (more than just parents and children). For many families, Christmas is the only time that they are all together (so it is often a time of conflict rather than harmony, in fact).

Parties on New Year's Eve, on the other hand, are usually for friends. Most people attend a gathering at this time and 'see in' the new year with a group of other people, often drinking a large amount of alcohol as they do so. In London, many go to the traditional celebration in Trafalgar Square (where there is an enormous Christmas tree which is an annual gift from the people of Norway).

In Scotland, where the Calvinists disapproved of parties and celebrations connected with religious occasions (such as Christmas), New Year, called Hogmanay, is given particular importance – so much importance that, in Scotland only, 2 January (as well as New Year's Day) is also a public holiday (so that people have two days to recover from their New Year's Eve parties instead of just one!). Some British New Year customs, such as the singing of the song *Auld Lang Syne*,

▶ The Christmas party

In thousands of companies throughout Britain, the last working afternoon before Christmas is the time of the annual office party, at which a lot of alcohol is often consumed. Sexual feelings, hidden throughout the year, come into the open. This is a problem for company bosses. By law, an employer is responsible for sexual harassment at work and may have to pay as much as £10,000 in compensation. The peak time for complaints of sexual harassment is in January – just after the annual office party. Many employers now insure themselves against claims for compensation at this time.

▶ Christmas dinner

The traditional meal consists of stuffed roast turkey with roast potatoes and some other vegetable (often Brussel sprouts). Other foods associated with Christmas are Christmas pudding, an extremely heavy sweet dish made of dried fruits (it is traditional to pour brandy over it and then set it alight) and Christmas cake, an equally heavy fruit cake, with hard white icing on top.

A scene from the pantomime 'Jack and the Beanstalk'

originated in Scotland. Another, less common, one is the custom of 'first footing', in which the first person to visit a house in the new year is supposed to arrive with tokens of certain important items for survival (such as a lump of coal for the fire).

As a well-known Christmas carol reminds people, there are twelve days of Christmas. In fact, most people go back to work and school soon after New Year. Nobody pays much attention to the feast of the epiphany on 6 January (the twelfth day of Christmas), except that this is traditionally the day on which Christmas decorations are taken down. Some people say it is bad luck to keep them up after this date.

Other notable annual occasions

Easter is far less important than Christmas to most people in Britain. Although it involves a four-day 'weekend', there are very few customs and habits associated generally with it, other than the consumption of mountains of chocolate Easter eggs by children. Some people preserve the tradition of eating hot cross buns on Good Friday (▷ *Calendar of special occasions*). Quite a lot of people go away on holiday at this time.

None of the other days of the year to which traditional customs are attached is a holiday, and not everybody takes part in these customs. In fact, many people in Britain live through occasions such as Shrove Tuesday, April Fools' Day or Hallowe'en (▷ *Calendar of special occasions*) without even knowing that they have happened.

There is one other day which, although many people do not mark in any special way, is very difficult to ignore. This is 5 November, the day which celebrates a famous event in British history – the gunpowder plot. It is called Guy Fawkes' Day – or, more commonly, Bonfire Night. At the beginning of the seventeenth century, a group of Catholics planned to blow up the Houses of Parliament while King James I was in there. Before they could achieve this, one of them, Guy Fawkes, was caught in the cellars under Parliament with the gunpowder. He and his fellow-conspirators were all killed.

▶ Panto

The Christmas and New Year holiday seasons bring with them a popular theatrical tradition. This is pantomime (often shortened to 'panto'), staged in hundreds of theatres and specifically designed to appeal to children. It usually involves the acting out of a well-known folk tale with plenty of opportunity for audience participation.

There are certain established conventions of panto. For example, the cast includes a 'principal boy' (the young hero), who is always played by a woman, and a 'dame' (an older female character), who is always played by a man.

The continuing popularity of panto is assisted by the fact that these leading roles are today frequently taken by well-known personalities from the worlds of television or sport.

St Valentine's Day and Gretna Green

Despite the unromantic reputation of the British, on this day every year about £7 million worth of flowers are delivered (orders from men outnumber those from women by forty to one), an extra 40 million chocolates are sold and greetings-card manufacturers collect £25 million.

Every St Valentine's Day, thousands of people travel to a tiny village on Scotland's border with England. Many of them go to get married, and many more couples go through mock wedding ceremonies. The village is Gretna Green. Its romantic reputation began in 1754. In England in that year, marriage for people under the age of twenty-one without permission from parents was banned. In Scotland, however, this permission was not required, and Gretna Green was the first stop across the border. The laws that brought fame to Gretna Green no longer apply. But its reputation is secure. In this small place, at least one couple gets married, on average, every day of the year. Weddings for St Valentine's Day have to be booked three months in advance.

Shrove Tuesday

This day is also known as Pancake Day. In past centuries, Lent was a time of fasting. Both meat and eggs were forbidden throughout the six weeks. The tradition was to eat up all your meat on the Monday before Lent, and all your eggs on the Tuesday – in pancakes. Now, the fasting has gone and only the eating remains.

Two events are associated with Shrove Tuesday. One of them is the pancake tossing contest (how many pancakes can you throw into the air and catch within a certain time?). The other is the pancake race. Contestants have to run while continuously tossing a pancake. Anyone who drops his or her pancake is disqualified.

A Guy Fawkes' night bonfire

At the time, the failure of the gunpowder plot was celebrated as a victory for British Protestantism over rebel Catholicism. However, it has now lost its religious and patriotic connotations. In most parts of Britain, Catholic children celebrate it just as enthusiastically as Protestant children – or, for that matter, children brought up in any other religious faith. (As with Christmas, most of the customs associated with this day are mainly for the benefit of children.) Some children make a 'guy' out of old clothes stuffed with newspaper several weeks beforehand. They then place this somewhere on the street and ask passers-by for 'a penny for the guy'. What they are actually asking for is money to buy fireworks with.

On Guy Fawkes' Night itself there are 'bonfire parties' throughout the country, at which the 'guy' is burnt. Some people cook food in the embers of the bonfire, especially chestnuts or potatoes. So many fireworks are set off that, by the end of the evening, the air in all British cities smells strongly of sulphur. Every year, accidents with fireworks injure or even kill several people. In an effort to make things safer, some local authorities arrange public firework displays.

Finally, one other day should be mentioned. This is a different day for everybody – their birthday. Once again, it is most important for children, all of whom receive presents on this day from their parents, and often from other relatives as well. Adults may or may not receive presents, depending on the customs of their family and their circle of friends. Many will simply be wished 'Happy birthday' (not, by the way, 'Congratulations', unless it is a special birthday, such as a twenty-first). Some children and adults have a party, but not all. Moreover, nobody, including adults, is automatically expected to extend hospitality to other people on this day, and it is not expected that people should bring along cakes or anything to share with their colleagues at work, although some people do.

Calendar of special occasions

New Year's Day* (1 January)
2 January is also a public holiday in Scotland.

St Valentine's Day (14 February)

Shrove Tuesday (Forty-seven days before Easter)

St Patrick's Day (17 March)
This is a public holiday in Northern Ireland.

Mother's Day (The fourth Sunday in Lent)
£50 million worth of flowers are bought for this day. Cards are also sent.

April Fools' Day (1 April)
It is traditional for people to play tricks or practical jokes on each other on this day. Children are the most enthusiastic about this custom, but even the BBC and serious newspapers sometimes have 'joke' (i.e. not genuine) features on this day.

Good Friday*
The strange name in English for the day commemorating Christ's crucifixion.

Easter Monday* (The day after Easter Sunday)

May Day* (The first Monday in May)
In Britain this day is associated more with ancient folklore than with the workers. In some villages the custom of dancing round the maypole is acted out.

Spring Bank Holiday* (The last Monday in May)
There used to be a holiday on 'Whit Monday' celebrating the Christian feast of Pentecost. Because this is seven weeks after Easter, the date varied. This fixed holiday has replaced it.

Father's Day (The third Sunday in June)
This is probably just a commercial invention – and not a very successful one either. Millions of British fathers don't even know they have a special day.

Queen's Official Birthday (The second or third Saturday in June)
It is 'official' because it is not her real one. Certain public ceremonies are performed on this day.

Orangemen's Day (12 July)
This is a public holiday in Northern Ireland only. In this way, the holiday associated with the Catholic part of the community (St Patrick's Day) is balanced by one associated with the other part, the Protestants (see chapter 4).

Summer Bank Holiday* (The last Monday in August)

Hallowe'en (31 October)
This is the day before All Saints' Day in the Christian calendar, and is associated with the supernatural. Some people hold Hallowe'en parties, which are fancy-dress parties (people dress up as witches, ghosts etc.). However, this day is observed much more energetically in the USA than it is in Britain.

Guy Fawkes' Day (5 November)

Remembrance Sunday (Second Sunday in November)
This day commemorates the dead of both World Wars and of more recent conflicts. On and before this day, money is collected in the street on behalf of charities for ex-servicemen and women. The people who donate money are given paper poppies to pin to their clothes. No politician would be seen on this day without a poppy!

Christmas Eve (24 December)

Christmas Day* (25 December)

Boxing Day* (26 December)
Explanations for the origin of this name vary. One is that it was the day on which landowners and householders would present their tenants and servants with gifts (in boxes), another is that it was the day on which the collecting boxes in churches were opened and the contents distributed to the poor.

New Year's Eve (31 December)

* Public holiday

QUESTIONS

1 Why, do you think, have the two traditional types of holiday (at seaside boarding houses and at holiday camps) in Britain become less popular in the last quarter of the twentieth century? Is the modern pattern of British holidaymaking the same as it is for people in your country?

2 What aspects of Christmas in Britain, and the customs associated with it, are different from those in your country?

3 In Britain, you are generally considered to be unfortunate if your birthday is in the last half of December. Why? What special days do you have in your country for individuals to celebrate which British people don't celebrate?

4 There is a science-fiction story in which beings from outer space fly over Britain one night and conclude that planet Earth is full of barbaric, cruel people. Which night was it? How did they form this impression?

SUGGESTIONS

- *A Christmas Carol*, by Charles Dickens (which features the famous character of the miserly Scrooge), paints a picture of the Victorian idea of Christmas, which is influential to this day.

Index